MONSTROUS
MARTYRDOMS

MONSTROUS
MARTYRDOMS

Three Plays
Eric Bentley

Second Edition

Lord Alfred's Lover
H for Hamlet
German Requiem

Northwestern University Press
Evanston, Illinois

Northwestern University Press
Evanston, Illinois 60208-4170

Second edition

Printed in the United States of America

10 9 8 7 6 5 4 3 2 1

ISBN-13: 978-0-8101-2086-0
ISBN-10: 0-8101-2086-0

Library of Congress Cataloging-in-Publication Data

Bentley, Eric, 1916–
    Monstrous martyrdoms : three plays / by Eric Bentley.
      p. cm.
    Contents: Lord Alfred's lover — H for Hamlet — German requiem.
    ISBN 0-8101-2086-0 (alk. paper)
    1. Wilde, Oscar, 1854–1900—Drama   2. Douglas, Alfred Bruce, Lord, 1870–1945—Drama
  3. Hamlet (Legendary character)—Drama   4. Swabia (Germany)—Drama I. Title.

    PS3552.E548M6 2003
    812′.54—dc21

                                  2003052666

"And if there is still one hellish, truly accursed thing in our time, it is our artistic dallying with forms, instead of being like [martyrs] burnt at the stake, signalling through the flames."

—Antonin Artaud

Contents

Foreword

An earlier collection of my plays is called *Rallying Cries*. The phrase "Monstrous Martyrdoms" strikes a different note. But the word *martyr* means witness, and traditionally a witness to something held to be supremely worthwhile.

Yet our modern martyrs are not witnesses to a faith in the supernatural. More often they are victims of those who believe in the supernatural. Characteristically they are victims of those who believe what is conventionally believed.

There is at least one martyr in each of the plays of this book. The least obvious one is my Hamlet, for he is not killed but, rather, sentenced to a death in life. Oscar Wilde, though he did not die on the stake or the scaffold, actually saw himself as a martyr. The phrase "Monstrous Martyrdoms" is his, but homosexuals continue to be martyred in the second half of the twentieth century.

German Requiem is my most ambitious Martyr Play. The two young people martyred in its last act stand for a generation, maybe even a world. "They even killed their own sons," Bernard Shaw said about the statesmen of World War I who did not withhold their own families from battle. Those who threaten war today threaten a much larger number—of both foes and friends. Perhaps the word martyrdom is losing its meaning as so often the dead bear witness to nothing good, and sometimes to nothing at all. The word *monstrous*, on the other hand, gains ever more monstrous relevance.

Acknowledgments

On *Lord Alfred's Lover*, my greatest debts are to the first three producers of the play: the Hippodrome of Gainesville, Florida, the Center Theatre of Buffalo, New York (an offshoot of the State University of New York at Buffalo), and the Stonewall Repertory Theatre of New York City.

On *H for Hamlet*, I am indebted, first, to Alexander Knox and Alfred Drake and, second, to Walter Centuori, who found the play worthy of revision and revival in the 1980s. (It was first published in his magazine *Pirandellian Studies* early in 1985.)

On *German Requiem*, unproduced at the time this book goes to press, I am indebted to actors who have taken part in preliminary readings; also to friends who have offered constructive comment, notably Richard Hall, Michael Bertin, and my son Eric Bentley, Jr.

E. B.

New York, 1985

LORD ALFRED'S LOVER

To Lamont

Anais Nin said it for me: "We write to lure and enchant our lovers. We write to serenade them. We write to taste life twice. We write . . . to explore all our secret and hidden selves . . . to rebel against the world . . . to throw bombs at it and destroy it . . . or to make a larger world."

CAST (in order of appearance)

Lord Alfred Douglas in 1945 . . . . Quentin Crisp
Young Lord Alfred Douglas ("Bosie") . . . . Matthew Conlon
Oscar Wilde . . . . Maxim Mazumdar
Constance Wilde . . . . Suzanne Hall
Robbie Ross . . . . Mitchell Sugarman
Lord Queensberry . . . . Callan Egan
Arthur Marling . . . . David Officer
Charlie Parker . . . . Christopher Consani
Freddy Wood . . . . Michael Gnat
Plainclothesman . . . . Nicholas Haylett
Cliburn . . . . Michael Gnat
Allen . . . . Nicholas Haylett
Edward Carson . . . . Nicholas Haylett
Sir Edward Clarke . . . . Callan Egan
Jane Cotter . . . . Suzanne Hall
Sir Frank Lockwood . . . . Christopher Consani
Adrian Hope . . . . Nicholas Haylett
Lord Rosebery . . . . Christopher Consani
Maurice Gilbert . . . . Kevin Christy

The cast as listed in the righthand column above is that of the first New York production, under the auspices of Stonewall Repertory Theatre in the winter of 1982–1983. The number of actors is eleven (ten male, one female), though the play had originally been written for a cast twice this size. Small parts indicated in the text but not listed above were read by the actor playing the older Lord Alfred Douglas, Quentin Crisp. Sometimes a slight adjustment of the text was indicated. The curious can compare the present, "adjusted" text with earlier editions published in 1978 and 1981.

Part One

PROLOGUE

Oscar Wilde died in 1900. Lord Alfred Douglas lived on until 1945. The latter is shown now on the stage in the last months of his life, ensconced in a comfortable armchair, no doubt before a warm fire, a glass of port in his hand. He is addressing someone but, in the theater, we do not see the person addressed, for we ourselves are occupying his space—the other side of the fireplace. LORD ALFRED, *therefore, seems to be addressing us but at the same time regarding us as a single person, whose identity is revealed in the opening lines.*

LORD ALFRED: Yes, Father Murphy, make yourself comfortable, take the chair—that one, yes—beside the fire. Port? *(He pours port wine.)* I'll have a drop myself. H'm. Don't suppose you often go home like this—with a confessee—straight from the confession box, eh? Unorthodox, what? And we are orthodox, you and I. Happiest papist in England, that's old Douglas, all for confession! How I must've bored you sometimes! Nothing to confess at my age. Being rude to the butler? Eating meat on Friday? Tonight I'm going to make it up to you. Confess the sins of a lifetime. Someone else's lifetime. Except—his life is mine, what? Your face tells me you've guessed: I'm talking about Oscar Wilde. What century is it, Father? I don't ask the date or the year. Just the century! The twentieth. H'm. 1900 was the year he died. Yes, Oscar took one look at the twentieth century and dropped dead. Clever feller, what? Two world wars, Lenin, Stalin. They said on the wireless today this Hitler only has weeks to live. 1945. Exactly one half-century since—

(He reads the lines of the JUDGE *from the last of the Oscar Wilde trials.)*

JUDGE: People who can do these things must be dead to all sense of shame. That you, Oscar Wilde, have been the center of a circle of

17

extensive corruption of the most hideous kind among young men, it is impossible to doubt. You shall be imprisoned and kept to hard labor for two years.

(The JUDGE *disappears.* LORD ALFRED *resumes.)*

LORD ALFRED: That's my story. The Ancient Mariner—always retelling his story—that's old Douglas. Summed it up this way once in some lawsuit or other—

(Voice heard over the loudspeaker system.)

LAWYER'S VOICE: Lord Alfred Douglas, is it true you now regret ever having met Oscar Wilde?

VOICE OF MIDDLE-AGED DOUGLAS (*which can be read by* OLD LORD ALFRED): Most profoundly.

LAWYER: Why is that?

DOUGLAS: He was a diabolical scoundrel.

LAWYER: Diabolical? You use the word rhetorically?

DOUGLAS: I use the word advisedly. He exercised a diabolical influence upon all Europe. Oscar Wilde was the greatest force for evil in the past four hundred years.

LAWYER: Since the Protestant Reformation?

DOUGLAS: Since Martin Luther. Precisely.

(The speakers are turned off. LORD ALFRED *resumes.)*

LORD ALFRED: *Mea culpa!* What? I should hate the sin, not the sinner? Just my point, Father. The sin, the heresy, vile pagan cult of which Oscar, alas, was high priest. What do they call it nowadays? Homosexuality, phew, what a word! We just called it being "so." Is he so? Yes, he's so, he's so! Second *mea culpa:* Oscar was converted to this heresy by me—the great, the catastrophic Oscar was all my fault! How'm I going to atone for that one, eh? I'll make a clean breast of it anyway . . . before kicking the bucket . . . . Beginning with that damned poem of mine.

(In a spotlight we see the young ALFRED [BOSIE] DOUGLAS.)*

BOSIE *(reciting):*

Two Loves

I saw two shadows walking on the plain
One sang the joyous love of boy and girl
And wore three chains of roses round his neck
But he that was his comrade wanly sighed.

He wore a purple robe o'erwrought in gold
With the device of a great snake whose breath
Was flame. "Why, sighing, dost thou rove," I asked,
"These pleasant realms?" Said he, "My name is Love."
Then the first shadow quickly turned to me
And cried: "He lieth! For his name is Shame.
My name is Love! I am *true* Love! I fill
The hearts of boy and girl with mutual flame!"
Then said the other shadow: "Have thy will!
I am the love that dare not speak its name."

(BOSIE, the young Douglas, disappears. LORD ALFRED, the old one, resumes.)

LORD ALFRED: Oscar Wilde, yes. Already a famous poet, critic, playwright, and, oh, yes, dandy. Didn't have "class," though. Irishman in London. Outsider, really. Didn't even have money, real money. Taste? In some things. Lovely house in Chelsea. Charming wife, delightful children. . . .

ONE

Oscar Wilde's home, 16 Tite Street, Chelsea. Oscar's library and workroom at present being invaded by his two little boys, CYRIL *and* VYVYAN.* *Although immaculately clad,* OSCAR *is on all fours doing animal imitations—a lion, a wolf, a horse. The boys enter into the game, one taking aim at the lion with an imaginary rifle, one mounting the horse, and so on. There is no sound during this pantomime save giggles of applause and animal noises. At a certain point,* CONSTANCE WILDE *pops her head round the door.*

---

*Since both the boys' lines were read in the New York production by old Lord Alfred, the latter also was given a long introduction to the scene as follows:
Oscar Wilde, yes. Already famous as poet and critic, still more famous as playwright, most famous of all as a character, a dandy. . . . We lords and ladies might have remarked that he did not have class. As an Irishman in London, he was indeed a bit of an outsider. Still, he did have what everyone wants: lovely house, lovely wife, lovely children. Adored being a father, and being made much of *as* a father in family rituals, Christmas, birthday parties. He himself had a birthday at the time my story begins. Also, as we shall find, at the time my story ends. Oh yes, Father Murphy, he always gave a good performance, starting with those animal imitations for Cyril and Vyvyan, his sons, then aged ten and eleven. (The lights have now come up on Oscar poised to tell a story. Constance enters and speaks.)

CONSTANCE: Robbie Ross is on his way up, Oscar. Boys, you must go back to the nursery.

CYRIL: Oh, mamma!

VYVYAN: Daddy was going to tell us a story.

CONSTANCE: It will have to wait now.

OSCAR: Why? Whose birthday is it anyway?

BOTH BOYS: Yours! Yours!

OSCAR: And the boys have given me this gorgeous pair of gloves in the choice of which I detect a fine feminine eye! (*Kisses* CONSTANCE.) On my birthday, I should have what I like most in the world—a distinguished audience! Why not a story for my boys, my wife, and . . . enter on cue, Robbie—my old friend Robbie Ross?

(ROBBIE *has indeed entered during this speech, and is being greeted by* CONSTANCE *and* OSCAR.)

ROBBIE: Aren't you going to shake hands, Cyril? Vyvyan?

CONSTANCE (*making them do so—a stiff, small-boy handshake*): Of course, of course.

OSCAR: Now everybody sit down while I do "The Happy Prince."

(VYVYAN *groans.*)

OSCAR: "The Selfish Giant."

VYVYAN: Again?

OSCAR: But those are my favorites.

CYRIL: Your best are those you make up as you go along.

CONSTANCE: I agree with Cyril. Take off from . . . the events of the day.

OSCAR: I've been reading *Dr. Jekyll and Mr. Hyde.*

ROBBIE: Rewrite it.

CYRIL: Yes. Is that the one about—?

CONSTANCE: Psst.

OSCAR (*slowly, thinking it out as he speaks*): The Strange Case of Mr. Jekyll and Dr. Hyde. Once upon a time, there was a man named Dr. Hyde. He was nice. He was nice looking, and he had a nice time. So the princes of this world hated him, and the chief prince commissioned a biography of Dr. Hyde which would be forbidding enough to act as a warning. The biographer linked niceness with wicked temptations. A nice time amounted to nothing more nor less than giving way to these temptations. So in the biography, Dr. Hyde lost his looks and became rather a fright.

CYRIL: Like Dracula?

OSCAR *(nodding):* "But this will only make people commit suicide en masse," said the chief prince, and he burned the biography saying to the biographer, "Get another idea." "Very well," said the biographer, "Dr. Hyde must have an alter ego."

VYVYAN: A what?

OSCAR: A second personality. Called Mr. Jekyll. We'll simply keep Dr. Hyde from public view. He must live only at night, and have his nice times then. By day, coming out at his front door, only Mr. Jekyll will be seen, and he won't be nice and have a nice time, he will be respectable and have a respectable time. Now, all the crimes of London, all the vices, can be imputed to Dr. Hyde! But Mr. Jekyll resembles the Invisible Man.

CYRIL: He isn't seen?

OSCAR: Because he looks like everyone else, behaves like everyone else, he is as blameless as he is inconspicuous.

VYVYAN: In-con-what?

OSCAR: Mr. Jekyll serves the purpose for which he was intended: to take the attention off Dr. Hyde.

CYRIL: Does it work? The biographer's idea?

OSCAR: What do you think?

VYVYAN: Dr. Hyde will be found out!

OSCAR: How?

VYVYAN: By accident.

OSCAR: Cyril?

CYRIL: Or because he steps out of line.

OSCAR: H'm?

CYRIL: Goes out by day.

OSCAR: Thank you, Cyril. That gives me an ending. As Dr. Hyde emerged from the house at daybreak, a dozen bullets from a dozen different directions converged upon his heart. For the princes of this world had that doorway covered night and day—

CYRIL: No! *Day* and day!

OSCAR: —by the twelve deadliest sharpshooters in the land. What's the matter, Constance?

CONSTANCE (*who has turned pale*): Oscar, I wish you wouldn't.

OSCAR: Wouldn't what, my dear?

CONSTANCE: Such violence! The children. . . .

ROBBIE (*smiling at* CONSTANCE): "Stories are well or badly written, that is all."

CONSTANCE (*shaking her head*): Boys, your father and Robbie want to talk.

OSCAR: Good night, Cyril. Vyvyan.

BOTH BOYS: Happy birthday!

(*As the children leave,* CONSTANCE *has an impulse to say something more but suppresses it and follows them. A longish pause.*)

ROBBIE: Why did you do that?

OSCAR: What?

ROBBIE: Tell that story.

OSCAR (*closing the door*): I'm inspired.

ROBBIE: You're possessed.

OSCAR: No, no, secrecy is the law of our life!

ROBBIE: I wouldn't care about one little story confined to our family circle, if you weren't doing that sort of thing all the time, everywhere. Dropping hints, talking too much, living in a style that is precious close to giving the whole show away.

OSCAR: You are scared, aren't you?

ROBBIE: For you, yes. The rest of us keep the secret.

OSCAR: All I can do to make good is adopt a tone that casts doubt on my veracity.

ROBBIE: The dandy pose.

OSCAR: And what is a dandy?

ROBBIE: You did close the door?

OSCAR (*nodding*): And, as *you* should know, this room is absolutely soundproof.

ROBBIE: A dandy is a euphemism for what our detractors call . . . a sodomite.

OSCAR (*blithely*): No! Dandies are accepted in society, and—what was the word again? (*making a mouth*) —sodomites are not. If one were a sodomite, and, accordingly, had to hide, one might well hide beneath the mask of a dandy: it would be congenial. It would enable one to employ some of the repertoire of the sodomite—the talk, the gestures—without going to prison for it. If a transvestite can keep out of prison by calling himself a female impersonator, he should obviously do so. That one impersonates a female is a guarantee that one is not one. Hence, if a dandy poses as a sodomite, that is a guarantee that he is not one.

ROBBIE: Cyril asked: does it work?

OSCAR: And agreed that it does—till Dr. Hyde steps out of line. Well, take our affair.

(ROBBIE *looks alarmed.*)

OSCAR: The door is closed. You and I were lovers for two years. Does the world know?

ROBBIE: If it does, we should head for North Africa. (*Pause.*) Constance smelled a rat.

OSCAR: The wrong rat. She thinks Dr. Hyde is sleeping with girls.

ROBBIE: Thinks *you* have mistresses? Nonsense.

OSCAR: A lady can hardly think thoughts that, in a lady's world, do not exist. The way you glower at me, Robbie. I'm deceiving my wife like other husbands! Like them, I should feel guilty?

ROBBIE: I just wonder how you can bear it. Not the "guilt." The strain. Of the Double Life.

OSCAR: Without which I would never have been your lover.

ROBBIE: It was when you were my lover that I learned what that strain was—at the breaking point all the time.

OSCAR: I didn't break.

ROBBIE: You haven't reached forty.

OSCAR: You want me to be you, dear boy. To be simply "so."

ROBBIE: There is something—impertinent—I want to tell you. You can hurl it—or me—through the window. . . .

OSCAR: Dear boy, I abhor physical exercise—

ROBBIE: I was your lover—and what I am now is even more—

OSCAR: The friend of friends—

ROBBIE: It's high time I got up my courage and said Oscar, you *are* "so." *Simply* so. Not one of "them." One of us. (*Pause.*) Now kill me.

OSCAR: I adore boys. But, my dear, dear, dear, Robbie, I also adore girls. Ladies. Even women. Am I not a father?

ROBBIE: May I be outrageous?

OSCAR: Outrage, darling, is my element.

ROBBIE: I want to ask an indiscreet question.

OSCAR: Answers are sometimes indiscreet; questions, never.

ROBBIE: When did you last sleep with your wife?

OSCAR: A question never asked before in Victorian England!

ROBBIE: But outrage is your element.

OSCAR: Who sleeps with his wife? Marriage, *mon cher*, is a pretext for adultery.

ROBBIE: Who is your mistress then?

OSCAR: All England is my mistress, not to bore you with my exploits in North America. I say yes to both continents and both sexes. I wish to experience everything. To ingest, as my friend Walt Whitman might put it, the universe.

ROBBIE: You wish to evade the issue.

OSCAR: Oh, you are *bright*, Robbie Ross, there is a grain of truth in what you say. But where does truth get you, King Oedipus?

ROBBIE: To tragedy.

OSCAR: Now, who and what is Oscar Wilde?

ROBBIE: You want me to say: a master of comedy.

OSCAR: Better than having my eyes put out! Through evasion of the issue to a happy ending—what a sound philosophy! Supposing I don't sleep with Constance. Supposing she has no—female rivals. For me Sodom is a place to visit, not to inhabit.

ROBBIE: A place to visit—with Lord Alfred Douglas?

OSCAR: Oh, I haven't seen Bosie—

ROBBIE: That's his nickname?

OSCAR: It means boysie, little boy, isn't that enchanting? I haven't seen him for months—

ROBBIE: You were running after him at Oxford a year ago!

OSCAR (*nodding*): And now he has sent me a poem which is a portent. I feel I'm on the brink of a Really Tremendous Affair.

ROBBIE: Look out for his father.

OSCAR: I already have.

ROBBIE: You've met?

OSCAR: Charmed the hind legs off him.

ROBBIE: A very eccentric chap. Fanatical atheist, incidentally.

OSCAR: He adored what *I* had to say about God! But let me show you the poem.

(OSCAR *produces it from a pocket. As* ROBBIE *starts to read it aloud, they disappear.*)

ROBBIE: "Two Loves. . . ."

(LORD ALFRED *resumes.*)

LORD ALFRED: The Scarlet Marquess—my father, eighth Marquess of Queensberry. Famous for the Queensberry rules of boxing. Famous for breaking the rules by which Queensberrys live. Famous for a bout with Oscar Wilde which left both contestants dead in the ring. It ended in death. It had begun in death: My brother's. My eldest brother—Drumlanrig—heir to the Queensberry title and secretary to none other than . . . Lord Rosebery. It was in all the papers: Dead at Twenty-seven. A hunting gun that went off accidentally . . . I can see Drumlanrig's funeral now. The carriages in the rain. Mother avoiding Father. And when the ceremony was over, Father pulling me to one side in the church to say—

TWO

In a side aisle of a church, BOSIE *is cornered by his father.*

QUEENSBERRY: You have been making the acquaintance of Mr. Oscar Wilde!

BOSIE: So have you. I introduced him to *you* a year ago at the Café Royal.

QUEENSBERRY: It's *that* Mr. Wilde?

BOSIE: When he found you were an atheist, he mounted a full-scale defense of God, Christianity, the Catholic Church, the whole shebang.

QUEENSBERRY: H'm! Well, now I have to warn you against him.

BOSIE: I don't understand.

QUEENSBERRY: Advise you . . . never to be seen with him.

BOSIE: That's absurd.

QUEENSBERRY: Maybe. Maybe not. It's just not worth taking chances.

BOSIE: Chances on what?

QUEENSBERRY (*hesitant*): On trouble . . . scandal.

BOSIE (*coldly*): I have no idea what you mean.

QUEENSBERRY (*bluntly*): There are rumors about him.

BOSIE (*on his high horse*): And for that he's to be ostracized?

QUEENSBERRY (*hating the big word*): Ostracized, my foot. I'm just saying: a family like ours can't afford another scandal.

BOSIE: Another?

(QUEENSBERRY *stammers, but no words come out.*)

BOSIE (*cuttingly*): Oh, you mean your own carryings-on with assorted young females of plebeian background!

QUEENSBERRY (*has an impulse to punch his son but lowers his raised fist*): It's not for me I speak. It's for the family. Don't stir up a hornet's nest by asking for details. A nod should be as good as a wink.

BOSIE: In a family as close and loving as ours!

QUEENSBERRY: A Douglas is still a Douglas!

BOSIE: Mr. Wilde has invited this Douglas to supper next Tuesday. And this Douglas has accepted.

QUEENSBERRY (*trying to speak "officially" now*): Bosie, as the head of the family, I must report to you my decision that all contact between us and this man Wilde is to end forthwith.

BOSIE (*mimicking the official tone*): Then I must report back that I am a big boy now and dine with whom *I* choose!

QUEENSBERRY (*quivering with contained rage*): No!

BOSIE (*ditto*): Yes!

QUEENSBERRY: Oh, you are willful!

BOSIE: I get it from you.

(Fearing that people will hear, QUEENSBERRY *opens a nearby door and drags* BOSIE *into a small vestry room.* QUEENSBERRY *has now got a grip upon himself.)*

QUEENSBERRY: I didn't want to say anything. It's wrong that I have to. But you won't take a hint.

BOSIE: Not that kind of hint.

QUEENSBERRY: Drumlanrig's death. (*Slowly, dully.*) Was *not* an accident.

BOSIE (*very much taken aback*): Wha-a-t?

QUEENSBERRY: The gun did not "go off accidentally."

BOSIE *(with a slow intake of breath)*: He shot himself? Why, in God's name—?

QUEENSBERRY: So Rosebery can be prime minister.

BOSIE: What?

QUEENSBERRY: Which he will be. If the Liberals win the election. But not if he is sleeping with your brother.

BOSIE: My brother was only his secretary, for God's sake—

QUEENSBERRY: In London, maybe. But how about Rosebery's retreat in Germany?

BOSIE: I don't know about such things.

QUEENSBERRY: I do. And I followed them there. With a dog whip in my trunk.

BOSIE: So you hounded him to his death.

QUEENSBERRY: The whip was for Rosebery. I was going to rescue my son from his clutches.

BOSIE: Only he rescued himself . . . is that it?—he removed himself from the scene so Lord Rosebery could move to number ten Downing Street. Is that it?

QUEENSBERRY: Potential blackmailers in attendance. A national scandal in the making.

BOSIE: Were they lovers, actually?

QUEENSBERRY (*spits*): That is no word for two red-blooded men.

BOSIE (*pertly*): Oh, you don't know about such things.

QUEENSBERRY: At least you will appreciate why our family is not ready for another scandal of that sort.

BOSIE: Mr. Wilde is not my lover.

QUEENSBERRY (*again reacting to the word*): Please.

BOSIE: I hardly know Mr. Wilde.

QUEENSBERRY: Tell me on your word of honor as a gentleman, as a Douglas, that Mr. Wilde is definitely not one of "those."

BOSIE (*blustering*): Mr. Wilde is a husband and a father!

QUEENSBERRY (*persisting*): Then give me your word.

BOSIE: It's not fair. A gentleman does not rat on friends—

QUEENSBERRY: You are not giving me your word.

BOSIE: I give you my word, I don't know.

QUEENSBERRY: Think I never heard the stories about you?

BOSIE (*unprepared for this, flushing*): What do you mean?

QUEENSBERRY: Even if I'd never had anyone keep an eye on you—

BOSIE: You've had people keeping an eye on me?

QUEENSBERRY: I receive a steady flow of anonymous letters—

BOSIE: And you accept anonymous letters as gospel?

QUEENSBERRY: Your carryings-on at Winchester meant nothing to me. Everyone does it. Oxford is something else. At Oxford, everyone stops doing it. But you didn't.

BOSIE (*hysterically*): If you're so sure I've gone to the dogs—

QUEENSBERRY: I will say nothing more about what you may do— privately. But when it's public, it's family business. Suppose we knew only one thing about Mr. Oscar Wilde, and it was that he lives in the flare and blare of publicity. It would suffice to tell us: keep away. We are not shopkeepers fascinated with other people's morals. We are noblemen interested in our own . . . honor.

BOSIE (*sobbing*): There's nothing dishonorable about Mr. Wilde!

QUEENSBERRY: That's as may be. Tarnish the Queensberry honor, and you'll have me to reckon with. The carriages are waiting.

(They disappear. LORD ALFRED *resumes.)*

LORD ALFRED: Oscar had *not* invited me to supper. I now invited him and slipped a copy of "Two Loves"—that damned poem—into the envelope. Oscar responded with a letter we would never hear the end of.

(OSCAR is seen, reciting.)

OSCAR: My own boy, your poem is quite lovely, and it is a marvel that those red, rose-leaf lips of yours should have been made no less for music of song than for madness of kisses. Your slim gilt soul walks between passion and poetry. I know Hyacinthus, whom Apollo loved so madly, was you in Greek days. Always with undying love, yours, Oscar.

(OSCAR disappears, and LORD ALFRED resumes.)

LORD ALFRED: The supper was good, Father, even in my opinion. Oscar was always satisfied as long as a meal cost a lot. Then followed—shall we say A Night With Oscar Wilde? At the Mitre Hotel, Oxford.

THREE

A bedroom in the Mitre Hotel, Oxford, though we cannot yet see it since pitch darkness reigns. We hear a clock striking three AM.

BOSIE'S VOICE (*out of the darkness*): Do you realize we've been naked together for two solid hours, and nothing has happened?

OSCAR'S VOICE (*from same*): You've been groping about quite a lot.

BOSIE: And you haven't?

OSCAR: I *had* to learn if you ever. . . .

BOSIE: Rose to the occasion? Never did. Had to learn if you . . . . *You* never did. What *is* the matter with us?

OSCAR: The balloon of balloons did not inflate. Which alone is sufficient grounds for divorce. Yes, even for Catholics.

BOSIE: Annulment!

OSCAR: That's the word. The Vatican will give us an annulment.

BOSIE: Me and Catherine of Aragon.

OSCAR: Oh, I could have you beheaded instead.

BOSIE: That was Anne Boleyn.

OSCAR: Never did know one queen from another.

(He is in a dressing gown now and has lit the gas. BOSIE *simply uses the eiderdown as his robe.)*

BOSIE: *Post coitum omne animal triste!*

OSCAR: "Sex makes the best of us a little sad!"

BOSIE: And lack of sex makes the worst of us a little sadder.

OSCAR: I have something to tell you. I prefer young boys.

BOSIE: Of the criminal classes?

OSCAR: Let us say from the ample bosom of the people.

BOSIE: Bayswater, not Mayfair.

OSCAR: Are you mocking me, Bosie? Can't you see anything good about an old queen who likes to merge with her people?

BOSIE: *Au contraire.* I can admit—now you have preceded me—that my preference is also for the younger generation and the lower classes.

OSCAR: Younger than you?!

BOSIE: Oh much, much. As near the cradle as possible.

OSCAR: But that's illegal, my dear Bosie! And is not civilization based on law?

BOSIE: Anything that's any fun is *against* the law. Even groping middle-aged men.

OSCAR: I was born in fifty-six!

BOSIE: Fifty-four.

OSCAR (*indignant*): You've been rummaging in Dublin birth records!

BOSIE: I'm a student of Oscar Wilde, a lady who lies about her age.

OSCAR: How long have you been at your illegalities? At your age, I was a virgin.

BOSIE: You didn't go to Winchester.

OSCAR: Winchester? So you've had the upper classes too?

BOSIE: After which I worked my way down the social ladder.

OSCAR: So at the tender age of—how old are you?

BOSIE: Twelve—

OSCAR: You've had all England! No wonder Britain is reaching out to Egypt, Africa, India! The South Seas await the arrival of Bosie Douglas with quivering—

BOSIE: Sphincters.

OSCAR: Is that the plural of Sphinx?

BOSIE: You are boy hungry.

OSCAR: After a night with you, darling, *naturellement*.

BOSIE: Let me be your procurer.

OSCAR: Procurator? Of Sodom and Gomorrah?

BOSIE: Find boys for you.

OSCAR: Your discards?

BOSIE: Fascinating female impersonators.

OSCAR: My own mother is one.

BOSIE: The best of the lot is Arthur Marling. He'll perform at Alfred Taylor's place tomorrow night.

OSCAR: Not Alfred Taylor the—

BOSIE: Exactly. On Little College Street.

OSCAR: I have a very important engagement tomorrow night.

BOSIE: No!

OSCAR: Seeing Miss Arthur Marling in the company of Lord Alfred Douglas.

BOSIE: Thank you. Now, about you and me—

OSCAR: The procurer and the procured for—

BOSIE: I begin to see how it will work out.

OSCAR: It will work out?

BOSIE: Yes. If we keep our trousers on.

OSCAR: At all times?

BOSIE: Just when we are alone together.

OSCAR: *How* will it work out?

BOSIE: Turning elsewhere to satisfy the body's needs, we shall turn to each other—

OSCAR: Our trousers tightly buttoned up—

BOSIE: In quest of the things of the spirit.

OSCAR: Lust with others? But for us—love?

BOSIE: Exactly.

OSCAR: My God, it sounds just like marriage!

BOSIE: Not a bit. The married hate each other. Look at my parents.

OSCAR: Look at *my* parents. They adored each other. From his or her separate bedroom.

BOSIE: And speaking of parents, we'll be father and son, too.

OSCAR: You'll be my father?

BOSIE: You'll be mine. The one I never had.

OSCAR: Thought he was still alive and kicking.

BOSIE: Kicking me. That's the trouble.

OSCAR: You have an irresistible bottom.

BOSIE: What did you say of those who rise at dawn, sound their hunting horns, and gallop off after foxes?

OSCAR: Nothing. My outdoor sport is chess in sidewalk cafés.

BOSIE: You called them "the unspeakable in search of the uneatable." (*With mock hauteur:*) My father, sir, is a master of hounds.

OSCAR: That's nothing. My father—a Dublin doctor—was in court for seducing a patient with the aid of chloroform.

BOSIE: I prefer your father to mine! But I'll take your father's son.

OSCAR: What do you see in him? Even at the customs in New York, he had nothing to declare but his genius!

BOSIE: So I've been to bed with a genius?

OSCAR: He didn't get you pregnant.

BOSIE: Oh but he did! With poetry! I'm going to be a great poet!

OSCAR (*declaiming*): "With the device of a great snake whose breath is flame!"

BOSIE: Oscar Wilde, you are the most wonderful man I have ever met. Never mind that I don't lust for you. I am beginning to worship you.

OSCAR: Pray continue. I adore being adored.

BOSIE: What do you see in *me*?

OSCAR: Nothing! Sorry—everything. You have the two things I value most.

BOSIE: Youth and beauty?

OSCAR: "Beauty *is* youth; youth, beauty. That is all we know on earth and all we need to know."

BOSIE: Not true. We need to know what love is.

OSCAR: Why?

BOSIE: I know what lust is. So, when I lust, I know what I'm doing. If

I'm going to love you, I need to know what I'll be doing. Shall we get some sleep now?

OSCAR: You're going to love me? In spite of . . . ?

BOSIE: Oh yes. Who cares about . . . ?

OSCAR: Well said. I think I'm going to love you too.

BOSIE: So . . . we shall find out what love is. Take your dressing gown off.

OSCAR: We'll find out what love is—if it kills us!

(They disappear, and LORD ALFRED *resumes.)*

LORD ALFRED: It did kill *him*, Father Murphy, and would have killed me, had I not seen the light, our holy Catholic light. Alfred Taylor's place, what a place it was! No windows—unless there was a window tucked away somewhere behind the thick pseudo-Turkish tapestries. Oh yes, we went, Oscar and I, would that we hadn't! For it was there that we met . . . well, just about everyone, the whole gang. Even someone I'd picked up at a nearby pub turned out to be one of the gang. I can see myself now, slipping into the back room to, shall we say, practice unnatural vice? I can see Charlie Parker—a gentleman's valet without a gentleman—sitting hopefully beside an empty chair. I can see Oscar having a good giggle with Arthur Marling, a transvestite who, in seeking fame, had only found a modest notoriety.

FOUR

(The lights have come up on these people, one by one, as they are named, and we are now in Alfred Taylor's place. Two rooms. One, a rather simple bedroom, nothing much more there but a large mattress, the other far more of a "production" in tacky Oriental vein, Chinese-y bric-a-brac all around, with a few Turkish motifs mixed in, such as a meerschaum on the floor and heavy carpeting to invite sitting cross-legged or reclining on the floor. If there were windows, one cannot tell where they would be, as the walls are heavily draped in cheap tapestries. Piano and small platform at the back permit this room to do duty also as a miniature theater. As the lights come up, BOSIE *is dimly seen making love with the new acquaintance, while, in fuller lighting,* OSCAR, *propped on cushions, is talking with* ARTHUR MARLING, *a London street urchin, at present dressed as such, very cute, completely unaffected in speech. There is a small table nearby, a single young man—an obvious*

"renter"—sitting at it, drinking, and waiting for someone to occupy a vacant chair that is at his side. Other such people are imagined to be present—beyond the fourth wall.

ARTHUR: So you are . . . a famous writer, Mr. Oscar?

OSCAR (*enjoying himself*): I have a . . . select circle of admirers.

ARTHUR: Are they *all* queer?

OSCAR: I wonder now. Isn't the Prince of Wales a womanizer?

ARTHUR: Is 'e one of your admirers?

OSCAR: Worships the ground I stand on!

ARTHUR: I'd 'eard about 'is late lamented son.

OSCAR: The Duke of Clarence?

ARTHUR: Everyone said 'e was queer. And heir to the throne of England! Jus' think, with him on the throne, we might all 'ave been made lords and ladies, an' I'd've been doin' a command performance at Buckingham Palace! I may make it yet to the 'ouse of Lawds.

OSCAR: So you're a famous actor, Mr. Arthur?

ARTHUR: I've performed for a prime minister.

OSCAR: Mr. Gladstone, I presume?

ARTHUR: Naow!

OSCAR (*hopefully*): Disraeli?

ARTHUR: 'Ow old d'you think I am?

OSCAR: I give up.

ARTHUR (*triumphantly*): Becoz—it's a *future* prime minister.

OSCAR: My heavens, you're a prophet, Arthur! Who?

ARTHUR; My lips is sealed, so 'elp me Gawd.

OSCAR: Give me a hint.

ARTHUR: I gave you one: 'ouse of Lawds.

OSCAR: Oh. Oh! Lord Rosebery?

ARTHUR (*grinning*): Turn around and don't look till I tell you.

(The lights dim a little on them and brighten a little on BOSIE *and friend, undressed.)*

BOSIE: Money? You want money for this? I had no idea you were a renter!

FRIEND: Out o' work at present. Just thought you'd like to 'elp a poor young feller out. A noble lawd like you. You *are* Lawd Alfred Douglas, ain't ya?

BOSIE: And what is your name?

FRIEND: Freddy Wood. If you don't propose to pay, we shall 'ave to refer this to Mr. Taylor when he returns.

BOSIE: Who's Taylor? Oh, yes. He's your pimp, isn't he?

FREDDY: Your language, me lawd!

BOSIE: Ponce?

FREDDY: Fancy man.

BOSIE: Anyway he's not here.

FREDDY (*turning nasty and placing his back against the door to the other room*): Hey, if you don't pay up, Mister Noble Lawd, I'm going to scream the 'ouse down!

BOSIE: Don't you do any such thing. The landlady would call the police.

FREDDY: Quite.

BOSIE: I've no money on me.

FREDDY: Oh, Oh! Then what are we goin' to do about it?

BOSIE: Let's see. I was wearing one of my flashier suits, would you like it?

FREDDY: Are you goin' to go 'ome naked?

BOSIE: I'll wear your clothes. Make a lark of it.

(They put on each other's clothes as they continue talking.)

BOSIE: Oscar will laugh his head off.

FREDDY: 'oo's Oscar?

BOSIE: Oscar Wilde. My friend in there.

FREDDY: Is 'e a lawd too?

BOSIE: He's a genius.

FREDDY: Some sort o' critter that comes out of a bottle?

BOSIE: A poet! An artist!

FREDDY: Rich?

BOSIE: He's above riches. But the rich flock to see his plays.

FREDDY: An' 'e don't get paid?

BOSIE: He gets paid quite handsomely. Let me help you with that cravat.

(As they finish dressing, the lights switch again, and we look at OSCAR and ARTHUR. ARTHUR has finished dressing and, in black and gold finery, looks like an authentic pretty girl, not a freak of nature.)

ARTHUR: You may turn around now, Mr. Oscar.

OSCAR (*having done so*): "What heavenly vision steals upon my sight?" Arthur, my pet, you are enough to re-arouse my interest in girls!

ARTHUR: Now I'm goin' to sing for you. That's my act.

OSCAR: You're a famous prima donna, too? Do you like your work, Arthur?

ARTHUR: More than anything in the world.

OSCAR: Even sex?

ARTHUR: Oh, Mr. Oscar, for me this *is* sex. Billy!

(The pianist, BILLY, strikes up. ARTHUR sings.)

Will you love me in December as you do in May?
Will you love me in the good old-fashioned way?
When my hair has all turned gray
Will you kiss me then and say
That you love me in December as you do in May?*

(BOSIE and FREDDY have now finished dressing. They emerge from the bedroom to join OSCAR and CHARLIE PARKER—the silent boy at the table—in the applause for ARTHUR.)

OSCAR: Arthur, you are the Queen of Little College Street! Who are your two princesses?

BOSIE (*attempting FREDDY'S accent*): 'Ello, Mister Toff. My oi toss you off? Freddy Wood, at your service!

FREDDY: An' I'm dear lil—what was the name?

BOSIE: Bosie.

---

* In the New York production this bit of the song did not provide enough time for Bosie and Freddy to finish dressing, so more of it was sung.

FREDDY: Bosie. Will you love me in December as you do in May?

(He throws OSCAR *a kiss.)*

OSCAR: Definitely! My God, all three of you are someone else!

ARTHUR: Isn't it the only way?

BOSIE: The truth of masks, the need of lies, Oscar dear, your theory!

OSCAR: I tell everyone: be yourself!

BOSIE: No one obeys. Not even you.

OSCAR: Touché.

ARTHUR: Bosie, sit down with Mr. Oscar while Freddy and Charlie and me do our song and dance.

(With OSCAR *and* BOSIE *as his audience,* ARTHUR *sings a verse of "Ta Ra Ra Boom De Ay."* CHARLIE *and* FREDDY *join in the refrain and dance. When the music and dancing are at their height, a long ring at the doorbell. Music and dancing stop.)*

ARTHUR: Freddy, see who that is. (*As* FREDDY *exits to the hallway,* ARTHUR *whispers to* BOSIE.) Get Mr. Oscar out by the back door, it's a raid.

BOSIE: How d'you know?

ARTHUR: I know the ring.

OSCAR: What about you, Arthur?

ARTHUR: Can you get some money to us? For a lawyer?

OSCAR: Of course.

ARTHUR: Now skedaddle.

BOSIE: Oscar, come.

(He pulls OSCAR *out through the other room. At the same time, a* PLAINCLOTHES OFFICER *enters, dragging* FREDDY *with him. Two uniformed constables place themselves in the doorway.)*

PLAINCLOTHESMAN (*looking round*): Ancient bloody Rome. Ancient bloody Babylon. 'ello. (*Walks over and lifts up the cloth on the little table. The renter who had been at the table is now hiding under it.*) 'oo are you?

CHARLIE: Charlie Parker. Gentleman's valet.

PLAINCLOTHESMAN: Lookin' for your gentleman, eh? (*His eyes light on* ARTHUR.) You! Call yourself a man?

ARTHUR (*trying in vain to take it light*): Well, er, not often, officer! (*Giggles.*)

PLAINCLOTHESMAN: No, eh? (*He tears* ARTHUR's *dress from the neck down to the knee.* ARTHUR *is wearing nothing underneath.*) Then where's your boobs eh? Hey, and what may that be stuck in the middle of your Mount of Venus? (*Turning to the two coppers.*) Put some decent clothes on 'im and bring 'im along. Bring 'em all along.

(*They disappear.* LORD ALFRED *resumes.*)

LORD ALFRED: Eighteen arrests. More port, Father Murphy? Oscar slipped Arthur Marling a few pounds for a lawyer. After two days in jail, all eighteen were released for lack of evidence. That evening, when Oscar returned with Bosie to his rooms in the Savoy Hotel, a certain person was waiting for them.

FIVE

The Savoy. On a chair, FREDDY WOOD. *Enter* OSCAR *with* BOSIE.

BOSIE: Freddy Wood! And still in my suit!

FREDDY: When was there a chance to change it? I've come 'ere straight from—

BOSIE: Aren't you going to thank Mr. Wilde for getting you out?

FREDDY: Oh, from the bottom of me 'eart.

OSCAR: Don't mention it, Mr. Wood. But do mention how you got in. You have the key to my suite at the Savoy?

FREDDY: Oi 'ave connections on the staff.

OSCAR: Oh. I wish *I* had. May one also ask what in God's name you want?

FREDDY: Well nah, that I'll 'ave to explain to Lawd Alfred alone.

BOSIE: Nonsense. Explain away!

FREDDY: I'm embarrassed.

BOSIE: You *could* just leave.

FREDDY: Oh no, I 'ave a tale to tell.

OSCAR: I adore tales.

FREDDY: You may not adore this one.

BOSIE: Sit down, Freddy.

FREDDY (*settling into a chair*): Thanks. H'm. Well, Lord Alfred, I'll be frank with you. When you gave me this 'ere suit, the pockets wasn't empty. Money? Naow. Letters. From Mr. Wilde 'ere to your noble self.

OSCAR (*flushing*): Good God, Bosie, is this how you treat *our* correspondence? Throwing it away with your old clothes?! (*Furious now:*) Don't you realize my letters are *literature*? Don't you realize—

BOSIE: Oh, shut up, Oscar (*pointing to* FREDDY'S *immaculate get up*). Those are not old clothes! Freddy stripped them from me at the point of a gun!

OSCAR: The point of a penis.

BOSIE: Anyway, your letters aren't lost, they're found, aren't they, Freddy?

FREDDY: Well nah, some of the stuff *in* these letters—

BOSIE: Now, Freddy, a gentleman does not read other people's letters!

FREDDY: I'm not a gentleman. A bad egg, that's me. And deep in debt right now. (*He coughs.*) Readin' these letters and makin' a note they come from a genie, I take 'em to some friends of mine—I thought they was friends—name of Cliburn and Allen, experts in (*darkly*) that sort of thing.

BOSIE: What sort of thing?

FREDDY: Professional "appraisers." Talked of just a couple of quid till they come to *one* letter. "That's 'ot," said Cliburn. "Red 'ot," says Allen, "thirty quid!"

BOSIE: But instead you have come here like an honest lad to return lost property. You shall have a reward! (*Silence.*) H'm?

FREDDY: Well, no, I don't 'ave the letters on me. Fact is Cliburn and Allen turned on me, threatened me somethin' awful . . . unless . . . I . . . .

BOSIE: Yes? Yes?

FREDDY: Get the thirty pound from you. In return for the letters.

BOSIE: Oh. Oh! Oscar, we've been had.

OSCAR: By the way, Mr. Wood, which was the letter your friends—or enemies—Cliburn and Allen—described as 'ot, red 'ot? May I see it?

FREDDY (*stopping his hand from completing the journey to his inside pocket*): I think I remember 'ow it starts. Yes, um, "My own boy, your poem is quite lovely, and it is a marvel that those red, rose-leaf lips of yours . . . ."

OSCAR: Stop! Bosie, my dear, Mr. Wood and I wish to be alone together!

FREDDY (*expostulating*): I didn't say—

OSCAR: Bosie?

BOSIE (*taken aback, but conceding*): Very well. (*He leaves the room.*)

OSCAR: Lord Alfred, you see, is a gentleman and young. I am neither, and I recognize in you an experienced, not unskillful, and probably quite incurable, liar.

FREDDY: Don't follow you, Mr. Wilde, sir.

OSCAR: Perfect example of the simple lie! It was impossible to fail to follow me. I said you were a liar. You replied that you did not follow me.

FREDDY: You're too clever for the likes o' me, Mr. Wilde.

OSCAR: Do Cliburn and Allen exist? If they do, do they have my letter? Did they ever? Come on, Freddy! May I call you Freddy? Tell me lies about Cliburn and Allen!

FREDDY: Well now, Mr. Wilde—

OSCAR: You may call me Oscar.

FREDDY: Well, as one non-gennleman to another, Hosker, wot does it matter to you where the thirty quid goes?

OSCAR (*whistles*): Good. Very good, Freddy. You are now prepared to drop Cliburn and Allen and agree with me that the thirty pounds are intended for the pockets of a single friend of theirs, if they exist, Mr. Freddy Wood.

FREDDY (*carefully*): I say again, wot does it matter to you where the thirty quid goes?

OSCAR: It's not where, dear, it's what. A Wilde—one of the Wildes of Ireland—cannot pay BLACKMAIL.

(*The word hangs in the air, then:*)

FREDDY: 'Ow about a Douglas o' Scotland?

OSCAR: Ireland and Scotland stand together against blackmail.

FREDDY (*crisply*): Then we shall 'ave to make these letters public!

OSCAR: We?

FREDDY: Cliburn and Allen—

OSCAR: They don't exist!

FREDDY: I shall give the letters to *The Times*.

OSCAR: Which couldn't print them.

FREDDY: I shall send them to the Queen—

OSCAR: Who will never receive them—

FREDDY: Oh, we'll find somebody. Let's think now—

OSCAR: Freddy . . . .

FREDDY: Yeh?

OSCAR: Freddy, did anyone ever tell you you were very attractive?

FREDDY (*thrown, this time*): Wot?

OSCAR: I didn't say you were a nice boy. You're wicked. You're dangerous. That's what's so exciting. Freddy, I want to go to bed with you.

FREDDY: You're coddin'.

OSCAR: "Coddin'"?

FREDDY: Wait a minute. Do you know the price of a steamship ticket to the good ol' USA?

OSCAR: I should. I've been there twice.

FREDDY: Not first class!

OSCAR: Well, the least one could do it for would be . . . by George, I have it—thirty pounds! You are planning to leave the country? What have you done, Freddy, murdered your grandmother?

FREDDY: I down't 'ave to answer that.

OSCAR: Suffice it that you are in trouble with the law?

FREDDY: Quite.

OSCAR: And when would you be leaving?

FREDDY: The next boat leaves ten days from now. (*Silence.* FREDDY *looks at* OSCAR.)

OSCAR: "Freddy gives Oscar significant look."

FREDDY (*with sudden cunning*): There is a way of satisfying both parties.

OSCAR: Is there?

FREDDY: I get thirty quid. You get me. An' no blackmail in the picture.

OSCAR: Just some rather expensive whoring.

FREDDY: I'll call on you—three times.

OSCAR: Ten pounds a tumble, eh? Queen Victoria would do it for less.

FREDDY: Four times. Final offer! Goin', goin' . . . .

OSCAR: You are so *bad*, Freddy. Of course, I could take you despite that fact.

FREDDY: You're not goin' to?

OSCAR: No, I'll take you *because of* that fact.

FREDDY: Honest?

OSCAR: Honest! "Evil, be thou my good!"

FREDDY: I don't understand.

OSCAR: That's all right. Hand over the letters.

FREDDY: What?

OSCAR: The letters are in your pocket. Hand them over.

FREDDY: H'm. I hand over the letters. You hand over the thirty quid.

OSCAR: I will. After our last . . . rendezvous.

FREDDY: Then that's when you'll get the letters.

OSCAR: H'm. What's to stop you, in the meanwhile, having copies made?

FREDDY: What use are they to me in America?

OSCAR: But if you left them with Cliburn and Allen?

FREDDY: I have some news for you.

OSCAR: H'm?

FREDDY: You were right. Cliburn and Allen don't exist.

OSCAR: H'm. Well, thank you, Freddy. H'm. Meet me Monday at eight.

FREDDY (*at the door*): Where?

OSCAR: The Florence Restaurant on Rupert Street. (*He shows* FREDDY *out.* BOSIE *reenters.*) You listened at the keyhole?

BOSIE: Of course.

OSCAR: How did I do?

BOSIE: You were robbed. The *pope* would do it for less.

OSCAR: I was buying my letters back.

BOSIE: What if Wood has played the joker in the liar's pack? The truth. Suppose Cliburn and Allen do exist.

OSCAR: We would get blackmailed *again*. Oh, dear! I wonder what Cliburn and Allen are like in bed.

(They disappear. LORD ALFRED *resumes.)*

LORD ALFRED: Well may you shake your head, Father, but at that time Oscar was the toast of the town. Every critic quoted his quips, every newspaper ran his photograph, not to mention the cartoons, oh, the cartoons! On top of the world, the high priest of the Homo Heresy could come on stage after the opening night of *Lady Windermere's Fan*—lighted cigarette in hand, and ladies present!— and talk down to the finest flower of London high society.

(OSCAR is seen, cigarette in hand, making a curtain speech.)

OSCAR: I have enjoyed this evening *immensely*. The actors have given us a *charming* rendering of a *delightful* play, and your appreciation has been *most* intelligent. I congratulate you on the *great* success of your performance, which persuades me that you think *almost* as highly of the play as I do myself.

(He disappears. LORD ALFRED *resumes.)*

LORD ALFRED: The cigarette, ugh! But, Father, Oscar got away even with that. Spent his life finding out what he could get away with! What do they call it—tragic rashness? But oh dear, *mea culpa, mea maxima culpa*, Bosie Douglas did not restrain him.

SIX

16 Tite Street. OSCAR, *sitting in the library with* BOSIE, *over wine.*

BOSIE: So Freddy left?

OSCAR: And must by now have reached the Land of Libertines.

BOSIE: You have rid us of our blackmailer—and in fine Uranian style!

OSCAR: What was the word?

BOSIE: Uranian.

OSCAR: The love that dare not speak its name?

BOSIE: Only now . . . we're beginning to dare!

OSCAR: If its name is Urania, no one will be much the wiser!

BOSIE: You're laughing at me. I prate of a new movement in history. You *are* that movement. Have been ever since—was it in '81?—you "walked down Piccadilly with a poppy or a lily in your medieval hand."

OSCAR: Only I didn't. Anyone could do that. The hard thing is to convince the world you did when you didn't.

BOSIE: Who but one of "us" would wish to convince the world of a thing like that?

OSCAR: You are leading up to something.

BOSIE: A question. Are you ready for the next step?

OSCAR: No. For me the last step but one is always one step too many. What *is* the next step?

BOSIE: When some distinguished Uranian comes right out with it— says, Yes, he is, and he's not ashamed of it either.

OSCAR: A little letter to *The Times*. "You all believe I'm practicing hideous unmentionable vices, the worst offences in the statute book, the most monstrous of sins against nature. I am. Join me Saturday at combined orgy and black mass. Your loving sister, Oscar Wilde."

BOSIE: Don't you think the day will come?

OSCAR: The Kingdom of Sod is not at hand! And you can keep your old cross and the rusty nails for somebody other than yours truly!

BOSIE: I expect the world of you.

OSCAR: Don't expect a Uranian world of me, I'm only a part time Uranian!

BOSIE: What do you expect from . . . that part of your time?

OSCAR: Oh, to dine with beautiful boys of bad character. They are gilded snakes and make me feel I'm a snake charmer! I lure the cobra! Make it spread its hood and sway to and fro in the air!

BOSIE: What about a snake's poison?

OSCAR: Just part of its perfection! I find these young scoundrels rather wonderful in their infamous war against life. Entertaining them can be an astounding adventure. It's like—feasting with panthers!

BOSIE: I can't wait to show you Algiers.

OSCAR: You really think I'll like it?

BOSIE: You'll love it!

OSCAR: Following your cock?

BOSIE: Oscar!

OSCAR: I can be coarse!

BOSIE: You're telling me I can be selfish—dragging *you* to Africa because *I* want to go.

OSCAR: And, of course, you're not?

BOSIE: No. My greatest pleasure is hearing someone say as we enter the Café Royal, "There goes Oscar Wilde with his boy."

OSCAR: Then I apologize.

BOSIE: And so do I.

(They embrace. A knock at the door. They pull apart.)

MANSERVANT (*entering*): A telegram for you, Lord Alfred. (*He hands it over and leaves.*)

BOSIE (*opening it*): My father's in London. Says he must see me *at once.* (*Shows telegram to* OSCAR.)

OSCAR: I'll fetch your coat. (*Wheels* BOSIE *around, kisses him.*) By the time you get back, I'll be reconciled to the African trip. (*The lights go down on a delighted smile from* BOSIE.)

SEVEN

LORD QUEENSBERRY'*s London flat. Hunting trophies. Photographs of boxers.* QUEENSBERRY, *seated with two small men who might be bookies by the look of them—sportily dressed, lower-class types.*

BOSIE (*entering*): Hullo, father. Oh, I thought you were alone.

QUEENSBERRY (*pointing to each little man in turn*): This is Mr. Cliburn, Bosie. This is Mr. Allen. (*The two little men have got up to bow.*)

BOSIE: Cliburn and—?

ONE OF THEM: Allen, sir, at your service.

BOSIE (*faintly*): So you exist.

QUEENSBERRY (*not catching this*): You've met?

BOSIE: No, no. Let's say, their fame goes before them.

THE OTHER LITTLE MAN: We're in business together.

BOSIE: Yes. And what business *is* that?

(*The two exchange a look.*)

QUEENSBERRY (*coughing nervously*): Messrs. Cliburn and Allen have brought to my attention a certain document.

BOSIE (*to both little men*): So it is you.

QUEENSBERRY: A letter to you from Mr. Wilde.

BOSIE (*sarcastic*): An original Wilde manuscript?

QUEENSBERRY: I shall give you the chance to affirm or deny its authenticity.

BOSIE: I see.

QUEENSBERRY (*handing him a paper*): In case you are tempted to tear it up, bear in mind that there are three witnesses.

BOSIE: Good God! (*Scrutinizing the paper:*) Ha. How much are they asking?

QUEENSBERRY: Thirty pounds.

BOSIE: Ah yes, thirty pounds—the going rate, h'm? Well, dear papa, you've been gypped. It's a forgery. (*Another look between* CLIBURN *and* ALLEN.)

ALLEN: But we ourselves paid— (*Cliburn shushes him.*)

CLIBURN: We are offering it in good faith.

ALLEN: We believed the gentleman who sold it to us.

BOSIE: D'you know Mr. Wilde's handwriting?

CLIBURN: Perhaps not.

BOSIE: Definitely not. Here is a real letter from him. (*Takes papers from his pocket, gives them to his father, who compares the handwriting.*) Are you going to have them arrested, daddy dear?

ALLEN (*without the look, this time*): I don't think you'll do that, me lord. False or not, the document would be read in open court.

QUEENSBERRY (*moving to the door and shouting through it*): James, my dog whip! And don't you try to escape. The doors are covered by my prize fighters.

CLIBURN: If this should prove not to be the original, we will return your money in due course.

ALLEN (*suddenly*): I don't agree to that.

CLIBURN: Leave this to me.

ALLEN: What difference does it make if it's the original or not? It's the contents they want, isn't it?

CLIBURN: I said leave this to me.

ALLEN: Fifteen is mine.

CLIBURN: If you don't shut your face—(*He raises a fist to his colleague.*)

BOSIE (*over the raised voices and the raised fist*): Silence! (*There is silence.*) Thank you. My dear friends, you have been outswindled by Mr. Freddy Wood, who collected his thirty pieces of . . . gold earlier. I'll give you ten pounds for this copy, I can't imagine why. Now get out. (CLIBURN *and* ALLEN *have calmed down, and revert now to their usual exchange of glances.*)

CLIBURN: Very well. (*He takes the money.*) If that's how you feel about it. (*They leave.*)

BOSIE: The company you keep.

QUEENSBERRY: And the company *you* keep.

BOSIE: If you mean Oscar Wilde, I am proud of it.

QUEENSBERRY: This is an accurate copy? "Red rose-leaf lips . . . ."

BOSIE: One of his prose poems, yes.

QUEENSBERRY: Your name is Hyacinthus? Apollo kisses you madly? And Mr. Wilde's love for you will never die!

BOSIE: But you "don't care" what I do in private. Have I been kissing Oscar Wilde *in public*?

QUEENSBERRY: You might as well have. They are passing the news to the stately homes of England, while—what's 'is name?—

BOSIE: Freddy Wood—he's in America—

QUEENSBERRY: America? Spreading the news around the entire world?

BOSIE: I tell you again: I am not having an affair with Oscar Wilde. He is my friend. I admire him. I won't say if I love him, such things are beyond your understanding, but you want to know if I'm sleeping with him. I am not. (*Silence.*) So please, father, is it all right if I *don't* commit suicide?

QUEENSBERRY: That's just what I'm trying to save you from—the fate of Drumlanrig.

BOSIE: So you get together with professional blackmailers to. . . .

QUEENSBERRY: They are not my only source.

BOSIE: Oh!

QUEENSBERRY: From a cousin of Mrs. Wilde's—

BOSIE: Which one?

QUEENSBERRY: Mr. Adrian Hope—

BOSIE: Oscar calls him the Forlorn Hope!

QUEENSBERRY: I hear that Mrs. Wilde is about to sue for divorce.

BOSIE: One hears that about Mrs. Everybody.

QUEENSBERRY: Not on these grounds.

BOSIE: What grounds?

QUEENSBERRY: Sodomy. With you.

BOSIE (*with a slow intake of breath*): Slander. Repeat it in public, and Oscar will sue you. I can't wait till he has you in the dock. In the jail. What a pity we don't have chain gangs like the Americans! Or galley slaves like our ancestors!

QUEENSBERRY (*quivering*): So this is the so-called male your mother claims is *my* son! I never believed her! I never believed this white-livered, smooth-faced, sicked-up-looking creature was mine! (*He is beside himself.*)

BOSIE (*as if noticing his father for the first time, turning on him*): Ha? So that's how you talk when you are real? Now you can ask *nothing* of me! And nothing is what you will get!

QUEENSBERRY (*roaring*): Stop, you! (BOSIE, *on the way out, stops in his tracks. Suddenly in a low icy voice:*) Nothing is what *you* will get. Your allowance will be stopped in the morning.

BOSIE (*venomously, as he turns on his heel*): What a funny little man you are!

EIGHT

16 Tite Street, as before. OSCAR WILDE *in his library, reading. Noise off: raised voices, scuffle, a door banging.* OSCAR *jumps up. His manservant* LANE *comes in holding his jaw,* LORD QUEENS-BERRY *on his heels, haggard, unkempt; his voice will reveal he has been drinking. He is breathing heavily after a scuffle in the front doorway.**

LANE: Sorry, Mr. Wilde, sir, but 'e forced his way in with a left 'ook to the jaw.

OSCAR (*smoothly*): The Marquess of Queensberry, I presume?

QUEENSBERRY (*thickly*): Send your man out.

OSCAR (*to* LANE): This gentleman, Lane, is by profession a boxer—with, as we now learn, a little burglary on the side. What do you have your eye on, Douglas? My blue china?

QUEENSBERRY (*directly to* LANE): Get out.

OSCAR: Remain within earshot, Lane. We may need a witness. (*LANE withdraws.* OSCAR *rudely, to* QUEENSBERRY:*)* What can I do for you?

QUEENSBERRY: Have you taken furnished rooms for my son in Piccadilly?

OSCAR: No.

QUEENSBERRY: Were the two of you kicked out of the Savoy Hotel for indecent behavior?

OSCAR: Of course not.

QUEENSBERRY: You won't deny writing the letter beginning: "My own boy, your poem is—"

OSCAR (*interrupting*): You—or rather he—bought a copy of a letter of mine for ten pounds. What of it?

QUEENSBERRY: You'd already bought back the original for thirty pounds, that's what.

---

* In the New York production, this incident was handled by having old Lord Alfred report: Having got himself very drunk indeed, my father decided to pay Oscar a visit. Confronted in the doorway of Number 16, Tite Street, by Oscar's manservant, he forced his way in with a left hook to the jaw.

OSCAR: My letters fetch a good price, even from me.

QUEENSBERRY: Mr. Adrian Hope says your wife is—

OSCAR (*coolly*): Are you insinuating you know things which, if revealed, would make trouble for me?

QUEENSBERRY: I don't say you are it. But you pose as it.

OSCAR: And the pose is the man. There is philosophy in you, Douglas!

QUEENSBERRY: Can we stop sparring? I'm desperate, Wilde. I do have Bosie's interests at heart. Whatever else you believe of me, believe that. My own plea to him failed, he's so loyal to you . . . . You are now the only person that can save him.

OSCAR: You aren't *appealing* to me by any chance?

QUEENSBERRY: If you *are* his friend—

OSCAR: I myself could choose to—?

QUEENSBERRY: Break off this relationship.

OSCAR: Marguerite Gautier to his Armand!

QUEENSBERRY: What?

OSCAR: A learned allusion. Queensberry, you are the most repulsive man I have ever met. You defame me to my dearest friend. You assault my manservant, break into my home, and insult me to my face. You then have the effrontery to appeal to my better feelings! It's my worser feelings *you* bring out. I shall now summon Lane and, if that's not enough, ask assistance from the Metropolitan Police. Leave us!

QUEENSBERRY: Look, Wilde, if I catch you and my son together, I will thrash you in public. I will advise hotels and restaurants that, if they admit you, I will come there and strike you in the face with my stick. I will hire bully boys to follow you and flog you within an inch of your life. I will hire detectives to find out the worst about you in the confidence that that worst will be enough, if not to hang you, as it certainly would have in happier days, then to put you through the ordeal of trial in a court of law and punish you with penal servitude. When, if ever, you emerge from that darkness, I will make England too hot to hold you. Even abroad you will have no rest, for, wherever you go, infamy will follow, and you will die— poor, miserable, sick, untended—long before your time!

OSCAR: Lord Queensberry's curse! My dear fellow, if you were determined to play Cassandra, you should have come here in drag.

QUEENSBERRY: Bugger! (*A long silence.*)

OSCAR: I do not know the Queensberry rules, my lord, but the Oscar Wilde rule is: shoot at sight.

(QUEENSBERRY *moves toward the door.*)

Part Two

LORD ALFRED: "Cassandra may be mocked but should not be ignored." We ignored her, Oscar and I. Took our North African holiday. Oscar hated it, was delighted to return ahead of me to attend the first night of *The Importance of Being Earnest* in London. I got back a couple of days later, though. Wired Oscar I'd meet him at the Café Royal at six o'clock.

NINE

The Café Royal. A corner table laid for two. OSCAR *sitting at it with* ROBBIE. *Café music throughout.*

ROBBIE: It's seven.

OSCAR: Punctuality is the thief of time. You're not still jealous of Bosie?

ROBBIE: One is always jealous of one's replacement.

OSCAR: I'm not sleeping with him.

ROBBIE: Replacement in your heart. Bosie's the most beautiful boy in London, and not the worst poet.

OSCAR: The best—present company excepted.

ROBBIE: Which leaves me with my receding hairline and my inability to even write a book about you.

OSCAR: The friend who doesn't write the book is a friend indeed! By contrast with dear Frank Harris who will publish a book full of fairy tales. Or dear Robert Sherard who will write and write on me and never discover I'm a fairy.

ROBBIE: Meaning you can fall back on me when Bosie has one of his tantrums.

OSCAR: Shelley fell upon the thorns of life. I fall on you.

ROBBIE: There he is at the door. I'll leave you alone.

OSCAR: At least say hello.

ROBBIE: Must I?

OSCAR: Yes, dearie. (*Stands up, extending his arms to* BOSIE *who has entered.*) Welcome back from darkest Africa! (*They embrace.*) And here is Robbie, dying to embrace you also.

BOSIE (*coolly*): How are you, Robbie?

ROBBIE (*just as coolly*): How d'ye do? (*They shake hands.*) I was just leaving.

OSCAR: But I forbade him to. (*All sit.*) Now tell us about your Arab boys.

BOSIE: One Arab boy. Chased him all the way to Biskra.

ROBBIE: Was he worth it?

BOSIE: Yes! Now, tell me about *The Importance of Being Earnest*!

OSCAR (*sarcastically*): Oh, you remembered? You dear thing!

ROBBIE: A triumph. The second Oscar Wilde triumph of the season. Two plays on at once. Both of which will run for centuries. Oscar holds the future of English drama in the palm of his hand.

OSCAR: That is a quotation. Obviously from someone of exquisite taste. But don't tell George Bernard Shaw.

BOSIE: What about my father?

OSCAR (*again sarcastic*): You remembered *him* too?

ROBBIE: He's the unforgettable man. Where were you, Bosie Douglas, when we needed you?

OSCAR: Who but you could handle the wild man of Borneo?

BOSIE: What's his latest?

ROBBIE: He was going to attend the opening and throw carrots and turnips at the actors. Oscar found out and got his tickets canceled. He prowled around the theater all evening, grinding his teeth and chattering like an ape.

OSCAR: He couldn't break in, though. There were twenty bobbies at the door!

BOSIE: And since then?

OSCAR: On the rampage at the Savoy, Willis's, Kettner's, warning them against us.

BOSIE: I know: let's sue him!

OSCAR: Sue him?!

ROBBIE: First he must commit a crime.

OSCAR: Yes. Is he Jack the Ripper by any chance?

BOSIE: Well, if he's libeling you all around town . . . .

OSCAR: Without committing his libels to writing, however. We can't prove it.

ROBBIE: May I venture an outsider's opinion?

OSCAR: You're not outside Fairyland.

ROBBIE: But suing people for *calling* us fairies is dangerous.

OSCAR: Fairies in glass houses . . . .

BOSIE: My father isn't "people," Robbie. He's an animal. In court, he'll lose as soon as the jury sees him. Anyone he accuses of anything will promptly become a hero.

ROBBIE: A live hero?

BOSIE: Put *me* in the witness box, and let me tell how he treated his family, how he hates women, how—

ROBBIE (*glancing across the room*): Someone's heading for this table.

OSCAR: The assistant manager from my club. Merriman.

MERRIMAN (*entering*): The manager asked me to give you this envelope, sir.

OSCAR: How very kind of you (*slipping him a tip which, from the man's expression, we guess to be large*). Good night, Merriman.

MERRIMAN: Good night, sir. (*He leaves.*)

OSCAR (*opening the envelope*): A visiting card in a club envelope? Oh, the card is your father's, Bosie! What's this he says?

BOSIE (*taking the card, reading*): "Oscar Wilde posing as a sodomite." Spelled som*domite. He never did learn to spell.

ROBBIE (*taking the card*): This is too much.

BOSIE: The tower of ivory assailed by the foul thing.

OSCAR: This man is out to destroy me. Spill my life on the sand.

BOSIE: Never! Let *his* blood flow!

OSCAR: Libel committed to writing! There really is nothing for it but a criminal prosecution.

ROBBIE (*nervously*): Oscar, Bosie, listen. There *is* a way out.

OSCAR: What?

ROBBIE: Tear that card up. Throw the pieces in the fire. Then it will never have existed.

BOSIE: My father's been harassing Oscar for six months. And now, because he couldn't throw his carrots and turnips, he sends this card. If it is ignored, he will think out some bigger outrage.

OSCAR: Bosie knows his father, Robbie

ROBBIE: Sue Queensberry. He may love it. It may give him the opportunity to *lynch* you. Think. He says you pose as a sodomite. You call him a liar. And then what? In self-defense he must show that you do pose as a sodomite.

BOSIE: And when the jury is not convinced?

ROBBIE: Even worse. Then Queensberry will instruct his lawyers to demonstrate that Oscar *is* a sodomite.

OSCAR: But they can't. My "affair" with Bosie happens to be platonic. I would read them a little lesson on *that*!

ROBBIE: Queensberry has made the acquaintance of Cliburn and Allen. Suppose he finds out that Freddy Wood was not only a tattletale and a blackmailer but a queer and a renter? Suppose he followed the trail that leads to Alfred Taylor's place, to Parker, to Marling?

OSCAR: Robbie, it is not just in boxing that there are Queensberry rules. Society protects itself by a network of such rules. I shall not be pursued down into the underworld: such things are not done. Lest others more important than I be exposed. We protect each other: there is a tacit but binding consensus.

ROBBIE: Binding? In sending this card, Queensberry has already broken that bond.

BOSIE: And will suffer the consequences. No jury will stand for it. They will support Oscar's contention that such a card is an outrage!

ROBBIE: Oscar, I appeal to you.

OSCAR: I have no alternative, Robbie.

ROBBIE: What will you tell your lawyer, Sir Edward Clarke?

OSCAR: About what?

ROBBIE: Whether you are it. Whether you even pose as it (*as* BOSIE *starts to expostulate*).

OSCAR: Robbie, do you find me guilty of anything?

ROBBIE: Of course not.

OSCAR: A confession of guilt is quite uncalled for, is it not?

ROBBIE: But you will be *lying* to Sir Edward—

OSCAR: If he is so misguided as to put questions that should not be put.

BOSIE: It's none of his business, Robbie! Incidentally, I came here to dine with Oscar . . . alone.

ROBBIE: I'm in a minority of one, it seems.

OSCAR: Your advice was . . . friendly. You will be there when I need you.

ROBBIE: Heaven grant you won't . . . need me.

OSCAR: Amen to that, dear boy.

BOSIE (*harshly*): Good night.

ROBBIE: Good night. (*He slips quickly out.*)

BOSIE: Phew! Robbie can really be difficult.

OSCAR: He loves me.

BOSIE: I worship you. Can we relax?

OSCAR: Better still, we can eat. And drink. I have a special wine for you. Waiter! (*He claps his hands.*) Guess the brand and the year.

BOSIE: I have a brain wave. Let's go away for a few days.

OSCAR: We just did. I loathed it.

BOSIE: This time it should be . . . Monte Carlo!

OSCAR: Nonsense, I have to arrange things with Clarke.

BOSIE: That will take one hour at most.

OSCAR: You think this case is so easy to win?

BOSIE: A walkover.

OSCAR: Monte Carlo is boring.

BOSIE: We'll play the casinos.

OSCAR: More boring still.

BOSIE: Not to me.

OSCAR: To me!

BOSIE: Oh, you can sit outside and write a masterpiece!

OSCAR (*loudly*): I don't want to go!

BOSIE (*sharply*): We're going! I will not be gainsaid!

(To dramatize this point he takes a wine glass and throws it on the parquet floor. WAITER, entering with the wine, witnesses this and is startled.)

WAITER (*to* OSCAR, *stammering*): Your . . . wine, sir. I've removed the cork.*

OSCAR: Thank you. We are rehearsing . . . a foolish melodrama!

(WAITER, sensing the electricity of storm, dumps the tray and withdraws fast.)

BOSIE (*who simmers down*): I'm sorry. And look. *(He reads the label on the bottle.)* Dagonet, 1880. The perfect wine. The perfect year.

OSCAR (*who has been pouring it, sighing*): To Monte Carlo!

BOSIE (*with the relaxed satisfaction of the victor*): Oh, thank you. You will come back from the Riviera rested—and spoiling for a fight!

(They drink.)

TEN

LORD ALFRED: Foolish melodrama indeed! Going away—again—at a time like that! And we did not ask, Father, what *he* would be doing in the crucial weeks before the trial. No: the criminal prosecution of the Eighth Marquess of Queensberry would simply be another of Oscar's triumphant—and comic—first nights. The elite of Victorian London turned out to see the author of *The Importance of Being Earnest* cross-examined by Queensberry's counsel.

The Old Bailey. OSCAR WILDE *under examination by* EDWARD CARSON, QUEENSBERRY's *counsel.* QUEENSBERRY *is in the dock.* BOSIE *is in the visitor's gallery with* ROBBIE.

---

* When Lord Alfred handles the Waiter's part, it is best to cut the Waiter's line and have Lord Alfred say: "I can still see the waiter's startled eyes as he brought Oscar the wine."

CARSON: You have given your age as thirty-nine. Were you born on October 16th, 1854?

OSCAR (*airily*): I have heard tell that I was!

CARSON: That would make you forty.

OSCAR: I despise arithmetic. But I do not pose as young.

CARSON: What do you pose as? (*Pause.*) A man unconcerned with morality?

OSCAR: I am concerned to make things of beauty.

CARSON: Have you read a story called *The Priest and the Acolyte*?

OSCAR: I have.

CARSON: Is it immoral?

OSCAR: Worse. It is badly written.

CARSON: A priest falls in love with a boy who serves him at the altar, and the boy is discovered in the priest's arms. Administering poison to the boy, the priest quotes the sacrament of the Church of England. Is that not blasphemous?

OSCAR: Blasphemous is not a word of mine.

CARSON: Here are some words of yours. "Advice to the Young." (*He reads.*) "Wickedness is a myth invented by good people to account for the peculiar attractiveness of others." You think that is true?

OSCAR: I rarely think what *I* write is true!

CARSON (*reading*): "If one tells the truth, one is sure, sooner or later, to be found out." Is that good for the young?

OSCAR: Anything is good for the young that stimulates thought.

CARSON: "Books are well or badly written, that is all."

OSCAR: The books that the world calls immoral are books that show the world its own shame.

CARSON: A perverted novel might be a good book?

OSCAR: I do not know what you mean by a perverted novel.

CARSON: Your novel *The Picture of Dorian Gray* is open to such an interpretation.

OSCAR: Philistines' views on art are unaccountable.

CARSON: The majority of persons are Philistines?

OSCAR: Oh, I have found wonderful exceptions.

CARSON: The love of the painter Basil Hallward for his model Dorian Gray might lead the ordinary individual to believe it has a . . . certain tendency?

OSCAR: *I* do not know the views of "ordinary individuals."

CARSON: Do you know what is natural? "I have never loved a woman: I suppose I never had time. I adored *you* madly, extravagantly, absurdly . . . ." Is this a natural feeling, one man to another?

OSCAR: It is natural for an artist to admire—love—a young man.

CARSON: Have you yourself known the feeling?

OSCAR: Dorian Gray is fiction.

CARSON: "I have adored you extravagantly . . . ."

OSCAR: Do you mean financially?

CARSON: Are we talking about finance?

OSCAR: I don't know *what* you're talking about!

CARSON: I shall make myself plain before I have done. Have *you* ever adored a young man madly?

OSCAR: I have never adored anyone—except myself. To love oneself is the beginning of a lifelong romance.

CARSON: Here is a letter you wrote to Lord Alfred Douglas. (*Reading:*) "My own boy. . . ." Why would a man of your age call someone nearly twenty years younger his own boy?

OSCAR: I was fond of him.

CARSON (*glancing at the letter*): Your own boy was also one "Hyacinthus"—whom Apollo loved—"so madly." Do you love Lord Alfred Douglas madly?

OSCAR: The letter is a prose poem.

CARSON: A "thing of beauty" beyond the Philistine understanding? (OSCAR *shrugs and smiles.*) Have you stayed in hotels with Lord Alfred Douglas?

OSCAR: Very respectable hotels.

CARSON: One of the "two loves"—in Lord Alfred's now notorious poem—is unnatural love, is it not?

OSCAR: No. It is not.

CARSON: Then tell us—let us hear it from the source—what *is* "the love that dare not speak its name"?

OSCAR (*looking across at* BOSIE, *after a careful pause*): The love that dare not speak its name in this century is such a great affection of an elder for a younger man as there was between David and Jonathan and such as Plato made the very basis of his philosophy. It pervades great works of art like those of Shakespeare and Michelangelo and, such as they are, my own letters to Lord Alfred Douglas. There is nothing unnatural about it. It is not a sensual love. It is the noblest form of affection and it repeatedly exists between an elder and a younger man, when the elder has intellect and the younger man has all the joy, hope, and glamor of life before him. That it should be so the world does not understand. The world mocks at it and sometimes writes insulting things about it on visiting cards.

(*Loud, prolonged applause.* CARSON *is frowning.* OSCAR *is smiling.*)

ELEVEN

In the chambers of Sir Edward Clarke. OSCAR, ROBBIE, *and* BOSIE *sit waiting. One of Sir Edward's* ASSISTANTS *comes in.**

ASSISTANT: Sir Edward Clarke will be with you in just a few moments, sir. (*He leaves.*)

OSCAR: Carson has talent.

BOSIE: You have genius.

OSCAR: He is science; I am art.

ROBBIE: This is the age of science, however.

BOSIE: Our devil's advocate speaks!

ROBBIE: Carson posed as the Philistine to maneuver Oscar into posing as . . . the other thing . . . in full view of the jury.

BOSIE: Oscar defended *platonic* love, that's the point. And people rose to their feet cheering.

(*The* ASSISTANT *comes in again.*)†

---

* Or Lord Alfred stands in for him with these lines:
  A victory! Oscar and Robbie and I met in Sir Edward Clarke's chambers that evening to discuss how the victory should be properly exploited. At least Oscar and I did.
† Or Lord Alfred:
  It was at this moment that Oscar was handed a document by Sir Edward's assistant.

ASSISTANT (*to* OSCAR): Sir Edward wants you to read this, sir.

(The ASSISTANT *withdraws.)*

OSCAR: With a wax seal, dear God. (*He breaks the seal, opens the envelope, glances over the couple of pages of documents.*) H'm. The Marquess has submitted some new entries in his plea. Now I *would* like to go to Monte Carlo! Read it, Bosie.

BOSIE (*taking the papers*): "John Sholto Douglas, Marquess of Queensberry, states that our Sovereign Lady Queen Victoria ought not further to prosecute him because the alleged libel is true. Oscar Fingal O'Flahertie Wills Wilde did solicit one Freddy Wood to commit sodomy with him—"

OSCAR: How in God's name does Queensberry know Freddy Wood?

BOSIE (*who has been reading on in silence*): He will put in the witness box Freddy Wood . . . Charlie Parker . . . Arthur Marling . . . Sidney Mavor . . . Freddy Atkins . . . Maurice Schwabe . . . Ernest Scarfe . . . Walter Grainger . . . Alfonso Conway. . . .

OSCAR (*who has jumped up*): The house is on fire! The roof is falling in!

ROBBIE: Queensberry must have worked on this for weeks: the weeks you two spent in Monte Carlo—

OSCAR: I said we shouldn't go!

ROBBIE: Brought Freddy Wood back from America. Hired detectives. Sent them to your haunts. Offered money in return for . . . cooperation.

OSCAR: He *has* pursued me down to the underworld. This is the end.

BOSIE: No, no, let him put these creatures in the witness box! Sir Edward Clarke will wreck them by revealing their record!

OSCAR: Your vote is against, Robbie?

ROBBIE: You are not sure to win. And if you lose!

BOSIE: To back down now would be to lose now.

OSCAR: He's right, Robbie. If Sir Edward is prepared to go ahead . . . .

*(*SIR EDWARD CLARKE *enters.)*

CLARKE: Good evening, gentlemen. Sorry to have held you after the long day in court, but— (*He indicates the documents.*)

OSCAR: Are you prepared to go ahead, Sir Edward?

CLARKE: Is that your wish?

OSCAR: What is the alternative?

CLARKE: We can withdraw the suit.

OSCAR: Thus conceding the libel was true.

CLARKE: It would be hard to give any other impression.

OSCAR: Again I have *no* alternative. I *must* ask you to proceed.

CLARKE: And I must ask you for the assurance that there is no substance to any of that (*gesturing toward the papers, awkward pause*).

BOSIE: Doesn't one's lawyer defend one, innocent or guilty?

CLARKE: If one is the defendant. Your father is the defendant. Which gives me the right to ask the plaintiff if he is free and clear.

BOSIE: Thank you.

CLARKE: Mr. Wilde?

OSCAR (*gesturing towards the documents*): That is all totally without foundation.

CLARKE: Then we can proceed—with every prospect of success.

TWELVE

The Old Bailey. CARSON *is again cross-examining* WILDE.

CARSON: You have denied the alleged intimacies and indecencies in *all* these cases?

OSCAR: I have.

CARSON: Even when a lad was with you in a hotel—the same room, the same bed?

OSCAR: Even then.

CARSON: You have not denied association with persons of a different station in life?

OSCAR: I recognize no social distinctions of any kind.

CARSON: And much younger than yourself?

OSCAR: I would sooner talk to a very young, perhaps idle, fellow than be cross-examined by distinguished gentlemen of advanced years.

CARSON: Would you talk to a street Arab?

OSCAR: If he would talk to me.

CARSON: And take him to your rooms?

OSCAR: Be it so.

CARSON: Give him an excellent dinner?

OSCAR: I do everything excellently.

CARSON: Champagne?

OSCAR: Iced champagne is a favorite drink of mine—strongly against my doctor's orders.

CARSON: Never mind your doctor's orders!

OSCAR: I never do.

CARSON: And after the wining and the dining?

OSCAR: Is that a question?

CARSON: This is a question: do you know Walter Grainger?

OSCAR: I do.

CARSON: How old is he?

OSCAR: When I knew him, he was sixteen.

CARSON: Was he a servant?

OSCAR (*nodding*): He waited at table.

CARSON: Did you ever kiss him?

OSCAR: Oh dear, no, he was a peculiarly plain boy.

CARSON: Ha?

OSCAR: He was so ugly I pitied him for it.

CARSON: Was that the reason you didn't kiss him?

OSCAR: You are insolent, Mr. Carson.

CARSON: Is that said in support of your statement that you never kissed him?

OSCAR: The question is childish.

CARSON: Did you put that forward as a reason you never kissed him?

OSCAR: Not at all.

CARSON: Then *why* did you mention that he was ugly?

OSCAR: If I were asked why I did not kiss the doormat, I should say because I do not like to kiss doormats.

CARSON: Why did you mention his ugliness?

OSCAR: You insulted me with an insulting question.

CARSON: Was that why you said the boy was ugly?

OSCAR: One says things flippantly sometimes.

CARSON: This was said flippantly?

OSCAR: Yes. Yes, this was said flippantly.

* * *

(CARSON *questions* CHARLIE PARKER.)

CARSON: Name?

PARKER: Charles Parker.

CARSON: Age?

PARKER: Twenty-one.

CARSON: Occupation?

PARKER: I *was* a gentleman's valet.

CARSON: You were?

PARKER: Later I was out of a job.

CARSON: Is it true you were arrested in a certain incident last year, Mr. Parker?

PARKER: Yes.

CARSON: Tell us about that.

PARKER: There was a police raid at Alfred Taylor's place on Little College Street. Eighteen arrests, myself among them.

CARSON: Was a Mr. Arthur Marling among them?

PARKER: Yes, he was.

CARSON: Who *is* Mr. Marling?

PARKER: A female impersonator. He was wearing a female garb of black and gold.

CARSON: Did Mr. Oscar Wilde supply money for the defense?

PARKER: Yes.

CARSON: How did you meet Alfred Taylor?

PARKER: On Piccadilly. He came up and spoke to me about the 'ores. "Why waste money on trash like that?" he said. "You could be makin' a mint!" I said, "If a gentleman with money took a fancy to me, I'd be quite agreeable."

CARSON: Did Taylor then introduce you to Mr. Wilde?

PARKER: Took me to dinner with 'im.

CARSON: A good dinner?

PARKER (*nodding*): With champagne! Brandy and coffee afterwards! Red-shaded candles on the table!

CARSON: Wilde paid?

PARKER: Yes, sir.

CARSON: And then?

PARKER: Wilde said, "You're the boy for me! Will you come to the Savoy Hotel?"

CARSON: Did you go?

PARKER: Yes, sir!

CARSON: Did you have more to drink at the Savoy?

PARKER: Liqueurs, sir.

CARSON: And then?

PARKER: Mr. Wilde asked me to go to the bedroom with him.

CARSON: What occurred in the bedroom?

PARKER: Mr. Wilde committed the act of sodomy upon me.

CARSON: And paid you for it?

PARKER: Yes, sir.

CARSON: How much?

PARKER: Two pounds.

CARSON: A fixed price?

PARKER: No. The week after, he paid three.

CARSON: Also for the act of sodomy?

PARKER: Well, 'e would ask me to pretend I was a woman, and he was my lover. I would sit on his knee while he played with my privates.

* * *

(CARSON *questions a female witness.*)

CARSON: "And committed the act of sodomy upon me," Parker's direct testimony. Mr. Wilde denies it. But he has not denied that some of the lads were in his bed. We will, therefore, solicit testimony from one who, from her daily labor, knows what happens in, and to, beds. Your name, madam?

COTTER: Jane Cotter.

CARSON: Occupation?

COTTER: Chambermaid at the Savoy.

CARSON: Did Mr. Oscar Wilde occupy one of your rooms?

COTTER: Yes, sir.

CARSON: Looking around this courtroom can you identify anyone as the Mr. Wilde you knew?

COTTER (*pointing*): 'im, sir.

CARSON: In what circumstances did you last see him?

COTTER: In Room 362, sir.

CARSON: Alone?

COTTER: There was a young boy with him.

CARSON: In bed?

COTTER: Yes, sir.

CARSON: A young boy of about what age?

COTTER: Sixteen, sir.

CARSON: Did you remark on this to anyone?

COTTER: I told the masseur.

CARSON: And he took a look?

COTTER: I *made* him look, sir.

CARSON: I shall call the masseur, my lord. (*Turning back to* JANE COTTER:) What else do you remember?

COTTER: Well, sir—

CARSON: Are you embarrassed?

COTTER: Yes, sir.

CARSON: **Well, ma'am, take your time, and tell what embarrasses** you . . . .

COTTER: It was the sheets.

CARSON: The bed sheets.

COTTER: Yes, sir. Mr. Wilde's sheets was stained in a . . . peculiar way.

CARSON: So peculiar you had to report the incident?

COTTER: To the 'ousekeeper, yes.

CARSON: Did she inspect the sheets?

COTTER: Yes.

CARSON: I shall call the housekeeper, my lord.

CLARKE: May I cross-examine, my lord?

JUDGE: If you will be brief.

CLARKE: My client suffers from a looseness of the bowels. Was there anything about the stains, madam, that would not be explained thereby?

COTTER (*confused*): Well, sir, really . . . .

CARSON (*jumping up*): My learned friend's interposition is absurd, my lord.

JUDGE: You *are* putting rather a strain upon the court's credulity, Sir Edward.

CLARKE: I request a moment to consult with my client.

JUDGE: Granted.

(CLARKE *and* OSCAR WILDE *whisper very briefly.*)

CLARKE: Mr. Oscar Wilde begs leave to withdraw the charges.

THIRTEEN

Sir Edward Clarke's chambers. SIR EDWARD *talks with* OSCAR, BOSIE, *and* ROBBIE.

OSCAR: What now?

BOSIE: My father gets a verdict of not guilty?

CLARKE: It can hardly be avoided. They have a dozen more such witnesses on hand. This is not the time for me to complain, Mr.

Wilde, of the slight warning you gave me of the testimony these people would provide. Suffice it now that we have lost. Why don't you go while the going's good?

OSCAR: Go where?

CLARKE: I needn't remind you of the Cleveland Street scandal.

OSCAR: Lord Arthur Somerset fled to France.

CLARKE: The authorities proved cooperative.

OSCAR: And?

CLARKE: Once Queensberry is declared not guilty, the government will move to prosecute you under the Criminal Law Amendment Act. But the goverment does not move swiftly. Leaves a gentleman an hour or two to catch a train to Dover. Then by boat to Calais, and he is free.

OSCAR: If yet again I have no alternative . . . .

CLARKE: Except to become the defendant.

OSCAR: On what charge?

CLARKE: Gross indecency.

OSCAR: If I lose?

CLARKE: Two years' hard labor. Social ostracism. Your reputation gone. Possibly your health and peace of mind.

OSCAR: I don't see how I could pay you, Sir Edward.

CLARKE: Relying upon the assurances you have given that all these accusations are without foundation, I would take your case without fee.

OSCAR (*wiping away a tear*): But if I have no chance as plaintiff, do I have a chance as defendant?

CLARKE: If I undermined the jury's confidence in the government witnesses, they would have to acquit you.

OSCAR: Robbie?

ROBBIE: You know what *I* think.

OSCAR: Bosie?

BOSIE: Sir Edward will undermine the jury's confidence in the witnesses!

ROBBIE: You are incorrigible.

BOSIE (*to* CLARKE): And I will destroy the jury's confidence in *Queensberry*! Put me in the box!

CLARKE: No, no, Lord Alfred—

OSCAR: Bosie! Was it a friend you were looking for when you met me?

BOSIE: What else?

OSCAR: I sometimes think it was a weapon against your father. Sir Edward, Robbie, Bosie, my decision is taken—France.

ROBBIE: Oh, thank God.

OSCAR: And, Bosie, you are coming with me.

(BOSIE *sputters a little and then is silent.*)

ROBBIE: I'll get your things from Tite Street. Wait for me in Bosie's suite at the Cadogan.

OSCAR: Thank you, Robbie. (*Forcing a half-smile.*) By midnight I shall be on the boat to Calais.

(*They disappear.*)

QUEENSBERRY,* *glass held high, is addressing friends and admirers gathered at a celebration. In the theater, the actor can face the audience, as if all the others were out front.*

QUEENSBERRY: Outside the Old Bailey, the whores danced and sang in the street! Miss Hosker had to slip out by a side door to avoid meeting them. For myself, well, the telegrams are still pouring in. I'll read you one. (*He does so.*) "Every real man in the city is with you. Now kill the bugger!" And here is my message to Miss Hosker. (*Again reading:*) "If the country allows you to leave, the better for the country, but, if you take my son with you, I will follow and shoot you down like a dog!"

(*Cheers and clapping, whistles and cries.*)

---

* But if the actor who played Queensberry earlier is now playing Clarke, it will be well to give this speech to old Lord Alfred, recasting it thus:

Outside the Old Bailey, the whores danced and sang in the street. Oscar had to slip out by a side door to avoid them. My father received congratulatory telegrams reading, for example, "Every real man in the city is with you, now kill the bugger!" My father also *sent* telegrams, including this one to Oscar: "If the country allows you to leave, the better for the country, but, if you take my son with you, I will shoot you down like a dog!" Meanwhile, at the Cadogan Hotel, near Sloane Square . . .

FOURTEEN

In the Cadogan Hotel. OSCAR *in a chair sipping hock and seltzer,* BOSIE *hovering.*

OSCAR: You're so nervous. Whose crisis is this, mine or yours?

BOSIE: I'm getting ready to say something.

OSCAR: Say it, dear boy.

BOSIE: I'm *glad* you're leaving for France.

OSCAR: What?

BOSIE: Robbie was right all along. I was wrong.

OSCAR: And here was I thinking you'd insist that I kill your father for you, commit vicarious parricide!

BOSIE: If it could have been done with a flick of the wrist! But I wasn't asking you to sacrifice *your* happiness.

OSCAR: Now *I'm* blushing—at the bad thoughts I've had about you. More hock and seltzer. Hock and hock is more like it.

(He pours hock and no seltzer. A knock at the door.)

BOSIE (*going to the door*): This will be Robbie with your things. Are you ready?

OSCAR (*having gulped some hock*): Ready? Oh yes, the readiness is all. (*He stands; he is wobbly.*) Good heavens, I'm drunk. I *never* get drunk! (*He sits down heavily.*)

ROBBIE (*in the room now*): I spoke with Constance. She's so happy you'll be out of it.

OSCAR: *Constance* wants me in France?

ROBBIE: She wants you at liberty. Of course.

OSCAR (*rather drunkenly*): Liberty or death!

ROBBIE: The warrant is out for your arrest. Scotland Yard will send its men here to serve it.

BOSIE: We must get you out before they arrive.

ROBBIE (*surprised, to* BOSIE): You want that?

OSCAR: Oh, yes. Dear Bosie has undergone a change of heart.

ROBBIE (*warmly*): Really? That's splendid of you, Bosie. (*To* OSCAR:) I held on to my cab. We can all go straight down.

OSCAR: I'm drunk.

ROBBIE: Bosie, help me drag him to the cab.

(OSCAR *lets himself be lifted to a standing position but then shakes both off a little ponderously yet without hysteria.*)

BOSIE: Oscar, you're not as drunk as all that.

OSCAR (*sitting down deliberately*): I am as drunk as I need to be. Sit down, children, and listen to papa.

ROBBIE: There just isn't time.

OSCAR: Allow me to correct you, Robbie. For better or for worse, time is what there is all too much of.

BOSIE: You're not changing your mind?

OSCAR (*to both*): May *I* speak my lines, darlings? Sit. (*They do so very nervously.*) To end the suspense, and so you won't be too upset when a certain knock is heard at the door, yes, I have changed my mind.

ROBBIE: You've decided to stay?

OSCAR: I have stayed.

ROBBIE: But why? Why?

OSCAR (*slowly*) "One of the most intriguing questions in the whole intriguing story of the late Oscar Wilde is why he declined the traditional way out and stayed to face a ferocious prosecution . . . ."

ROBBIE: Oscar, my God, are you bent on self-destruction?

OSCAR: In love with my own downfall? A Frenchman has said such things about me.

ROBBIE: You've been in touch with your mother. I think she has more to do with it.

OSCAR: Never retreat! Never give up! Her Hibernian creed.

ROBBIE: And just now that *is* self-destructive. To avoid retreat as an artist—destruction as an artist—you must get away from all this! (OSCAR *is silent.*) Then, why? (OSCAR *is silent.*)

BOSIE: Robbie, step into the other room a moment. (ROBBIE *hesitates.*) Trust me. (*They exchange a look, and* ROBBIE *goes.*) I said stay here, and you decided to go to France. I said go to France, and you decide to stay here. No longer pushed by me, you wish to show me you can do it on your own. You wish to show me how much you love me. But how much do you love me? How much do I love you? We never found out. And it did kill you. Or it will, if you let it. But I won't let you let it—I'm going to get you into that cab downstairs.

(He talks and moves as if he would do so, but OSCAR *is unmoved, literally and figuratively.)*

OSCAR *(unhurried)*: One theory, of course, is that Wilde was in the grip of an uncontrollable infatuation with Lord Alfred Douglas . . . .

BOSIE: Or, under the influence of hock, supposed that he was . . . !

OSCAR (before BOSIE *can continue trying to get him out of the hotel)*: Bring Robbie back in. *(After a hesitation, and recognizing he has failed to budge* OSCAR, BOSIE *lets* ROBBIE *back in.)* Robbie, Bosie, I'm staying. Not, so to speak, for the reasons given. All I know is it's something I have to do. Oh dear, I hope I'm not a martyr to some sacred cause!

BOSIE: Oscar—

OSCAR: The affair we never had, Bosie, we never *shall* have. This may be good-by forever.

BOSIE: Not on your life! I shall be at your side! Now Sir Edward will *have* to put me in the witness box.

OSCAR *(firmly)*: He has said no. I say no now. Bosie, you will leave the country before the new trial starts.

BOSIE *(blustering)*: No, no, no—!

(A knock at the door, quiet but commanding.)

OSCAR *(to both)*: You may kiss me good-by. *(He kisses* ROBBIE *first, then* BOSIE, *a shade more lingeringly, by which time the knock has been repeated loudly.)* Open the door.

(ROBBIE does so, and two men walk past him into the middle of the room. The one that entered first picks out OSCAR *and addresses him.)*

RICHARDS: Mr. Oscar Wilde? *(He produces a badge.)* Inspector Richards of Scotland Yard. I hold a warrant for your arrest.

BOSIE *(interposing coldly)*: I am Lord Alfred Douglas. There was something—a business matter—I had not quite finished telling Mr. Wilde.

RICHARDS *(crudely)*: You have one minute.

BOSIE (*stiltedly*): I only wanted to add, Mr. Wilde, that the, er, unfinished business between us is now . . . finished.

OSCAR (*entering into the artificial tone of this*): Then may I wish you Godspeed, my dear Lord Alfred, on your journey to . . . was it France?

BOSIE: Yes. Thank you. Thank you very much. It's good-by as you say. Good-by, did you say forever?

(*As* OSCAR *is led off, they all disappear.* LORD ALFRED *resumes.*)

LORD ALFRED: Oscar was now defendant in a case entitled Regina versus Wilde. Queen versus Queen: a little queen from Merrion Square, Dublin, had taken on the Queen of Great Britain and Ireland, Empress of India. What was that, Father Murphy? Yes, yes—another judge and jury received the same evidence as before. Sir Edward Clarke summed up for the defense.

FIFTEEN

The Old Bailey. SIR EDWARD's *closing speech to the jury.*

CLARKE: The crime with which the defendant is charged is the gravest of all offenses: the ultimate sin against nature. Men guilty of this offense suffer from erotomania, a form of absolute madness, the insanity of the perverted sexual instinct. We all agree, do we not, gentlemen? What then would you think of a man who insisted on bringing his case before the world when he knew himself to be *guilty* of the gravest of offenses, knew also that a dozen witnesses could testify to this? Is Mr. Wilde such a man, or is it not rather to those who claim to have been witnesses that we should turn our attention? Wood and Parker and their kind are shameless creatures who live by luring men to their rooms on the pretense that illicit pleasures will be provided upon arrival. Their victim, unless he is prepared to face disgraceful charges, must pay a large sum of money. Rather than incur even the breath of such scandal, a man pays—an *innocent* man pays . . . . So I ask you, gentlemen, can you find Mr. Oscar Wilde guilty on the evidence of such witnesses?

(*They disappear.* LORD ALFRED *resumes.*)

LORD ALFRED: They couldn't—they didn't—find him guilty. Or not guilty. End of case? Not quite, Father. That evening Edward Carson received a visit from the solicitor general of Great Britain—

SIXTEEN

In CARSON's *chambers.* CARSON *at his desk. A man entering.*

CARSON: Sir Frank Lockwood? Since when does a modest barrister receive a call from his solicitor general?

LOCKWOOD: How d'you do, Mr. Carson? (*They shake hands.*) As for your question, let us say: when that barrister, however modest, has achieved a brilliant victory for the Crown.

CARSON: Not one, surely, that has very much significance *to* the Crown?

LOCKWOOD: You think not? But the hour is late. May I go straight to business?

CARSON: Please! (*Gestures to him to sit.*)

LOCKWOOD (*sitting*): I have come to seek your advice.

CARSON: On the Wilde case? It is over, surely?

LOCKWOOD: That is the issue. It is over. Unless we—the Crown—reopen it.

CARSON: Try him again?

LOCKWOOD: Yes. Do you advise it?

CARSON: No.

LOCKWOOD: Why not?

CARSON: Well, it would come as a great relief—to the whole country—to put this distasteful business behind us, don't you agree?

LOCKWOOD: *I* might agree, but what about Queensberry? Is *he* ready to let matters rest?

CARSON: Queensberry lives now for vengeance and more vengeance. But I am not his creature.

LOCKWOOD: You want to let up on this Wilde fellow?

CARSON: Yes. Even in Queensberry's interests. He is bringing disgrace upon himself and upon us all.

LOCKWOOD: *He* represents us all?

CARSON: Yes. He may be a cad, *the* cad. But he is still a member of the club.

LOCKWOOD: The club. Ah, yes.

CARSON: But?

LOCKWOOD: It would be a relief to put the distasteful business behind us, but would it be behind us? I am afraid, my dear Carson, it would still be ahead of us and squarely in our path.

CARSON: Who is "us"? The Liberal government?

LOCKWOOD: In the first instance.

CARSON: I need hardly remind you that I am no Liberal. As for your Liberal prime minister, Lord Rosebery, there is a rumor, is there not of a retreat in Germany where he spends his leisure time in exclusively male company . . . It is even said that he was as obsessed with Lord Alfred's elder brother as Wilde now seems to be with Lord Alfred—

LOCKWOOD: Forgive me, Mr. Carson, we cannot be interested in what you surmise or even what you might know. But for the prime minister, at this point, to let up on Oscar Wilde might be thought to indicate leniency in such matters, and such leniency might in turn be thought to have . . . its reasons.

CARSON: I see.

LOCKWOOD: The Crown will, therefore, continue to prosecute Wilde, and the Crown wishes you to do the prosecuting.

CARSON: I'm against it, but you wish me to do it?

LOCKWOOD: Having in mind your unequalled mastery of this case, having in mind the now historic fact that your dazzling defense of Queensberry *became*, as the whole world knows, the prosecution of Wilde.

CARSON: Well, well. I do have to remind you I'm a Conservative. My dear Lockwood, when you lose the coming election on account of these . . . rumors, we win.

LOCKWOOD: We all put country before party, do we not? H'm? Let's say then, to use your cynical expression, we acknowledge membership in the same club? No? Then let me remind you that the Conservative party also has its . . . rumors.

CARSON: Nothing doing, Lockwood. You'll have to find someone else to pull your chestnuts out of the fire.

LOCKWOOD: That is final?

CARSON: Don't tell me it is a possibility you had not allowed for?

LOCKWOOD: The alternative is not preferable—openly placing in the lists against Wilde the highest legal officer in the land.

CARSON: That would be yourself? (LOCKWOOD *nods.*) Is it even *proper*? For the solicitor general—?

LOCKWOOD: Oh, it is proper. The question is: will *you* stay within the bounds of propriety? (CARSON *is slightly disconcerted.*) Or do we have to fear that you might spread those rumors on which, as you say, your party might ride to power?

CARSON (*catching on*): Ah! Well, as *you* say, my party also has its . . . rumors. No, I shall not betray the club.

LOCKWOOD: Thank you, Mr. Carson. Events can now take their course.

(They disappear. LORD ALFRED resumes.)

LORD ALFRED: "At the Sessions holden for the Central Criminal Court at Justice Hall, Old Bailey, in the Suburbs of the City of London on the 25th day of May in the year of Our Lord one thousand eight hundred and ninety-five: Regina versus Oscar Wilde."

SEVENTEEN

The Old Bailey, LOCKWOOD *summing up.*

LOCKWOOD: Mr. Wilde has had the benefit of a most able defense from my learned friend Sir Edward Clarke, yet all this learning and ability could only find one point—a single point—that might seem calculated to weaken the case against him. It is that some of the witnesses are criminals. I might remark in passing that a man can be judged by the company he keeps. The defendant is a man of culture, his associates should not have been criminals and illiterate boys. Sir Edward has warned you against reaching a verdict which would enable the detestable trade of blackmail to rear its head unblushingly in this city. Gentlemen, I ask you to take care lest, by your verdict, you enable another vice, just as abominable, to raise its head: were it not that there are men willing to purchase vice in the most hideous form, there would be no opening for these blackmailers to ply their calling. Turning to the misconduct in the Savoy Hotel, the defendant has given no explanation save that the disgusting condition of the sheets might be attributed to an ailment of the bowels. You, My

Lord, have pointed out how unlikely an attribution that was. Testimony was given by the chambermaid and the masseur of a boy in the defendant's bed. Are the chambermaid and the masseur blackmailers? Of course not. And if my learned friend had wished to contest their account, he would have called as a witness the only other person present: Lord Alfred Douglas. Or were there reasons for keeping Lord Alfred out of this courtroom? I will suggest, gentlemen, that there was a simple, overriding reason. Finally, the case for the prosecution not only does not depend on any witnesses alone, it rests on the direct evidence of the relationship between the defendant and Lord Alfred. The letter to Lord Alfred which the blackmailers described as hot, well, we have been asked to believe it is a prose poem that you and I, gentlemen, are too low to appreciate. We appreciate it at its proper value: somewhat lower than the beasts. What father would not try to save his son from—worse than bestiality? Mr. Wilde himself had to concede that the fateful words "posing as a sodomite" were justified. Clear, untainted, unchallenged evidence has been presented that there *was* such a pose, grounded in just those acts of gross indecency for which I now ask you, gentlemen, to condemn the man.

JUDGE: Gentlemen of the jury, do you find the prisoner at the bar guilty or not guilty of an act of gross indecency with Freddy Wood?

FOREMAN: Guilty.

JUDGE: Do you find him guilty or not guilty of an act of gross indecency with Charlie Parker?

FOREMAN: Guilty.

JUDGE: Do you find him guilty or not guilty of an act of gross indecency with a male person unknown in Room 362 of the Savoy Hotel?

FOREMAN: Guilty.

JUDGE: Oscar Wilde, you shall be imprisoned and kept to hard labor for two years. People who can do these things must be dead to all sense of shame.

Note: A second intermission can be avoided here, but the actor playing OSCAR *will not have time to change into prison clothes unless* LORD ALFRED *is provided with extra lines. In the New York production, he prefaced Part Three with the following:*

In Reading Gaol by Reading Town
There is a pit of shame
And in it lies a wretched man
Eaten by teeth of flame.
In a burning winding sheet he lies
And his grave has got no name.

Part Three

EIGHTEEN

LORD ALFRED: Reading Gaol. That's where they put him. Half the day picking oakum. Half in solitary. Know what he said, Father Murphy? "If this is how the Queen treats her prisoners, she doesn't deserve to have any." H'm. The lord of language—silenced. The lover of high living—fast living, oh dear yes—now in a cell, thirteen feet by seven, the light a naked gas jet, the lavatory a small tin chamber pot.

(OSCAR is seen, his head in his hands. A knock.)

OSCAR: Who is it?

VOICE: I am the prison chaplain, Wilde.

OSCAR: What do you want?

CHAPLAIN: I shall be coming twice a day for your solace and edification.

OSCAR: Thank you.

CHAPLAIN: In your home, did you say morning prayers?

OSCAR: I'm afraid we did not.

CHAPLAIN: You see where you are now! Read this tract.

(The ticking of a clock is heard, quite loudly, till the next scene begins.)

NINETEEN

Prison. Visitor's room. A table. ROBBIE ROSS seated at one side. OSCAR is brought in by a WARDER and is allowed to sit across the table from ROSS. WARDER sits at the end of the table.

OSCAR: The age of miracles is not past.

ROBBIE: Your presence was always a miracle. Now more than ever.

OSCAR: I was doomed to see visitors only through the bars of a cage, but Warder Martin here has won us the privilege to meet so. (*He indicates the table and chairs.*)

ROBBIE: That is very kind of you, Warder Martin.

WARDER: If you gentlemen have business, do it. The time limit is ten minutes.

OSCAR (*to* WARDER, *indicating* ROBBIE): He looks after my money, my property.

ROBBIE: I am here to tell you that you have no money, no property, any longer.

OSCAR: My plays—

ROBBIE: Both successes have been taken off the boards.

OSCAR: I thought they were running them without the author's name in the program?

ROBBIE: Not any more. Your books have vanished from the book shops. Your income is nil.

OSCAR: It makes prison sound like a refuge.

ROBBIE: It won't be. The court awarded Queensberry his costs. To get some part of them, he will have you declared bankrupt. There will be a proceeding.

OSCAR: No, no, there I can correct you. Bosie promised he and his brother Percy would help.

ROBBIE: Percy says you pulled the wool over his eyes, never letting him know about . . . those witnesses.

OSCAR: Bosie, though . . . .

ROBBIE: His father did cut off his allowance. He has no money now.

OSCAR: He could raise it! From his mother or someone! Everyone he knows is rich! (*Trying to calm himself:*) Tell me I exaggerate, Robbie.

ROBBIE: I am not the ideal mediator for Bosie.

OSCAR: Ha?

ROBBIE: My advice always ran counter to his.

OSCAR: Your advice was prudent—as became the friend of friends. Still, Robbie—Bosie, too, is a friend.

ROBBIE: He is not! When will you see that? He—

OSCAR: Not? What is he up to?

ROBBIE: The old imprudence: again seeking to use you as a weapon. In the cause of . . . Uranian Emancipation!

OSCAR: What?

ROBBIE: Sending pronunciamentos to magazine editors—with compromising letters of yours in them.

OSCAR: That's illegal.

ROBBIE: In England, yes. But he's in touch with French magazines.

OSCAR: I won't allow it! Which letters are they?

ROBBIE: Any that support his case for (*he glances at* WARDER) . . . "Uranians." (*To* WARDER:) May I read from a magazine?

WARDER: Unless what I hear is improper.

*(*ROBBIE *takes a clipping out of his pocket. At the other side of the stage, in a spotlight,* BOSIE *is seen, reciting as follows.)*

BOSIE: In France, I am rightly regarded as the child that Oscar Wilde loved. Had I lived in Athens at the time of Pericles, the conduct which has led to my disgrace would have resulted in my glory. We must blame Christianity for the reversal of public opinion and for the persecution of the excellent persons who are in truth the salt of the earth. Oscar Wilde is a martyr to progress. I love him, I admire him, I associate myself with him in everything. (BOSIE *disappears.*)

OSCAR: Not content to land me in Reading Gaol, he will make a mockery of me before all Europe! That boy is the true son of his father! I am beginning to hate him.

*(*OSCAR, ROBBIE, *and* WARDER *disappear. The clock ticks.* LORD ALFRED *reappears.*)*

LORD ALFRED: And no wonder. He couldn't sleep. Couldn't eat the food. When he did eat it, it gave him diarrhea. Lost twenty pounds in two weeks. Couldn't stay on his feet. Took a bad fall and damaged his ear. It was never to heal. An abscess formed that killed him by degrees . . . his dreams were nightmares. He had hallucinations. Entertained thoughts of suicide.

TWENTY

Prison. Visitor's room. CONSTANCE *is seated where* ROBBIE ROSS *had been. The* WARDER *brings* OSCAR *in. The*WARDER *goes to his place at the end of the table.* OSCAR *for the moment remains transfixed in the doorway.*

WARDER: You have fifteen minutes, Mrs. Wilde, ma'am.

OSCAR: What we did not find time to say in twelve years of married life, we must now say in fifteen minutes. (*Silence falls again.*) Say it, say it, Constance. Pour your heart out. The opportunity may never come again. (*Silence.*) The Bible mentions a sin for which there can be no forgiveness, and you have discovered what it is: that a father should ruin his two innocent children, blight their future, while deceiving and betraying the equally innocent young wife, year in, year out, so that now, if she were to review her married years, she would have to reconstruct it all day by day, asking, so where was he really going that morning, whom was he really seeing that afternoon . . . .

WARDER: You must sit down, Wilde. (*Pause as* OSCAR *sits.*) I think Mrs. Wilde might prefer it if I stepped out for a moment.

OSCAR: Are you permitted to?

WARDER: No. But I will.

OSCAR: You are a saint.

WARDER: 'Ardly, but thank you, sir.

(The couple are left alone. OSCAR *is weeping.)*

CONSTANCE: You really are the most disarming man in the world. You make a person rethink everything, even a person who doesn't think at all very often. I didn't come here to reproach you. And yet I did. I bring bad news. I wanted to hit you over the head with it.

OSCAR: Bad news comes so often, I may manage to be bored by it.

CONSTANCE: I gave instructions no one else should tell you. Came from Italy to tell you myself. Oscar, your mother passed away last week.

OSCAR: No! Mother—I killed her. That's what you mean?

CONSTANCE: It's what I was going to mean. Oh, Oscar, I have seen you that way all these months: the destroyer of your family. In your presence, it all seems unreal.

OSCAR: Did she die peacefully?

CONSTANCE: Yes, yes.

OSCAR: Bless her! There has been no love like hers. The nearest was . . . you.

CONSTANCE: You did love me, then?

OSCAR: Have you doubted that?

CONSTANCE: Then what went wrong?

OSCAR (*arriving at an idea, suddenly*): I have been insane these last four years!

CONSTANCE: Have been? It is over?

OSCAR: Over! Over forever!

CONSTANCE: Bosie Douglas has announced your intention of rejoining him.

OSCAR: What? Is that true? Constance, I now know—I have learned it in this purgatory—Bosie is my enemy! He can "announce" what he will! I shall never see him again!

CONSTANCE: What? Can I believe that?

OSCAR: If he were in this room now, I would kill him with my bare hands.

CONSTANCE: I didn't know . . . . If you have put all that insanity behind you, if you have put that beast Bosie behind you, you are a new man now!

OSCAR: Just the man who married Constance Lloyd and made her twice a mother! Can the unforgivable sin ever be forgiven?

CONSTANCE: You have repented, haven't you?

OSCAR: I *am* repenting.

CONSTANCE: Then I have good news. A message from my cousin Adrian Hope.

OSCAR: Have you turned to *him* for advice?

CONSTANCE: "Oscar could be released early from Reading if he would write the home secretary that he had seen the error of his ways."

OSCAR: Released early? I have prayed for that!

CONSTANCE: Repeat to the home secretary what you have said to me:

you were insane for four years, that way of life *is* insane, those people are depraved, diseased. And you have come to your senses. "A modern form of recantation," Cousin Adrian calls it, "the only argument the government could possibly listen to."

OSCAR: They will release me—soon?

CONSTANCE: They could.

OSCAR (*after a pause*): If I do this, and they release me—look me in the eye, Constance—will you take me back? (*Silence. She weeps.*) Your turn to cry! Then don't answer me. Not now. I will write the home secretary.

(He reaches for her hands across the table and kisses them. CON-STANCE *returns his gaze, half caught in it, daring for a moment to hope infinity, afraid too, skeptical. The clock ticks.)*

TWENTY-ONE

LORD ALFRED (*hogging the port without offering any to Father Murphy*): Rejection of that beast Bosie. Recantation of the Homo Heresy. He'd picked up that word "erotomania" from Sir Edward Clarke, who got it from the doctors, I suppose, what? The "alien-ists." They're the priests nowadays, what? Hear what Oscar wrote to the home secretary.

Prison, OSCAR *in his cell.*

OSCAR: Though the four years preceding my arrest were the most brilliant of my life, I was suffering from erotomania in its most horrible form. It made me forget my wife and children, my social position in London, my European distinction as an artist, the honor of my family, nay, my very humanity, and left me a helpless prey of absolute madness. For, of all modes of insanity, the insanity of the perverted sexual instinct is the most dominant in its action on the brain. It taints the intellectual as well as the emotional energies. It clings like a malaria to soul and body alike. But, released now, I would strive to recreate the life of a quiet student of letters. Sanity, balance, and wholesomeness can thus be restored to my soul.

(The clock ticks between scenes.)

TWENTY-TWO

Prison. Visitor's Room. CONSTANCE *has a man with her.* WARDER MARTIN *places* OSCAR *opposite them, then slips out.*

CONSTANCE: Cousin Adrian wants to speak to you, Oscar.

ADRIAN: It is too late, Cousin Oscar.

OSCAR: For . . . ? (*Stammering.*)

ADRIAN: For what you . . . proposed.

OSCAR (*to* CONSTANCE): For me and you to . . . .

ADRIAN: It is *too late.*

OSCAR (*turning on him*): You make Constance's decisions for her now?

ADRIAN (*quietly*): Constance!

CONSTANCE (*speaking on command*): I agree with Cousin Adrian. It's a dreadful thing to say, I know, Oscar, but our confidence in you is, er, shaken. I . . . .

ADRIAN (*prompting*): Go on.

CONSTANCE: I couldn't *trust* you enough after . . . after . . . . (*She can't continue.*)

ADRIAN: Trusting you for twelve years and finding her trust misplaced.

OSCAR: But, Constance, I told you . . . .

CONSTANCE: You hate Bosie. And those other . . . beasts. You have said good-by to all that!

OSCAR: And what I wrote the home secretary . . . .

CONSTANCE: You had been crazy . . . you had contracted a terrible disease . . . !

OSCAR: All of which is now behind me.

CONSTANCE: You would try to change . . . yes . . . but, er . . . . (*She falters.*)

ADRIAN (*stepping into the breach*): We have consulted experts on that disease, that form of . . . insanity. They—we—respect your change of . . . intention, but expert opinion—alienists who have given their whole lives to this study—is that you are unlikely to succeed. It is a . . . leprosy, a . . . cancer, for which there is no cure.

OSCAR: Constance?

CONSTANCE: I don't know, Oscar. But even if the doctors are wrong . . . I wouldn't know, now, how to begin again. It *is* too late.

(Silence.)

OSCAR: Then I have only the children left.

*(*CONSTANCE *flutters and gasps.)*

OSCAR: When I get out. Is Adrian working out the arrangements on that too? Custody. Six months with you, six with me? Or will you take Vyvyan, and I, Cyril? Cyril is . . . my particular friend.

(Silence.)

CONSTANCE *(nervously)*: In here . . . you lose touch, Oscar.

OSCAR: With what?

ADRIAN *(to* CONSTANCE): Tell him.

CONSTANCE: Oscar, what we have come here for . . . Adrian offered to come alone but I thought you should hear it from me . . . . *(Swallowing.)* The custody of the children will be entrusted to me.

OSCAR: Alone? To you alone?

ADRIAN: Of course.

OSCAR: I won't give my consent! *(Silence.)* My consent is not needed? My refusal has no legal force?

ADRIAN: Psychologists have studied the children of . . . broken homes . . . where the father is . . . one of those. Such children have suffered damage to the brain.

OSCAR *(as a feeling of helplessness overcomes him, muttering)*: My children are mine.

ADRIAN *(relentless)*: Such damage to Cyril and Vyvyan must not be risked. They must never know what happened. They will be placed in a good Christian school—outside Britain—under a new family name. In that way, schoolfellows who may hear of this . . . scandal will not connect them with it, and all the boys themselves will know is that their father disappeared.

OSCAR *(his head bursting, his consciousness "spaced," manically reiterating)*: My children are mine! My children are mine!

(They disappear. LORD ALFRED *resumes.)*

So Oscar went rip-roaring mad, and wrote me a hundred-page letter— De Profundis the wretched Ross called it—saying I was the source of all his troubles and he would never see me again. What rot. As the whole world knows, he would rush back into my arms at the earliest opportunity. To each his lies and libels! To each his fantasies! What did happen to Oscar in those last days at Reading? I have a recurring fantasy—would you like to hear it, Father Murphy? It is that England's gay prime minister, Lord Rosebery, came to Reading and confronted England's most notorious homosexual . . . he called himself . . .

TWENTY-THREE

Governor's office in Reading Gaol. A stranger, promptly identified as MR. HIGGINS, *is sitting there alone, as* OSCAR *is shown in by* WARDER. HIGGINS *gives the latter a signal to leave.*

HIGGINS (*completing* LORD ALFRED's *sentence*): Higgins. My name is Higgins. The home office has received your petition. I have been instructed to inform you that the answer must be in the negative.

OSCAR (*not quite absorbing this, cupping an ear in one hand*): What was that?

HIGGINS (*finding his own words now*): There is nothing else for it. You will serve the full sentence.

OSCAR: Did you think I was lying?

HIGGINS: What *I* think is not in question, Mr. Wilde: I am . . . the messenger boy.

OSCAR (*as if he hadn't heard this*): I have repented what I did, what I was. He whom I loved, perversely, I now loathe. She whom I foully betrayed I love once more, if in vain.

HIGGINS (*beginning to tell him this is not his business*): Mr. Wilde, really—

OSCAR: No easy matter: Repentance. Recantation.

HIGGINS: Mr. Wilde, again I—

OSCAR: They think it was an empty gesture, do they? Galileo declaring the sun moves round the earth?

HIGGINS (*smoothly*): I am willing, if you wish, to drop the messenger role. What I say now, Higgins of the home office has not said.

OSCAR: What is the point? Your news is final, I assume?

HIGGINS (*nodding*): And your petition was the final appeal. Above the home secretary you cannot go.

OSCAR: Then you and I have nothing to discuss. (*Silence.*)

HIGGINS (*gently*): It seems you not only *hoped* your petition would succeed, you actually *assumed* it would, is that true?

OSCAR (*slowly*): That is true.

HIGGINS (*evenly*): Why *was* that?

OSCAR: I was *told* so.

HIGGINS: By?

OSCAR: By my wife. Who had it from a man whose name, at least, is Hope. (*Silence.*) And what was I requesting? A few months deducted from a sentence. I was appealing to high authority: above public opinion, above all middle-class prejudice. I groveled on my belly. What more is needed? What more is possible? (*Having been speaking, as it were, to the world, he now focuses on* HIGGINS.) Please don't *answer* my questions, Mr. Messenger Boy.

HIGGINS: You amaze me, Mr. Wilde. I wonder what your understanding now is of . . . all that has happened.

OSCAR (*with unwonted crudity*): I am in Reading Gaol for being queer. For which I repented. Denounced all queers. Agreed that queerdom is a psychosis, but asked, "Now I have sworn off my former life, vowed to lead another one, have a little mercy!"

HIGGINS: You have gone through a lot.

OSCAR: What amazes you?

HIGGINS: Your idea of the home office, the government, Imperial Britain . . . . What happened in the last trial?

OSCAR: I lost.

HIGGINS: Why?

OSCAR: Lockwood got a British jury to believe the truth. Is that what's so amazing?

HIGGINS: And who is Lockwood?

OSCAR: Solicitor general.

HIGGINS: The government, then.

OSCAR: I've heard there was politics in it.

HIGGINS: Was there *anything else* in it?

OSCAR: The Liberals couldn't afford to be soft with sodomites; they had some in their own ranks.

HIGGINS: On the lower echelons?

OSCAR: Oh, I heard . . . on the highest.

HIGGINS: Ah!

OSCAR: Ah?

HIGGINS: Evidently, it is not *forbidden* to be queer.

OSCAR: All the more reason that I might expect a little . . . mercy.

HIGGINS: And you ask why you amaze me! Let me go back to the trial *before* the last. I disagree with those who think you were self-destructive. You came within an inch of victory. If *that* jury, instead of throwing up its hands, had awarded you the verdict, what would your victory have meant?

OSCAR: Victory would have meant permission to exist—for me and . . . .

HIGGINS: Every other . . . sodomite?

OSCAR: It would have reversed the previous trial and ruled that the Queensberrys of this world may *not* send such messages.

HIGGINS: And, if even a lord is prevented by law from remarking that someone poses as a sodomite, when that someone *is* a sodomite, that someone may be said to have got away not only with sodomy but with the right not to have it remarked upon, even by a lord. Do you see now what your crime was?

OSCAR: What my crime was has been stated ad nauseam by Queensberry, Carson, Lockwood, the judge . . . by the world's press!

HIGGINS: And who reads "world's press"? The world's middle class. Philistia. Talking to them, one talks their language, puts on a show in a style of theater that is all theirs. And what is their speciality? One may learn the answer from the works of . . . Mr. Oscar Wilde. The middle-class speciality is *morality*, which, as that author has wittily demonstrated, is founded on *hypocrisy*. You have, therefore, gone over the heads of the actors and the audience of that show—to the men at the top. The top of the world. The pinnacle of power. Good. Your crime, in their eyes, can hardly be a vice which a great many of them also practice. Your crime must then be . . . . (*He pauses to let* OSCAR *finish the sentence.*)

OSCAR: The breaking of the eleventh commandment, "Thou shalt not be found out"?

HIGGINS (*smoothly continuing as if he himself had made this last remark*): The breaking of which commandment is a threat to their authority. Your claim to *respect* that authority is thereby shown to be empty and idle. They must, to the contrary, use their authority to stop you once and for all.

OSCAR: My crime was to make some highly placed sodomite shake in his shoes?

HIGGINS: And with him other persons at the pinnacle of power. You threatened a whole social order by threatening one of its basic rules. That rule is not heterosexuality. It is the tacit agreement to—just as an example—keep it dark if you are not heterosexual—to commit yourself to a double life.

OSCAR: As if I hadn't led it! At Oxford! On my American tours! In London with Robbie . . . . But how is it I can tell *you* such things?

HIGGINS: You have nothing left to lose. You *have* been stopped. And, er, by whom?

OSCAR: Oh, by the people I . . . repented to.

HIGGINS: And what is repentance but a child's ruse to get himself kissed and hugged by father or mother? You *are* a child, Oscar—

OSCAR: Oscar!

HIGGINS: That is more than half your charm. But we have put away childish things.

OSCAR: We?

HIGGINS: The modern state. Godless, impersonal, impervious. It cannot concern itself with children's cries of repentance. If there is an obstacle in its path, it removes that obstacle. A juggernaut, if you will, but the juggernaut was primitive like the stake, like the cross. The state is subtle. No fires, no nails through the hands. Our middle class, as also our conformist masses, are more impressed by a slight whiff of scandal. What an opportunity then, for a statesman, to pen the scandalous headline that will be carried by every newspaper in the country to descend as decisively as the guillotine upon the neck of its victim! You requested a few months deducted from a sentence. A small request, but how can the state even begin to consider it, having set in motion the machinery of liquidation—through scandal to ostracism and exile!

OSCAR: Lord Queensberry's curse!

HIGGINS: No new life awaits you on your release. No home. No homeland. Your children will have other names. You will have another name again. Living nowhere, in the company of no one, yourself No-one, No-thing, Non-entity . . . . (OSCAR *is weeping*.) I have said too much.

OSCAR (*almost as if he could manage a normal tone of voice*): Better men than I have heard the news, "You will be shot at dawn." Am I the first to be told, "You were shot yesterday"? (*He rises unsteadily to his feet*.) All that repentance business—beside the point! Ridiculous! (*Silence.*) May I go now?

HIGGINS: I will call the warder.

(He moves towards the door but stops when OSCAR *speaks.)*

OSCAR (*in a dead voice*): I don't know who you are, Mr. Higgins, but I know what you are. (*Silence.*) You're a successful one, and I'm an unsuccessful one. Ha? (*Silence.*) Is your answer the answer? Are you any more at peace in your heart of hearts than this miserable prisoner of Reading Gaol upon whom you have pronounced a nameless doom?

(Their eyes meet. The clock ticks. HIGGINS *opens the door and calls through it.)*

HIGGINS: Warder!

(They disappear. LORD ALFRED *resumes.)*

LORD ALFRED (*now drunk and reckless*): Penniless after Reading, Oscar got a monthly allowance from his wife on condition that he never see me again, and I got an allowance from my mother on condition that I didn't see *him* again. What could we do, when he got out, but fall into each other's arms and forfeit the money? Big to-do in the world press. When we shared a double bed in a Naples hotel room, it shook the Empire from London to Melbourne. Only we weren't fucking. (*This isn't his usual tone, and, we may imagine, Father Murphy gasps.*) Doing sex, I should say. Just tried to be, well, what? Loving friends? As in days of yore. Managed it for a week or two. But we were somewhat different people now and ready to realize that whatever love is, we were not really . . . compatible. Had been in love with . . . ideas of each other. Phantoms, phantasies. *My* phantom of the Great White Father. Not patron saint, Patron Genius. His phantom of . . . well, among other things, "a slim gilt soul walking between passion and poetry." I returned to my family's world and their estates in the country, even my father's part of it, all huntin', shootin', and fishin'. Oscar returned to

HIS world, the big, bad city, the rich and famous and, equally, the poor and outrageous and, if London was closed to him now, then Paris. Next I knew, less than two years had passed, he was dead in a Paris hotel room, leaving unpaid bills. Even his funeral wasn't paid for. I took care of all that. (*He stops as if that should be the end of his story. Resuming:*) What was Oscar's death to me? A liberation? I now said goodbye to . . . all that. (*He hurriedly pours himself what's left in the carafe, offering no port to Father Murphy. His hand shakes.*) Got married. Became a father. Wrote a memoir explaining that Oscar was . . . homosexual but that I was a Douglas and a gentleman. Included photos of wife and son. (*He sighs.*) Wasn't too good at this. Left the wife. My son—mental trouble, you know—had to put him away in one of those "homes." Where to turn? If not, Father, to our Holy Catholic Church? I converted. Why? Well, mostly to declare myself celibate, totally abstinent. As my confessor, you happen to know—but daren't tell anyone—that I cheated once in a while. But not often, hm? Holy Bosie! And there endeth my off-the-record super-confession. (*Silence. Is this silence an accusation?*) A bit confusing, I suppose. Didn't end quite as it began, I suppose. Turned around at some point. Is that what you're telling me? (*Silence.*) Very well, I lied about Oscar in that book. And in other books that followed. But I wasn't lying when I denied sex with Oscar, we never . . . or hardly ever . . . Well, oh yes, I lied when I denied sex with the other chaps—"all the boys of Oxford and half of those of London," as one dear friend put it. I lied when I denied . . . pimping for Oscar, how would he have found those lads without me? So, Father, I have now confessed everything. Everything I did. Everything that happened. Yes? (*Silence.*) I can read your mind, you goddamned Jesuit. What one *didn't* do is still a reality, *the* reality, if it is *there:* Inside. Do you know, Father, *inside*, I think I was *queer* from the day I was born. Yes. So my life since Oscar died has been one long pretense. Not a life. A death. For as you have guessed—if you didn't know all along, you damned Jesuit—I am queer right now. Queer and utterly unable to turn over any damned new leaf. (*The carafe being empty, he grabs an open bottle from the sideboard and pours wine for them both. His tone changes.*) In prison, Oscar repented his homosexuality, or thought he did, but when he got out, he repented that repentance, recanted that recantation. "Queensbury's charge *is* libel now," he said: "I do not pose as a sodomite, I *am* a sodomite." No double life now. No hiding behind Constance. No hiding behind (*He points to himself*) a slim gilt soul walking between passion and poetry. But instead? "Passion with the *mask* of love will be my consolation." With the boys of the Paris boulevards. (*Another change of tone: a touch of nostalgia now for the days of yore.*) I can see him now in his last days in that tatty hotel, drinking champagne—dying as he had lived, beyond his means—he said that, predicting from his deathbed that *the road will be red with monstrous martyrdoms but the criminal law amendment act will be repealed and we shall win.* You don't think of Oscar on a deathbed. (*Savagely:*) I'm on a deathbed. I've been on my deathbed for forty-five years. (*Nostalgically, again:*) You think of Oscar at a gay bar, that's what the young folks call them nowadays, his last birthday dinner, responding to a toast, his name is now Sebastian Melmoth—

EPILOGUE

Kalisaya Bar on the Boulevard des Italiens, Paris. Accordion music. Laughter. A dinner is just ending. OSCAR *is in the place of honor. In the theater, the guests are the audience, to whom* OSCAR *will address an after-dinner speech. Beside* OSCAR *is a beautiful teenage* BOY, *flauntingly gay in dress and deportment. The* BOY *jumps on his chair and claps his hands for silence.*

BOY: Messieurs-Dames! Les messieurs qui sont dames! Et les dames qui sont messieurs! (*Laughter, cries of "En anglais, s'il vous plaît!"*) En anglais? (*He will speak English with an accent.*) Thank you, thank you, everyone. I shall now ask our guest of honor to respond. Messieurs-Dames, I give you Monsieur-Madame Sebastian Melmoth! (*Applause as* OSCAR *rises to his feet.*)

OSCAR (*ad-libbing*): Little boys, Maurice, should be obscene and not heard. What do you think of Maurice, everyone? Eyes like the night! A scarlet flower for a mouth! The most beautifully curved lips in Paris! But his eyelashes are a shade too long. There once was a man who kept committing the gravest of all offenses, but he repented and was born again. You people—if anyone—can guess what happened next, can't you?

VOICE (*calling out*): He was caught in bed with a pageboy?

OSCAR: Correct! And the righteous said unto him, "Didst thou not vow, O Man, to turn over a new leaf?" And the man replied: "How can I turn over a new leaf before getting to the bottom of the page?" (*Loud applause, which* OSCAR *grandly acknowledges in the manner of a professional artiste.*) And when Jesus came to the city, he heard sounds of revelry, and saw there a youth following a harlot. And Jesus said to the youth, "Why lookest thou on this woman with lust?" And the youth answered, "I was blind and thou gavest me sight: what else should I look at?" And Jesus turned to the woman and said: "But why art thou walking in the way of sin?" And the woman answered: "Because it is pleasant, and my sins are forgiven— by thee." (*Murmurs of appreciation, warmer but more restrained applause, silence.*) Once upon a time there was a Child of the Sun who was brought up among the Children of the Earth. So people thought of him as a Child of the Earth. He even thought of himself as a Child of the Earth. Sometimes, however, he behaved in the manner of the Children of the Sun. And when he had done so once too often, the Children of the Earth locked him up in a dungeon, dropping a little hint that, should he repent, they would let him go free and, born again, he would *become* a Child of the Earth and live happily ever after. Well, he not only pretended to repent, he went to all the trouble of really repenting. He now hated himself—his original self—hated all Children of the Sun, including his friends, including his very best friend. Did the Children of the Earth let him go free? Did they? (OSCAR *appeals to his audience.*)

VOICE: Like Hell they did.

OSCAR: "No," they said, "Thank you so much for kissing the emperor's foot." I'm mixing my stories! (*Low key again.*) He served out his long term in the dungeon and, upon emerging, was not born again nor was he happy ever after. He came to a premature end, which is also the official end of the story.

(The tale is received with understanding, rather quietly. OSCAR *takes the white handkerchief from his breast pocket to wipe his perspiring brow; he has let himself go completely in telling this, his last story of the evening. Then steady applause starts, and* OSCAR *raises a hand for silence. He now drops all theatrical airs and speaks with simple conviction and deep feeling.)*

OSCAR: Unofficially, I wish to add that he was not *un*happy ever after, nor did he *wish* any longer to be born again. "Once is enough, sometimes too much," he said, "and one is what one is." "Only the worth-less," he also said, "can be reformed. People who can do *these things* must be dead to all sense of shame." And he resolved to live *so*— (OS-CAR *picks up this word and seems to offer it to his audience by bringing thumb and index finger together.*) "so!"—unsaved, unregenerate, impenitent, shame-less! Declining to be shamed by a shameful world.

H FOR HAMLET

For Gordon Rogoff

Vesti la giubba e la faccia infarina . . .

CHARACTERS
(eight men, two women)

Martin, alias Bernardo
Jimmy, alias Francisco
Jack, alias Reynaldo
William, alias Shakespeare
Curtis Browne, alias Hamlet
The Honorable Hugh Simpson, alias Attendant, alias Claudius
Mrs. Simpson, alias Gertrude, alias Ophelia
Susie Simpson, alias Ophelia
Dr. Theodor Sturm, alias Polonius
James H. Denmark

The place is Northern Long Island.

The time is "Now": 1920, 1950, 1980?

The play can be produced with either one or two sets. For further details, see the text itself.

Act One

The scene is laid in the hall of Elsinore, a castle on Northern Long Island, presumably built by an admirer of Shakespeare in the age of Jay Gould and Commodore Vanderbilt. The hall very much resembles the kind of setting Hamlet *often receives in our time: behind and beside the two thrones on the dais, all is curtains, archways, dark corridors, and chiaroscuro. The only eccentric feature is the presence—opposite the thrones—of two statues. One, as we at once perceive, is of* HAMLET *himself; the other as we might easily guess, of* OPHELIA. *Both figures seem to be about twenty years old. They are sculpted naturalistically (George Segal style) and, in production, must be exact likenesses of the actors playing* CURTIS BROWNE *and* SUSIE SIMPSON, *respectively.*

When the curtain rises, the stage is empty. The hall is dimly lit in the manner of modern atmospheric lighting men: we can't see much but we hear everyone else whispering: "Isn't it wonderful?" Silence. Then, from the shadows, a voice, casual and cool.

VOICE: Hey, Bernardo! Where's that damn light switch?

SECOND VOICE (*in the same manner*): What do you want the light switch for, Francisco? He should see it as it always is.

THIRD VOICE: Pitch dark in the middle of the morning! Are there no windows in here?

FIRST VOICE: Not a one, my dear!

SECOND VOICE: The existence of a light switch is top secret.

FIRST VOICE: And we'll treat you like a VIP. Got the switch now, Bernardo?

SECOND VOICE: Hold on to your seats! (*Short pause.*) Let there be light! (*General harsh white light comes on, and the owners of the voices are revealed. The first voice comes from* JIMMY, *the second from* MARTIN, *the third from* JACK. JIMMY *and* MARTIN *are*

*Bohemian sons of respectable middle-class families who had be-
come roommates in Greenwich Village until the need for cash put
them on the road to Elsinore. It was summer stock they tried first.
They are actors—members of Equity, as they will soon proclaim—so
here we find them, dressed for* Hamlet, MARTIN *as Bernardo,*
JIMMY *as Francisco. As for* JACK, *as we soon learn, he is a
newcomer and is being shown the ropes by the other two.* JACK's
*background is very different. He is from out west, and everything in
the east still makes his eyes pop and his mouth drop open. Naturally,
the other two enjoy teasing him. When the lights go on, there is a
pause while* JACK *gazes at the hall in astonishment.*)

JACK: Gee!

JIMMY: Of course, this isn't how you should see it. Not the right
lighting at all.

MARTIN: He doesn't even know electric light exists. (*He indicates
that the "he" referred to is off in the direction of the wings.*)

JIMMY: Uses candles, torches, lanterns . . . .

JACK: Gee! (*Growing used to his astonishment, he turns from the hall
to his two companions.*) And you fellows—guess I haven't really
seen you yet. Which of you is which?

MARTIN: I'm Bernardo.

JIMMY: I'm Francisco.

JACK: What?

MARTIN: And this is the Royal Council Chamber at Elsinore!

JIMMY: Or, if you like, the Prince's Bedchamber at Elsinore.

MARTIN: It kind of jumps around—unit set, see what I mean?
Depends what scene (*pointing again to the wings*) he has in mind.

JIMMY: Bedchamber, Council Chamber, Closet Scene . . . .

JACK: Hey, stop a minute, you said Elsinore?

JIMMY: Didn't you know? The place is an exact replica of the one in
Denmark.

MARTIN: "You are welcome to Elsinore."

JIMMY: Got it now?

JACK: But that's some *other* play.

JIMMY: What?

JACK: Didn't I see that one in Seattle? About the Oedipus complex or something?

MARTIN: "Let the bloat king tempt you again to bed . . . ."

JIMMY: "Pinch wanton on your cheek, call you his mouse . . . ."

JACK: But that isn't *Macbeth*.

JIMMY: *Macbeth*?

MARTIN: *Macbeth*!

JIMMY: This is *Hamlet*, my dear.

MARTIN: The melancholy Dane!

JIMMY: "The glass of fashion and the mould of form!"

MARTIN: "The observed of all observers"—

JACK: Hey, well, why didn't Mr. Browne tell me this when he hired me?

JIMMY: Mr. Browne?

MARTIN: Oh, he'd think you already knew!

JIMMY: You knew you were replacing Malcolm, my dear!

JACK: But Malcolm's a character in *Macbeth*!

MARTIN: You *are* mixed up. Malcolm was his *real* name. Malcolm Jones. In here he was Horatio.

JIMMY: Oh boy, what a part!

JACK: Well, Malcolm did quit, didn't he? I mean: the real Malcolm really quit?

MARTIN (*to* JACK): Malcolm Jones quit. But what could we tell *him*? He suspected dirty work. A plot—to remove Horatio—his best friend—

JACK: But Mr. Browne didn't say a word of all this—

MARTIN: He had something else to think of. His mother died.

JACK: His mother?

MARTIN: Died. Last week.

JIMMY: "When sorrows come they come not single spies/ But in battalions."

JACK: But—

JIMMY: You're in trouble, aren't you, my dear?

MARTIN: Too bad we can't say *you're* Horatio.

JACK: What *is* my part?

JIMMY: We don't know!

JACK: You don't know?

MARTIN: Well, um, Reynaldo.

JACK (*weakly*): Reynaldo?

JIMMY: "Where's Reynaldo?" he says.

MARTIN: And answers his own question.

JIMMY: "Off in Paris," he says, "off in Paris again. He should be here!"

MARTIN: We looked him up. Servant to Polonius, the book says.

JIMMY: Just that, servant to Polonius.

MARTIN: Another nonentity.

JACK: Another?

MARTIN (*glumly*): I'm—Bernardo.

JACK: Bernardo?

JIMMY: He.

JACK: What?

MARTIN: He. That's what it says. Bernardo, he.

JIMMY: "He comes most carefully upon his hour" and all that!

JACK: Who are you again?

JIMMY (*haughtily*): Francisco.

    (*Awkward pause.*)

MARTIN: But Malcolm had a real part. Horatio!

JIMMY: "Give me the man that is not passion's slave"—

MARTIN: "And I will wear him in my heart of hearts"—

JIMMY: As he did Malcolm.

    (*Another pause.*)

MARTIN: What a waste!

JIMMY: We're professionals, you know.

MARTIN: Members of Actors Equity.

JIMMY: Veterans of summer stock and the subway circuit.

JACK: Gee! Why did you quit—for this?

(Pause.)

JIMMY: Shall we tell him the awful truth?

MARTIN: Occupational unemployment.

JIMMY: We had to eat.

MARTIN: For that matter, what brings you here, my good man?

JACK: Well, gee, I guess I saw Mr. Browne's ad in the paper—

JIMMY: You have to eat too! Tsk, tsk, tsk.

MARTIN: Where are you from, brother?

JACK: Out west. Idaho.

MARTIN: What?!

JIMMY: But how divine!

MARTIN: This your first job in the East?

JACK: Yeah.

(JIMMY giggles.)

JACK: You guys aren't bitter, are you?

JIMMY: Are we, Bernardo?

MARTIN: We're frustrated, that's what.

JIMMY: Bernardo!

MARTIN (*to* JACK): Not the way he means. What *I* mean is: we wear these damn costumes—then we never go on stage.

JIMMY: Bernardo calls that Form without Content!

MARTIN: Form without Content. "Bernardo and Francisco"—

JIMMY (*sighing*): —"gentlemen of the guard"—*not* a nice thing to be!

MARTIN: Worse still to act—

JIMMY (*to* JACK): Now he's going to philosophize.

MARTIN (*darkly*): A real gentleman of the guard hasn't much of a part, that's true, but he doesn't *know* he has a part at all, see? It isn't a part, it's life, see what I mean? He's in the battle of life, championing his interests, fighting his rivals and so forth. But we—

JIMMY: We're frustrated! (*Before* MARTIN *can protest:*) Your own word, my dear!

MARTIN: Dressed up like this—for what?

JIMMY: For what, indeed?

MARTIN: We're puppets locked away in a closet!

JIMMY (*to* JACK, *indicating* MARTIN): Isn't he just great? (*Before* MARTIN *can speak:*) But you exaggerate, my dear Bernardo, we do have lines. We have to *improvize* lines—in character too!

MARTIN (*disgusted*): That's nothing.

JACK: Nothing?! You call it nothing? How am *I* to speak in character. I've been working on *Macbeth*. Bet you I could do any part in the play—

MARTIN (*cutting him down*): Well, now you're Reynaldo.

JIMMY: Servant to Polonius.

MARTIN: The nosy Parker he sent to Paris to follow Laertes to the whorehouse—

JIMMY: Bernardo knows everything! We have twenty-seven different editions of *Hamlet* in there—

MARTIN: I use the Variorum.

JIMMY: But first we'll give you a few pointers.

MARTIN (*swinging* JACK *round to face the statues*): Who are they, for instance?

JACK: How would I know?

JIMMY: That's *him*. An exact likeness.

MARTIN: That is, it *was* an exact likeness. Twenty years ago.

JIMMY (*indicating the other statue*): And who do you think she is?

JACK: His girl friend?

MARTIN: "The most beautified Ophelia . . . ."

JIMMY: "A vile phrase . . . ."

JACK: What?

JIMMY: "Beautified is a vile phrase."

JACK: But anyone can see these are modern statues!

MARTIN: Think so?

JIMMY: "There are more things in heaven and earth, Reynaldo,/Than are dreamt of in your philosophy."

MARTIN: You think they're out of place?

JACK: Well, yes.

MARTIN (*gloomily*): They'd certainly be out of place if they were real statues.

JACK: If they were . . . . But if they aren't real statues, what on earth are they?

MARTIN: Oh, they're statues—

JIMMY: For a died-in-the-wool materialist like you—

MARTIN: But for *him*?

JACK: For him? (*He gapes at the statues.*)

JIMMY: "Look now upon this statue, now on that!"

MARTIN: Images!

JIMMY: Heard of Shakespeare's images, my dear?

JACK: Well, um—

JIMMY: Here they are!

MARTIN: What do you see when you look in a mirror?

JACK: Myself!

MARTIN: Wrong.

JIMMY: An image, my dear!

JACK: Gee, you fellows—

MARTIN: Well, here are two such images. Living images in a world which— (*He shrugs.*)

JIMMY: Well, you'll soon see.

JACK: Phew! A guy could go crazy in here!

MARTIN (*frowning*): Crazy?

JIMMY (*indignant*): Crazy?

JACK: Yes, er— Well, you know what I mean.

MARTIN: Ahem.

JIMMY: You don't know much philosophy, do you?

JACK: I guess not.

JIMMY: You'll learn some here.

JACK: You guys sure picked up a lot.

MARTIN: Well, living in the company of the Immortal Bard—

(But MARTIN *is interrupted by a hurried opening of a door, and in comes an elderly man in the clothes of a twentieth century butler. He looks like a seedy Greenwich Village poet.)*

MAN (*weakly*): Now shut up a minute everybody—

JACK (*pointing at the butler's clothes*): He can come in *here*?

MARTIN (*catching on to this*): Intruder from the twentieth century, avaunt!

JIMMY: Avaunt and quit our sight! Course, it could be an ambassador from Norway, you know, we never did get protocol on that—

MARTIN: Go, Voltimand! I sternly bid thee go!—

JIMMY: Yes, get thee to a nunnery—

MARTIN: And be a breeder of sinners—

JIMMY (*to* JACK): Must have been *lovely* in those nunneries.

MAN: Francisco, shut your silly little trap and listen—

MARTIN: But thou art not allowed within these walls—

JIMMY (*to* JACK): He thinks Shakespeare wrote that lousy line! (*To* MAN:) Therefore be gone, thou haught, insulting man! (*To* JACK:) What do you think of that one?

MARTIN: Are you still there, truepenny?

JIMMY: Give him some light, away!

JACK: But who is this?

MARTIN: William. But what's in a name?

JIMMY: In costume, he's the Immortal Bard himself!

WILLIAM (*trying to be haughty*): When you've all quite finished! Mr. Browne is here!

MARTIN: To see how Junior's doing (*indicating* JACK).

WILLIAM: No, no. He's not alone—

MARTIN: Girls?

JIMMY: You know what *they* are, don't you, Reynaldo?

WILLIAM: No, no, not girls!

MARTIN: Ladies, then? Friends of Mr. Browne?

JIMMY (*to* JACK): Mr. Browne goes in for that sort of thing.

WILLIAM: Yes, his fiancée—

MARTIN: But he's engaged to—

JIMMY: Miss Susie Simpson. Daughter of—well, not *the* Simpsons,— exactly—but *those* Simpsons.

JACK: What Simpsons?

JIMMY: You'll know soon enough.

MARTIN: Who are the others?

WILLIAM: There's her mother—Mrs. Simpson.

MARTIN (*an explosion*): What?

JIMMY: Mrs. Simpson?

MARTIN: Mrs. Simpson—here? (*Urgently.*) Who are the men?

WILLIAM: There's Mr. Simpson—

MARTIN: Mr. Simpson—!

JIMMY: The Honorable Hugh?

WILLIAM: That's what they tell me, Mr. Browne's the only one of 'em I ever saw before—

MARTIN: Anyone else?

WILLIAM: Yes—

JIMMY: Another girl?

WILLIAM: A man. Middle-aged fellow. Foreign looking.

MARTIN: Who is he?

WILLIAM: They call him doctor . . . .

MARTIN: Another psychiatrist!

JIMMY (*to* JACK): They keep trying to cure *him*, see?

WILLIAM: Only this one's different.

JIMMY: Really! (*To* JACK:) Psychiatrists—I love them all!

MARTIN: Of what school? Freud? Jung? Wilhelm Reich?

WILLIAM: Mr. Simpson said he was a law unto himself. Mrs. Simpson said, "That's shocking." And Mr. Simpson replied, "Why not? His speciality is Psychodramatic Shock Treatment."

MARTIN: What?!

JIMMY (*almost winking at* MARTIN): We'll shock the pants off him before he's through!

MARTIN: No Form without Content about this!

JIMMY: Maybe we'll learn what Content without Form is like!

WILLIAM: Well, I guess it's no use trying to tell you guys anything—

JIMMY: But you did come to tell us—

WILLIAM: That they'll be coming in here right away—

MARTIN: In here?

JIMMY: Mrs. Simpson?!

MARTIN: High tragedy I call this!

JACK: I don't get it—

JIMMY: Why, that's Mrs. Simpson (*pointing to the statue of* OPHELIA).

MARTIN: That *was* Mrs. Simpson—

JIMMY: She was the model, see?

MARTIN: His girl friend as you put it—

JIMMY: So if *he* sees the real Mrs. Simpson, you can expect fireworks—

WILLIAM: Is he still asleep?

MARTIN: Sure—in there (*pointing off stage*).

WILLIAM: If he wakes up, you'll have to hold him there a while.

JIMMY: Are you joking?

MARTIN: He has the strength of ten when he's wild.

JIMMY: And there's only us three.

WILLIAM: Then tie him up while he's still asleep. (*They are amazed.*) Mr. Browne's orders. You should have let me get 'em out when I first came in. Now go into him. Go on. Go on. I can't keep them waiting any longer.

(*The three attendants leave.* WILLIAM *goes to the door on the other side and admits a young man who seems so much the Princetonian good fellow and socialite that the black mourning-band on his arm strikes a discordant note.*)

YOUNG PRINCETONIAN: Everything under control, William?

WILLIAM: Yes, Mr. Browne.

BROWNE: Good. (*He returns to the door he entered by and brings in the three Simpsons whom we have just heard about. Also the psychiatrist.*)

BROWNE's *fiancée*, SUSIE SIMPSON, *is of course the exact likeness of the statue of* OPHELIA, *lean, wanting but a touch to be haggard and gaunt, with big staring eyes; and yet the likeness would escape the casual observer, as* SUSIE *is rather obviously modern, wears flat-heeled shoes and a raincoat, and chews gum. The gum-chewing is of course one of her excesses; it is not "in character" for this Bryn Mawr girl except insofar as rebellion against parental gentility is the essence of her character.*

In MRS. SIMPSON *we see the queenly woman against whom* SUSIE *is, though she may not know it yet, rebelling. Queenly at any rate by the standards of Park Avenue and the ladies' clubs, she has an ample facade and has made heroic efforts, perhaps too evident, to keep it in repair. "A veritable Valkyry," said a romantic columnist. "Her face is made of plaster and it's peeling," SUSIE explained to a girl friend, who replied: "I know someone just like her—remember the dowager in the Marx Brothers' pictures?" But that is only how the young see her. The middle-aged may deny that she is even . . . middle-aged.*

Though the title of the HONORABLE HUGH SIMPSON *would indicate that its owner is an Englishman, it would indicate wrong. He was an Englishman; but now all that's left is the name. He is both an American and an Honorable, a combination that would be too much for most men, and is certainly too much for him. Nature never intended him for an Englishman either; he is too short. But he is married to a tall woman all the same; so we must credit him with courage, or rather we must credit with courage the man he once was. Who would ever guess now that they called him Bantam Cock at Princeton long ago? Today* SUSIE's *friends are just as rough on him as on her mother. One of them has been forbidden the Simpson house because he had said rather too loudly at a party: "Susie, come over here and leave that mousy little man alone!" However, it was* MRS. SIMPSON *who did the forbidding, and secretly at that, for* MR. SIMPSON *makes rather a thing of being a butt;* MRS. SIMPSON *likes him to be her butt, not everyone else's.*

DR. THEODOR STURM's* *beard is rather a disappointment—a*

---

* Pronounced German-fashion: "Shtoorm."

goatee, a mere wisp of grey hair. But there are red hairs among the grey, and the head makes up for everything by being perfectly enormous, an effect nonetheless shocking since his body is rather below the normal size. Shocking: the word shock, as WILLIAM *warned, is inseparable from* DR. STURM. *Until he arrived in New York, shock treatment was an archaism like mesmerism or blood-letting. "But why must everything be in Latin?" as he wisely says. "Psychiatry is the baby of the sciences, it must speak the common language of men. To give my method a Latin name would be to combine pretentiousness with obscurity. I like the term Shock Treatment. It gives people a shock. And since it is not sufficiently explicit I call it Psychodramatic Shock Treatment . . . ." What he means by this, he will have ample opportunity to explain.)*

BROWNE: Come in, Doctor.

*(*STURM *enters, followed by* SIMPSON. *Pause.)*

STURM: *Ach so!*

SIMPSON: What do you think of it, Doctor?

STURM: *Kolossal!* But you've seen it before.

SIMPSON: Not for twenty years. You like it?

STURM (*with gusto*): I . . . appreciate it. A marvellous demonstration. Subjectivity objectified! Psychosis symbolized in three-dimensional solids! But, of course (*he raises a warning finger*), nothing will cure this—except perhaps—I say perhaps—

SIMPSON: Well, what?

STURM: Shock Treatment.

SIMPSON: What?

STURM: Psychodramatic Shock Treatment.

SIMPSON: Oh. Oh, yes, of course.

(Awkward pause, ended by a noise at the door and the entrance of MRS. SIMPSON.*)*

MRS. SIMPSON (*irritably*): My dear Hugh, I do wish you wouldn't go wandering off— (*She sees* STURM.) Oh, I'm so sorry, Dr. Sturm— (*Turning to him, her attention is suddenly seized by something behind him.*) Ah! (*An intake of breath.*) So there it is! (*Calling out through the door she has left open.*) Susie, Susie!

SUSIE (*entering*): You've found it?

MRS. SIMPSON: Look!

SUSIE: Hey!

MRS. SIMPSON: It's not me at all, don't you see, it's you!

BROWNE: I was right, wasn't I?

SUSIE: A statue of me!

MRS. SIMPSON: No one could ever guess . . . . Hugh, you look at this, will you? We need an objective witness. Is it Susie or isn't it?

SIMPSON (*not looking*): It isn't.

MRS. SIMPSON: That's his idea of paying me a compliment. What do *you* say, Doctor?

SIMPSON (*to the* DOCTOR): Careful now! (*The* DOCTOR *starts to speak.*) Careful!

STURM: But what's the danger, for Heaven's sake?

MRS. SIMPSON: Ignore him, Doctor. He's a clown.

SUSIE: We call him the last of the English comedians.

SIMPSON: Better watch your step, Doctor.

STURM: Why, Mr. Simpson?

SIMPSON: Because you're skating on thin ice, old boy.

STURM (*laughing it off*): Ah, you speak symbolically . . . chimneys, spires, swords, umbrellas . . . all symbols of . . . . But where were we? Oh, yes. You are wrong, my friend. There's nothing surprising in this, it's natural. This girl resembles her mother. *Voilà tout!*

SIMPSON (*in a Shakespearean tone*): The ice cracks, breaks, gives way!

MRS. SIMPSON: What are *you* talking about?

SIMPSON: The doctor says the phenomenon is not surprising, it's natural. Then why are you surprised, my dear?

MRS. SIMPSON: Because it is *not* a statue of my daughter. It may be natural, but I'm taken aback.

SIMPSON: I'm not.

MRS. SIMPSON: We can't all be as bright as you, can we?

SUSIE: Oh, this bickering! (*To the* DOCTOR:) They do it all the time!

Much Ado About Nothing!

SIMPSON: Better than *Hamlet*, anyway, my dear.

SUSIE: Why?

SIMPSON: It's a comedy!

SUSIE: Pshaw!

SIMPSON: What's the matter with you? It's your mother that was surprised. You took it in stride.

MRS. SIMPSON: Obviously! She just sees herself! She doesn't think of it as me!

STURM (*who hasn't been listening*): Poor statue! It cannot escape! It can't get out of here!

SIMPSON: You don't say.

STURM: It is glued to that distant moment which Susie never knew but which—to Mrs. Simpson—means gestures, looks, smiles, that are not *in* the statue at all—

MRS. SIMPSON: That's what I was trying to explain. It isn't as if I were forever giving way to my feelings—

SIMPSON: No it isn't, is it, my dear?

MRS. SIMPSON: All right, I have none, I have no feelings. But when I do feel something, when it just comes to me, just happens, spontaneously, why must he spoil it for me, why must he always—

SUSIE: Oh, for Christ's sake!

SIMPSON: Let her talk. Give a horse its head, that's *my* motto.

BROWNE: Hugh, really!

SUSIE (*to her father*): Why didn't you stay home with your copy of *Punch*?

BROWNE: Hugh, we really must stick to the point. You know why we're here. Dr. Sturm is going to—

STURM: Precisely! (*Going cheerfully to the task.*) Now let's see if we can't clear things up. This statue of you, Mrs. Simpson. How does it come to be here? Did you give it to him—before?

MRS. SIMPSON: No, no. I was a mere school girl. I wasn't even engaged to him. I sent it to him several years after the accident. His sister asked me to.

BROWNE: My mother, that is. After his parents died, Mother and I were the only relatives he had left.

STURM: And your mother—(*Pointing to the mourning band.*)

BROWNE: Mother died a month ago, yes. Now he only has me . . . Mother saw him a week before she died, and came home in quite a state. She kept saying he could be cured.

STURM: What had given her that impression?

BROWNE: He'd said strange things to her.

STURM: Such as?

BROWNE: I wish I knew. Anyway, when she read about you in the *Times* a few days afterward—

STURM (*brightening*): Ah, you read about my work?

BROWNE: Yes, she said: "We must try him, Curtis." So I postponed the wedding—Susie and I were to have been married—

STURM: One question. Why wouldn't you brief me on all this before?

BROWNE: Mother said: "He must see Elsinore first. Let him breathe the air of Elsinore; then tell him."

STURM: I see. Your mother had the theatrical flair too?

BROWNE: Call it that.

STURM: I shall. It is admirable. Never, in a lifetime of psychodramatics, have I had so much assistance. Take the statue of Ophelia—

MRS. SIMPSON (*loudly*): Oh, leave the statue alone. (*Before he can retort.*) It's my fault, I know. Only—when I first caught sight of it—I was, well, bowled over.

STURM (*ready to pounce*): Exactly.

MRS. SIMPSON: It's a long time since I saw it, that's all.

BROWNE: That's true. It must have been here fifteen years!

MRS. SIMPSON: More than that. So, Doctor, please—

STURM: But, my dear Mrs. Simpson, how do you know *what* my view of the statue is?

MRS. SIMPSON: I'm sorry. Go on.

STURM: *Nun also.* I attach a certain importance to these statues. When were they made? Before the fancy-dress ball—or after?

MRS. SIMPSON: Why, before, of course.

STURM: That is to say, when he was quite . . . normal, quite sane? And did *he* suggest having them done?

MRS. SIMPSON: No, no. We were all having our pictures painted. He had a sculptor friend, so—

STURM: Ah, so everyone intending to go to the ball—

SIMPSON: Was having his picture done. Even me, by the way.

MRS. SIMPSON: It was rather thrilling. We could hardly wait for our costumes.

SIMPSON: We were going to have an exhibition. All the pictures in one room—with the two statues. But everyone wanted to keep his own picture—

MRS. SIMPSON: And my statue—I let *him* have it—

STURM (*pouncing*): Ah! He asked for it?

MRS. SIMPSON: Did he? I don't think so. I can't recall. It could have been his sister, Curtis's mother (*indicating* BROWNE)—

STURM: One other point. The idea of the ball—was it his?

SIMPSON: Of course not. It was my idea!

STURM: Now please, Mr. Simpson—

SIMPSON: But it was my idea. I remember exactly. It was summer. We were all on Long Island. At least twenty of us from Princeton. I'd come over from England only the year before, I'm English-born, you know . . . . We drove past this place one afternoon. It was obviously unoccupied. So I said, let's see if we could rent the place for a fancy-dress ball.

STURM: Ah! And he said: "Since it's called Elsinore, let's all be characters from *Hamlet?*"

MRS. SIMPSON: He did not! We never mentioned that word—

SIMPSON: You know about his name, don't you, old boy?

STURM: James Denmark.

SIMPSON: James *H.* Denmark.

STURM: H.?

MRS. SIMPSON: H. for Hamlet. The family name being Denmark, his parents in the theater, they were tempted and they fell, they called him Hamlet. A bitter cross to bear! None of us ever mentioned it. (*Turning to* SIMPSON.) It *was* your idea! No one else would have dreamt of—

SIMPSON: He said: "All right, what play?" I said: "Hamlet."

MRS. SIMPSON: He showed embarrassment. He looked at Hugh without flinching. He said: "All right, I'll play the prince if you"— and he turned to me—"will play Ophelia"—

STURM: He was in love with you, h'm?

MRS. SIMPSON: "So we're to be lovers?" I said. He replied: "Hamlet and Ophelia are implacable enemies."

SIMPSON: Of course he was in love with her. He gave her no peace. And she gave him no peace either.

MRS. SIMPSON (*stung*): What peace did you give either of us for that matter?

STURM: You were after her at the same time?

SIMPSON: I came, I saw, I conquered. Do you know why? I didn't ask to be taken seriously.

STURM: You didn't . . . ?

MRS. SIMPSON: That's a jab at me, Doctor.

STURM (*bewildered*): At you?

MRS. SIMPSON: And why beat about the bush? I have a . . . difficulty. (*Pause.*) I can't give myself.

STURM: Ah! I see! You—

MRS. SIMPSON: Oh, I can take my clothes off and (*looking across at* SIMPSON) that's enough for some. But I stay . . . detached. I look at a man's behind beating up and down between my thighs and I ask myself: what could be more absurd? I think of other things. Shall I dye my hair red? Red for passion? . . . They say women are made for love—how many women? It's men who drag love into everything, can't be alone with you five minutes without starting something. Love, love, love, love, love, love, love—most dreadful of the four-letter words! Grabbing your waist, clawing your neck, slapping your backside, squeezing your breasts, men make me vomit. *He* was different. Withdrawn. *He* never came at a woman mouth open and arms flailing. He went softly to bed like a wounded soldier, and all the women that knew him would have been glad to follow, so many Florence Nightingales.

STURM: You pitied him?

MRS. SIMPSON: Is it pity a woman feels for a wounded warrior? No. It is admiration—and gratitude that he enables her to be . . . useful.

STURM: Then you took *him* seriously?

MRS. SIMPSON: Almost. He was different. I was different too. Intolerant—of my home, my parents, Bryn Mawr, Northern Long Island, everything . . . . We could have been rebels together. Together we could have said, goodbye to all that, to hell with it! But he, too, looked into my eyes . . . .

STURM: He too?

MRS. SIMPSON: There comes a moment when a man takes you in his strong, strong arms and gazes deep into your eyes.

SIMPSON (*softly*): That's her cue to laugh, don't you know.

MRS. SIMPSON: That's my cue to laugh. Right in their silly faces. But why did I have to do it to *him*? I didn't dislike him. I was scared. When he looked into my eyes—he—he—

STURM: He looked into what our primitive forebears called your soul, *ja*?

MRS. SIMPSON: He looked where my soul was supposed to be—and found a blank.

SIMPSON: Come, come, my dear, you know that isn't—

MRS. SIMPSON: So I laughed. Everyone always laughed at him, and I laughed. I hate myself.

SIMPSON: Well, my dear, today they laugh at *me*—

MRS. SIMPSON: For quite the opposite reason! His dream was to be great, princely, heroic. Your affectation is—

SIMPSON: Self-abasement.

STURM: Self . . . ?

SIMPSON: Abasement, Doctor. They laugh in my face. He preferred having them laugh behind his back, I don't.

MRS. SIMPSON (*remorsefully*): It isn't true. I shouldn't have said that. You see, Doctor, how I take it out on my husband? It's disgusting, the way I treat him . . . .

SIMPSON: I wouldn't say that, my dear. All women take it out on all men, don't they, Doctor? I needn't take them seriously—they needn't take me seriously.

MRS. SIMPSON: You took me seriously at one time. (*To* STURM:) He was possessive, madly jealous—

STURM: Aha! So he (*pointing offstage*) wasn't the only unruly one?

MRS. SIMPSON: *He*? But *he* wasn't unruly at all?

STURM: No abnormal traits?

MRS. SIMPSON: He was . . . the most spiritual man I've ever met. He lived in a world of his own, a world apart.

STURM: Aha! A case of chronic alienation.

SIMPSON: He was a strange fella. Cold-blooded, don't you know.

MRS. SIMPSON: No, no, he was *full*-blooded, overflowing with creative energy . . . .

STURM (*To* SIMPSON): What do you mean: cold-blooded?

SIMPSON: He was, well, forever watching himself.

STURM: Lack of spontaneous emotion.

SIMPSON: I dunno. Maybe he had, what did you call 'em? Spontaneous feelings, but he watched *them* too. Yes, he'd fight with his own feelings, pick a quarrel with himself . . . .

MRS. SIMPSON: He once said: "Know what's wrong with me? I'm allergic to my own hormones."

SIMPSON: But he couldn't stop looking at himself, don't you know. He tried! That was why he took up acting. He said he'd "escape into other people."

STURM: He intended to be a professional actor?

SIMPSON: He adored the theater.

MRS. SIMPSON: And loathed it. His parents were actors, stars in fact, he hated the ballyhoo. "If there's anything I hate," he said, "it's a public figure. My favorite line is 'Far from the madding crowd's ignoble strife'."

STURM: Interesting! He wanted to act—but in private—and, here, he has his wish!

MRS. SIMPSON: What are you getting at, Doctor?

STURM (*briskly*): Tell me about the accident.

(Pause.)

SIMPSON (*in a changed voice*): What do you wish to know?

STURM: The facts. That's the staircase he fell down?

SIMPSON: Yes.

STURM: And he landed about here—on the back of his head?

MRS. SIMPSON (*as* SIMPSON *turns away*): Yes, I was here at the foot of the stairs, it was horrible . . . .

SIMPSON: Not that we . . . knew what was wrong, of course. Just a fall. Then he was carried upstairs to lie down.

MRS. SIMPSON: You couldn't tell anything had happened: no blood, no bruises—

SIMPSON: We thought he'd just fainted, of course—

MRS. SIMPSON: About two hours later he re-appeared.

SIMPSON: We were all in here. Every character in the play except him—

STURM: *Hamlet* without the Prince of Denmark, ha?

MRS. SIMPSON: His face as he entered! I saw the whole thing in a flash.

SIMPSON: Oh, come, my dear, none of us had the least—

MRS. SIMPSON: Oh, you were all behaving like lunatics—

SIMPSON: We were trying to speak in character. Improvising, don't you know. Great fun. *He* joined in—

MRS. SIMPSON: Until—at a certain point—we realized he was playing his part—in earnest!

STURM: Ah! So he joined in—?

SIMPSON: Yes, yes. We took for granted he'd recovered and was just acting—as we were—only better, I told you what a fine actor he was—

MRS. SIMPSON: Some of them started teasing him. One of them shouted, "The duel scene, the duel scene!"

SIMPSON: At that moment he drew his sword and let out a great yell. We were thunderstruck. You could have heard a pin drop.

MRS. SIMPSON: He rushed towards Hugh with his sword drawn, it looked like sure murder . . . .

SIMPSON: Then, just as suddenly, he stopped in his tracks. "The duel scene?" he said, "I don't know it."

STURM: That makes sense. He hated the play, tried to keep away from it . . . .

MRS. SIMPSON: Not now. For more than a month he'd thought of nothing else.

SIMPSON: He knew the whole thing by heart, duel scene included. He was crazy, that's all.

STURM: But, excuse me, wasn't Hamlet crazy too?

SIMPSON: I'm sure we could discuss *that* till doomsday, old boy.

MRS. SIMPSON: *He* was crazy, isn't that enough?

SIMPSON: And duel scene or no duel scene, James Denmark had disappeared leaving—

STURM: H. for Hamlet!

SIMPSON: Exactly.

STURM: And this place?

BROWNE: Mother bought it for him—to keep him happy.

SIMPSON: Quite a story, isn't it, Doctor? My wife grows old but our daughter takes her place on that pedestal. My hair turns grey but after twenty more years, *he* is still twenty, he is still here, he is still Hamlet. The age of miracles isn't past, what?

MRS. SIMPSON (*nervously*): What do you think, Doctor?

STURM (*solemnly*): Yes, um, what do I think? No, my friends, the problem is not an easy one. On the other hand—

(*But all of a sudden,* JACK *rushes back in; sees everyone, stops short.*)

JACK: Oh, pardon me!

SUSIE (*with a little scream*): Is that—Hamlet?

MRS. SIMPSON: That?!

BROWNE (*at once*): No, no, no!

STURM (*annoyed at being interrupted*): Then who on earth is it?

SIMPSON: A refugee from Elsinore, by George!

BROWNE: Oh, he's just one of the kids I hire to take parts in *Hamlet* and "sustain his illusion"!

JACK: Gee, I'm sorry, Mr. Browne!

BROWNE: You should be. My orders were to keep out of here.

JACK: Yes, I know, Mr. Browne. But I'm quitting! I can't stand it any longer.

BROWNE: But you started just this morning!

JACK: Yes, Mr. Browne. And I'm not cut out for this sort of thing!

MRS. SIMPSON (*to* BROWNE): I thought you said he was quite calm.

JACK: It's not him, ma'am, it's . . . Bernardo and Francisco! They're the ones who're crazy, Mr. Browne. I come here for the first time and . . . .

(A knock. The door opens slightly. MARTIN *and* JIMMY *appear in the doorway.)*

MARTIN: May we come in—

JIMMY: Dear Mr. Browne?

BROWNE: Okay, come in. But what is this, what goes on?

SUSIE: Christ, it gives me the creeps! *(She starts to go.)*

BROWNE: Susie, please don't go!

(She stops.)

MARTIN: Mr. Browne, this young man from the Wild and Woolly West—

JACK: Better make it snappy, I'm leaving.

JIMMY: Reynaldo, you ought to be ashamed of yourself.

MARTIN: As I was saying, Mr. Browne, this young man is, um—

JIMMY: Gumming up the works?

MARTIN: Right. Got *him* terribly excited.

JIMMY: He's just *storming* up and down, and I'll bet he *insists* on coming in here.

MARTIN: He always comes in here to storm up and down.

JIMMY: Now Bernardo has an idea!

MARTIN: Yes. If I could just announce your visit, it'd be a distraction for him.

JIMMY: Who are you all? That's the question.

MARTIN: Yes: in the play. Have you prepared certain roles?

BROWNE: Well, no, not really . . . .

SIMPSON: I say! We don't have to talk the lingo, do we?

STURM: My Shakespeare is a little rusty!

MARTIN: No, no, he seldom quotes the play.

JIMMY: Only when dictating his memoirs . . . .

MARTIN: Or at moments of great stress. No, he lives the part in modern English.

SUSIE: Oh, this is too much, I'm going. Mother, you come!

STURM (*apprehensive*): He still has that sword?

BROWNE: No, no. Susie, don't be childish. You wanted to see him—

SUSIE: I didn't! It was mother!

MRS. SIMPSON: And I still want to! I insist on it!

SIMPSON: Do we *have* to dress up?

MARTIN: Oh yes, sir. You see how *we're* dressed, that's the only sort of clothes he ever sees—

JIMMY: He'd think he was having a surrealist nightmare, poor dear!

MARTIN: What's more, he'd think it was his enemies' doing—

JIMMY: He's quick to suspect dirty work!

STURM: Aha! Persecution mania!

BROWNE: Now, please keep calm everyone! Nobody need see him except Dr. Sturm.

STURM (*still apprehensive*): I do not insist on seeing him alone, no—?

BROWNE: You'll have these two young men, of course.

STURM (*relieved*): Ah! And Mrs. Simpson said—

MRS. SIMPSON: Yes, I did, I do insist on seeing him!

SUSIE: Don't be silly, mother, let's get out of here!

MRS. SIMPSON: Susie, you don't understand. (*To* MARTIN:) I shall pretend to be his mother, Gertrude.

MARTIN: Hey, that could be dangerous!

SIMPSON: Let her be Ophelia then—she was, last time.

MRS. SIMPSON: Don't be ridiculous.

MARTIN: I guess you'll *have* to be Gertrude, ma'am. Jimmy, get the costume, will you?

JIMMY: How about our guest from New York City (*indicating* STURM)?

BROWNE: I thought he could do Polonius.

JIMMY: What a *divine* idea! But mind you don't hide behind the arras!

STURM: You're sure he doesn't still have that sword?

MARTIN (*tapping his weapon*): This is the only sword in the house. I'm never without it.

JIMMY: We keep it between us in bed like Siegfried and what's her name.

BROWNE: Okay, that's settled. You and I can be going, Susie. You too, Hugh.

SIMPSON: No, no, man and wife are one flesh, my boy!

MRS. SIMPSON: Oh, you and your jokes!

SIMPSON: Can't I see him if I wish? Old friends and all that?

MRS. SIMPSON: Friends!

SIMPSON: Acquaintances then.

MARTIN: Well, Mr. Browne, it wouldn't hurt to have another man.

BROWNE: Okay, okay.

JIMMY: Then the Honorable Hugh will need an honorable part?

SIMPSON: What about King Claudius?

JIMMY: *You're* looking for trouble, you are.

SIMPSON: You're speaking to the ex-president of the Princeton Fencing Club, my lad.

BROWNE: That's really rather foolish, Hugh. Couldn't you be some nonentity? "Attendant on the Queen," or something?

SIMPSON: You sum up my life, old boy. A nonentity, Attendant on the Queen. (*He bows to his wife.*)

BROWNE: All set then?

MARTIN: Um. Mr. Browne, there's one thing we haven't told you.

JIMMY: Oh, dear!

(Pause.)

BROWNE: Well, out with it!

MARTIN: *He* isn't always the same person nowadays.

BROWNE: What?!

MRS. SIMPSON: He's Hamlet, isn't he?

SIMPSON: Have to be Hamlet in *this* setting!

MARTIN: He's Hamlet sure enough—

BROWNE: Then why in God's name—?

JIMMY: But, you see, Mr. Browne, there were *two* Hamlets.

MARTIN: Father and son.

BROWNE: And he thinks—?

JIMMY: Three guesses!

MARTIN: Shut up, Jimmy. Yes: he thinks he's Old Hamlet once in a while.

JIMMY: And we prefer that, really.

MARTIN: It's better for him. No tragedy.

JIMMY: Just a nice old cuckold who died in a garden.

MARTIN: He's calmer that way.

BROWNE: And today?

MARTIN: It was young Hamlet who got in that rage. But now he's repentant . . . . Well, we'll see.

JIMMY: I wouldn't be a bit surprised if he's taken out the grey wig and turned into the old man.

BROWNE: Hadn't we better make sure?

MARTIN: Yes. (*To* JIMMY:) Go see what goes on. Jack, you bring the costumes.

(JIMMY *and* JACK *leave.*)

BROWNE: Meanwhile, we can go. Come on, Susie.

(BROWNE *and* SUSIE *leave.*)

STURM: He does not like Polonius, *hein*?

MARTIN: Which he? The prince doesn't. The king does.

STURM: *Ach so!*

SIMPSON: And what am *I* supposed to do, my good man? Just stand around?

MARTIN: Sure. Keep behind Mrs. Simpson.

MRS. SIMPSON (*to her husband*): Why couldn't you have left?

SIMPSON: Don't get so excited, my dear.

MRS. SIMPSON: Oh, leave me alone.

(JACK *returns with the costumes.*)

MARTIN: Oh, good.—Now, this cloak is for Mrs. Simpson.

MRS. SIMPSON: Wait, I must take my hat off.

(*She does so and gives it to* JACK.)

MARTIN: Put it over there, Jack. (*He prepares to place the royal crown on her head.*) May I?

MRS. SIMPSON: Heavens, are there no mirrors in Elsinore?

MARTIN: Only secret ones. Officially we don't like to see ourselves. Jack, take the lady to a secret mirror.

(MRS. SIMPSON *takes the hat back and goes out with* JACK *who carries crown and cloak. Meanwhile* STURM *and* SIMPSON *are putting the robes of Polonius and an attendant, respectively, around their street clothes.*)

SIMPSON: Not bad costumes, not bad at all! Being crazy is rather a costly habit, what?

MARTIN: Oh, yes, the stuff cost plenty. We have a wardrobe like the Metropolitan Opera. Why— (*But here* MRS. SIMPSON *re-enters.*)

SIMPSON (*struck*): I say! You're hot stuff, old girl!

MRS. SIMPSON: You look ridiculous!

SIMPSON (*indicating* STURM): What about him?

MRS. SIMPSON: Oh, he'll do. But you're ridiculous!

STURM (*to* MARTIN): Ahem. I suppose you often present people to him?

MARTIN: Well, there've been quite a few. Especially in the old days.

STURM: And they always had to be characters from *Hamlet*?

MARTIN: Oh, sure. But we'd repeat the same character any number of times. The girls *all* pretended to be Ophelia—

MRS. SIMPSON: Ah! There were girls too?

MARTIN: Quite a lot of them at one time.

SIMPSON: I say! What a lark! In costume?

MARTIN: Sure.

MRS. SIMPSON: What kind . . . were they?

MARTIN: All kinds. So long as they served the purpose.

(*The other door opens and* JIMMY *slips quickly in. He gives a sign for all conversation to stop.*)

JIMMY (*grandly*): His Majesty the King!

(JAMES H. DENMARK enters as OLD HAMLET. The grey hair is obviously a wig. The face underneath it is not young, yet it is a baby face and would be pretty still were it not for the deep-set haunted eyes that dominate it. His cheeks are rouged. He is clad in the traditional black suit of YOUNG HAMLET. He makes for the throne, and then stands erect in front of it looking at MRS. SIMPSON. Pause.)

HAMLET (*very quietly*): Welcome my Queen! Right welcome to Elsinore! (*To MARTIN, who is at his side:*) Isn't that my brother Claudius?

MARTIN (*also in an undertone*): No, Majesty, just an Attendant on the Queen.

HAMLET: No, no, it's Claudius. And that's Polonius. (*Suddenly.*) Polonius, how is your daughter?

STURM: Huh? Oh, yes, very well, very well.

HAMLET: And now, our Queen, what news from Norway?

(MRS. SIMPSON starts to speak.)

HAMLET: He's a fox, that Fortinbras. Should we offer him scorn and defiance? (*Indicating SIMPSON.*) What does he think, your Attendant? He'd patch up a peace, would he? But at this time I should speak no ill of Norway. The world needs peace. (*Moving over to SIMPSON.*) Were you with the Queen in Norway, noble sir? (*Before SIMPSON can answer.*) I'm so glad. Some people think I'm a bad king—weak—with a weakling for a son. They think my brother would be preferable, do you agree? There are worse rumors. About my brother and my queen. What a vulgar triangle that would make, eh, all jealousy and revenge! You don't believe it—do you?

SIMPSON (*fumbling*): Um, no, no I don't—

HAMLET (*quickly*): Don't you?—Polonius, you see through all this, huh?

JIMMY (*prompting*): Say yes.

STURM: Yes. Yes.

HAMLET: Then why didn't you report it?

JIMMY (*prompting*): You were going to.

STURM: I . . . was going to.

HAMLET: Polonius—the man who was going to. That's how you see yourself, isn't it? Don't fret, old man, it's the same with all of us. Fixed in some conception of ourselves as in a suit of armor. But note this, Polonius, while you keep a grip on yourself, holding your stick, fingering your beard, tapping the floor with one foot, something is slipping away unnoticed, slithering down your sleeves, gliding off like a serpent. That something is *life*, Polonius. (*To* SIMPSON:)—Did you wish to be born, did you will your own birth? No. But once born, I bet you started wishing and willing then, didn't you? You said: "I'll marry the queen," didn't you? (*To* MRS. SIMPSON:) How about you, lady? Have you ever taken a look at the thing you have willed yourself to be? Not for a long time? But one day, many years ago, do you remember, Queen? That day . . . . You do remember.

MARTIN: Your majesty—

HAMLET: How we cling to our idea of ourselves! Like a man who dyes his hair to stay young. No one is fooled, h'm? We all know it's hair dye, h'm? Take yours, Queen. Very good dye, of course, beautiful tint, but who are you kidding? Yourself? At most, your image in the glass. Oh, it's quite a deception, I see that, you're in disguise . . . . (*She starts. He smiles.*) I don't mean the crown on your head, I don't mean your royal cloak, I mean you wish to fix a memory in your mind—the memory of your hair as it was one day long ago when you looked in the glass and admired it, the memory, the fading image, of your youth, the dark tresses of your youth. That's *one* way memory works. (*Turning suddenly on* SIMPSON.) There is another way, ha? You're *not* trying to hang on to anything. You'd be glad to get away from something. But you can't, can you? The past lives on. Weirdly. Those things happened, we suppose they happened, but how? When? In a dream? Don't think I'm protesting: my own memories are like that. But don't worry: it'll be the same tomorrow with our memories of today. (*A sudden rage assails him. He whips off the grey wig, revealing a head of hair none too uniformly dyed blond. All present are alarmed.* MARTIN *and* JIMMY *have started to move to him and stop him. He raises an arm. Even his voice is younger.*) It is I, Hamlet the Dane!

MARTIN (*the only one still in full command of his resources*): Yes, your majesty!

JIMMY (*with difficulty*): King Hamlet!

HAMLET (*with anger*): Think I'm an idiot? Not *King* Hamlet! *Prince* Hamlet!

MARTIN (*aside to* SIMPSON *and the others, as* HAMLET *sinks down on the throne with his head in his hands*): We must pretend it's just after his father died. He suspects nothing. Nothing has happened. (*Giving a sign to* JIMMY.)

JIMMY: My lord!

HAMLET: Yes, good Francisco?

MARTIN: Your lady mother waits.

HAMLET: But why is my uncle with her?

JIMMY (*swallowing*): The queen has come to comfort you, my lord.

HAMLET: Pardon, good mother! And, good uncle, pardon! I am . . . troubled. This is a decisive moment—or is it?

MARTIN: Yes, my lord, it is. The king your father died yesterday.

HAMLET: I understand. I think I understand. What happens next?

MARTIN: Nothing, my lord.

HAMLET: "Nothing will come of nothing, speak again." (*Switching to* STURM:) What do you say, Polonius? (*Before he can speak.*) How's your daughter? Why didn't you bring her along? (*Screaming.*) I have to see your daughter!

MARTIN: Yes, yes, my lord. (JIMMY *is prompting, inaudibly.*) Ophelia will shortly wait upon you.

HAMLET: She will? (*He is amazed.*) No rash promises, mind! (*Turning to the statue of* OPHELIA.) There: Ophelia. You can't dress up some farm girl and make me believe . . . . (*To the* SIMPSONS:) Know what my problem is? Everybody agrees I have one. Well, is it here (*pointing to his head*), is it there (*pointing to the statue of himself*)? Or is it in the rope that connects the two?

MARTIN: Can we serve you, my lord?

HAMLET (*impudently*): Yes. Cut me loose from that statue. (*Pause.*) I'm tied to it hand and foot, don't you see? Cut the cord for me, will you? I want to *have* the life I missed, every moment of it. What makes you think I can go on being twenty forever? (*Switching to* STURM:) Ask your daughter that question, because if we could go on being twenty forever, that might be a solution. (*Abruptly, to* SIMPSON:) Or not?—what do *you* think? (*Becoming abstracted at once.*) I humbly take my leave. (*He starts to make his exit. As he does so,* SIMPSON *moves toward the throne where the wig has been left and is about to lay his hands upon it when* HAMLET *wheels around and screams.* SIMPSON *is petrified.* HAMLET *comes back for the wig, hides it in his doublet, and, looking* SIMPSON *and* MRS. SIMPSON *over, smiles, bows, and makes a stately exit.* MRS. SIMPSON *is so disturbed she falls onto the nearest throne, almost fainting.*)

Act Two

SCENE 1

Afternoon of the same day.

A room adjoining the hall of Act One, possibly to be staged in front of a curtain, possibly on a section of a turntable, which is set in motion, as described below, when the scene changes to Act Two, Scene Two.

On stage DR. STURM *and the* HONORABLE HUGH SIMPSON *in the midst of a rather heated argument.* MRS. SIMPSON *seems lost in thought.*

SIMPSON (*trying to cut it short*): In any event, Doctor, that's my impression!

STURM (*trying to hold his temper*): Impression, yes, Mr. Simpson, but after all, excuse me, an impression is at best a peripheral and subjective phenomenon and, as for the impressions of an outsider, a layman, well—

SIMPSON: But, Doctor, what about the things he said himself? They're not, what did you say? peripheral and subjective? I was quoting his exact words— (*appealing to the silent figure of* MRS. SIMPSON) wasn't I, my dear?

MRS. SIMPSON (*recalled from reverie*): What? Oh yes. But, if I may say so, my dear, he meant just the opposite—

STURM (*almost shouting his exasperation*): He was referring to these clothes! (*They are still wearing their disguises.*) *Mein Gott,* the whole thing is infantile.

MRS. SIMPSON (*taking umbrage*): Well, if that's how you feel!

STURM (*still more exasperated*): In the strict, scientific sense: this is a case of infantilism! (*Getting control of himself.*) It is also extremely

130

complicated.

MRS. SIMPSON: It seems to me absurdly simple.

SIMPSON: I thought it was pretty clear myself.

MRS. SIMPSON: Oh, but *you're* completely wrong—

SIMPSON: Or perhaps *you're* completely wrong, my dear—

STURM (*ending what is almost a hubbub*): Quiet! I must ask you both to be quiet! May I explain?

SIMPSON: Well, if you must, old boy.

STURM: Mrs. Simpson?

MRS. SIMPSON: Oh, please!

STURM (*clearing his throat*): In this type of insanity—I won't bother you with Latin names—but—in everyday parlance—the psycho-path—I avoid the words mad, insane, crazy, lunatic, depraved, deranged—the psychopath is infantile. He can see through a dis-guise—our disguise, for instance—and yet (*very emphatically*) at the same time accept it—entering into the game, as it were. Simple, isn't it? But also—upon the other hand—complicated. Because this type of . . . psychopath watches himself as if he were another person . . . not himself, as he says, but just an image—And this particular psycho-path has actually succeeded in making another person of himself—the statue! (*He points offstage.*)

SIMPSON: He said something of the sort.

STURM (*nodding*): He has removed the mirrors and recreated his own image in three dimensions. Now here *we* come—more three-dimen-sional images—also characters from *Hamlet*. But don't think he couldn't see through a trick like this. He saw there was something different about us, something different in *our sort* of make-believe. They're cunning, this type, they're suspicious. He saw through us, he tried to take us into his confidence by that rouge on his cheeks—as much as to say, "It's only a play, I'll show you it's only a play!" Yet he did not recognize us—

MRS. SIMPSON: There you're wrong, Doctor. He did recognize us.

STURM: No, no, impossible.

SIMPSON: For once I agree with you, Doctor. (*To* MRS. SIMPSON:) I'm afraid you're overwrought, my dear.

MRS. SIMPSON (*ignoring her husband and trying to convince* STURM):

He recognized me, I tell you. Don't you remember when he came close to me? He recognized me.

SIMPSON: But it was his (*indicating* STURM) daughter he was babbling about—

MRS. SIMPSON: And who is Polonius's daughter? Ophelia. And that was me.

SIMPSON: Then what about the "dark tresses" he mentioned?

MRS. SIMPSON: You have a short memory. How long have I been a blond?

SIMPSON: You think *he* remembers?

MRS. SIMPSON: I'm really a brunette, Doctor, like my daughter, that's why he started talking of her—

SIMPSON: But he doesn't know her, he's never seen her—

MRS. SIMPSON: That's just what I mean. He wasn't thinking of any daughter, he was thinking of me as I was then.

SIMPSON: My dear, if you aren't careful, you'll be as crazy as he is. (*Turning to* STURM:) You say *I* oughtn't to have come, what about my wife?

MRS. SIMPSON: He was talking to me, about me, there was nothing else in his mind—

SIMPSON: Isn't that funny? I had the impression that his chief interest was getting in all those digs at me. All that about his brother Claudius—how did it concern you, my dear?

MRS. SIMPSON: Oh, it did. He was *old* Hamlet—and I wasn't Ophelia, I was Gertrude—his unfaithful wife. Which makes you his rival.

SIMPSON: Holy Moses, Doctor, this thing's catching. The old girl's going off her rocker.

(*As* MRS. SIMPSON *starts vehemently in again, the* DOCTOR *tries to be the diplomat.*)

STURM (*clearing his throat*): Now, Mrs. Simpson, please! And Mr. Simpson, really! We know of course (*he is lecturing*) that everything in life is significant—everything is symbolic—but, at the same time, we musn't make the mountain from the molehill, *hein*? The arrival of two people had been announced to him: the Queen and Polonius. When he found someone *with* the Queen, why, of course he was disturbed. I was telling you: suspicion is one of the symptoms of—

SIMPSON: Exactly! He suspected I must be the villain. Why should she imagine he recognized her?

MRS. SIMPSON: I imagine nothing. Some things are unmistakable. That look, I don't say it lasted more than one second—

STURM: It's true, there are lucid intervals—

MRS. SIMPSON: And the look wasn't all. There was an undertone to his talk. He was full of regret for his life, for my life, full of horror at the terrible thing that happened to him, holding him here like this—tied as he said to that statue in there—trying to be Hamlet, staying young forever!

SIMPSON: Yes, and what for? *Why* did he sell you such a bill of goods?

MRS. SIMPSON: What reason are you thinking of?

SIMPSON: He was making love to you. At it again—after twenty years! (*To the* DOCTOR:) A grand passion, what?

MRS. SIMPSON: So you're *still* possessive, you're *still* madly jealous!

SIMPSON: Rubbish, my dear.

MRS. SIMPSON: After all this time? Can't you feel some pity?

SIMPSON: Splendid thing, pity, in its way! That's why he's going all out for yours! Thinks it might work the miracle no doubt—

(*Again anticipating an outburst from* MRS. SIMPSON, STURM *steps in.*)

STURM: Now, um, as to miracles, Mr. Simpson, I am no miracle worker, *hein*? No. This plan we agreed to—

SIMPSON: Oh, we agreed to it, did we?

MRS. SIMPSON: Of course we did.

STURM: Well, call it *my* little plan—that you've agreed to let me try out—on (*with a wave of the hand toward the next room*) our friend here. What are the postulates of the diagnosis, and, *ipso facto*, of the cure?

SIMPSON: Crikey!

MRS. SIMPSON: Quiet!

STURM (*undeterred*): The fundamental postulate of the diagnosis is that our friend—though not depraved, deranged, lunatic, crazy, insane, et cetera—is psychotic. His particular psychosis—I won't trouble you with the technical name for it—takes the form of a delusion. Of being Hamlet. That presents us with a certain problem —let's not make too much of it—it is common enough—in the Psychodramatic Sanatorium we have almost every great man of history: Napoleon, Caesar, Charlemagne, yes, with all due respect, even Jesus Christ. Can we blame our friend if he chooses to be Hamlet? The question is—one of the questions, anyway—the question of the hour, as it were—is—

SIMPSON: To cure him?

STURM: Correct. We have here a case of one personality superimposed upon another. Hamlet upon James Denmark. Maybe triple personality: two Hamlets upon James Denmark! Now this new personality—double or triple as the case may be—has come—this is my diagnosis—into a state of unstable equilibrium . . . .

MRS. SIMPSON: Oh!

STURM (*turning to her*): But that is *good*, dear lady. That is our chance. If the second personality is firm and stable, what can we do? Nothing. There is no heel of Achilles. No. We have to strike at moments of unstable equilibrium. If one only knew when they would occur! We've had luck, Mr. Simpson. Our forebears would have called it Providence, dear lady. Today—in the case of our friend here—is the moment to strike, as I told you, the moment when our shock treatment will—

MRS. SIMPSON (*irritably*): Yes, yes, Doctor, I understood the first time, but why aren't they back?

STURM (*knocked back on his heels*): Back? Who?

MRS. SIMPSON: Curtis and Susie, of course. *You* sent them on this strange errand—

SIMPSON: They can't find the dress, that's all. A dress you haven't worn for twenty years—

MRS. SIMPSON: I told them exactly where it is.

STURM (*having recovered his balance*): They will find it.

SIMPSON: What good will it do? The dress she (*indicating his wife*) wore as Ophelia twenty years ago won't—

STURM: Now, please, both of you, don't fret. We have a great opportunity. The battlements of his delusion are trembling as from an earthquake. One push and they'll fall like the walls of Jericho.

SIMPSON: So what are you doing with him, Doctor? Razing him to the ground?

STURM: Ts, ts, ts. It is his second personality—the false one—we shall destroy. He will then revert to the first.

SIMPSON: Will he?

STURM: Look. It's like a stopped clock. Shake it up, and it starts again. Where? Why, where it left off. It's as if no time had passed. It's as if—

(At this point, CURTIS BROWNE *enters.)*

MRS. SIMPSON: Curtis! Isn't Susie with you?

BROWNE: Yes, of course.

STURM: You found the dress?

BROWNE: She's trying it on.

MRS. SIMPSON: How was it, was it—?

BROWNE: Wonderful. Just like new. Hold on one second, you'll see.

MRS. SIMPSON *(shuddering)*: I feel strange.

(Here JACK *enters with an effort at being a formal attendant.)*

JACK *(standing to one side of the door)*: The Lady Ophelia, daughter to the Queen!

*(SUSIE *enters in a perfect* OPHELIA *costume exactly resembling that of the statue of Act One.)*

SUSIE *(passing the bowing* JACK*)*: Daughter to Polonius, silly!

SIMPSON *(for the first time really spontaneous)*: Susie? But it's *not* Susie!

MRS. SIMPSON: God in Heaven! It's the statue come alive!

STURM *(very interested)*: *Wunderbar!*

(A pause while they all look.)

SUSIE *(embarrassed)*: Well, say something. And, mamma, we'll have to do something with this waist, I can hardly breathe.

MRS. SIMPSON *(swallowing)*: Yes . . . yes . . . hold still . . . these pleats!

SUSIE: I'm suffocating! Can't we get on with the act?

STURM (*cutting in*): No, no, no! We must wait till dark.

SUSIE: I can't hold out *that* long!

MRS. SIMPSON: Then why did you put it on now?

SUSIE: Oh, I dunno. I guess it just looked tempting.

MRS. SIMPSON: At least you could have asked me to help you, look at these creases—

SUSIE: They're centuries old, what could you do?

STURM: Come, come. The creases are quite invisible from a distance. The illusion is perfect. Now, allow me. (*He positions* SUSIE *a few feet from her mother, so that he and the audience see them as a pair.*) That's it. (*He stands back to look. To* SIMPSON:) You see?

SIMPSON (*uncooperative*): See what, old chap?

STURM: The march of time!

SIMPSON: Oh, I see. Before and After—that sort of thing.

MRS. SIMPSON: "Crabbèd age and youth." It's a disaster.

STURM (*seeing he has put his foot in it*): No, no, Mrs. Simpson, that isn't what I meant, it's a matter of the dress, it's—

SIMPSON: Don't make matters worse, Doctor. The ladies are only a couple of decades apart: between that dress and the twentieth century there are hundreds of years.

STURM: *Sehr gut!* Psychodramatic shock treatment will make him jump the abyss of centuries.

SIMPSON: Suppose he falls in?

MRS. SIMPSON: Hugh!

SIMPSON: Shock treatment is dangerous at the best of times, but when you ask a man to jump centuries! You'll need a basket to pick up the pieces.

MRS. SIMPSON: So you do pity him?

SIMPSON: No, my dear, I pity *him* (*indicating* STURM).

STURM: Come, come, Mr. Simpson. Our friend, after he jumps, will *realize* it's *twenty* years, not hundreds. You are acquainted with the initiatory rites of the Aztec priesthood?

SIMPSON: I've forgotten the details.

STURM: The initiate is blindfolded. He walks forward. The voice of the priest is heard. "You will now jump into infinite space," it says. The initiate gets into position, takes a deep breath, jumps. But to his surprise the further bank of infinity is reached almost at once. His eyes are uncovered, and he sees that he has jumped one single step down the staircase.

SIMPSON: Goodness gracious!

STURM (*triumphantly*): Shock treatment! All very sound! The initiate will be a bigger and better person.

SIMPSON: Dr. Sturm, do you really believe all this stuff?

MRS. SIMPSON (*to get* STURM *out of this hole*): Ignore him, Doctor. Explain what you want us all to do.

STURM (*with relish*): Yes. The first thing, remember, is for you (*to* MRS. SIMPSON) to change.

SIMPSON: What, again?

STURM: You haven't been following, my dear Simpson! (*To* BROWNE:) You found the other dress?

BROWNE: Oh, yes.

SIMPSON: Oh. Oh, yes!

STURM (*to* MRS. SIMPSON): You will change into the other dress— which (*to* SIMPSON) is identical with this one (*pointing to* SUSIE's).

SIMPSON: So there'll be two Ophelias.

STURM: Quite. What is drama? Life all over again in make-believe: to see drama is to see double. *Sehr gut.* What is psychodramatic shock treatment? To exploit the psychology of drama for the purpose of healing—that ye may have life and have it more abundantly. He will see two Ophelias at once. He will see two Hamlets at once—himself and Browne. Psychodramatic Tableau! Two couples, two generations! A double image of his delusion! His brain reels. The trembling edifice of his illusion totters and falls. You've heard of men being shocked into insanity? That happened to him twenty years ago. What you will see today—if the gods are propitious—is a man shocked back into sanity.

SIMPSON (*to* MRS. SIMPSON): You really can swallow all this, my dear?

MRS. SIMPSON: Dr. Sturm is a great psychiatrist.

BROWNE (*to* JACK): You, bring Martin in here, will you? (JACK *leaves.*) Now, Doctor, you want him to think the visitors have left—Gertrude, Polonius, and the Attendant he thinks is Claudius?

STURM: Yes, we must all pretend to take our leave. And he must feel absolutely certain we've gone. I want him to feel the loneliness of the human situation.

(JACK *returns with* MARTIN.)

BROWNE: Martin, the visitors are leaving . . . .

MARTIN: Yessir.

BROWNE: What shall we tell him? Which Hamlet is he? What does he want to be told?

MARTIN: Oh, he's still young Hamlet. We could tell him his mother is going on a journey with Polonius.

STURM: Will he believe that?

MARTIN: I think so, sir. He's quiet now.

STURM: So I can go in there and tell him?

MARTIN: Yessir. Just one point though. He's worried. He keeps saying Ophelia doesn't love him, never did love him. That's not correct, is it?

STURM: Quite *in*correct. He's forgotten the play.

SIMPSON: Did he ever know it, my dear Doctor? He's Hamlet, not Shakespeare.

MRS. SIMPSON: Ophelia loved Hamlet but Hamlet didn't believe it. He thought she was just pretending—

STURM: Very significant!

SIMPSON: You could bring him a message from your daughter, couldn't you, Doctor? A valentine and all that sort of thing?

STURM: I shall make a point of mentioning Ophelia's love for him.

MARTIN: I know: why not have Mrs. Simpson wear her Ophelia costume now?

STURM: No, no! He must see Gertrude go. Then the sight of Ophelia must be a big surprise. The only Ophelia he's seen in twenty years is that statue—

MARTIN: Oh, no, sir. The women I told you about—

SIMPSON: They all said they were Ophelia, Doctor.

MARTIN: Well, *we* said they were Ophelia.

STURM (*worried*): Did any of them resemble that statue?

MARTIN: Not really, sir.

STURM (*reassured*): Then ours will be the first that ever did. Simpson, we're all right. Let's go into him.

MARTIN: Maybe just you—or you and the lady—

STURM: Correct. You and I can put it to him, can't we, Mrs. Simpson?

MRS. SIMPSON: I hope so.

(*Exeunt* MARTIN, STURM, *and* MRS. SIMPSON.)

SUSIE (*fretting*): Curtis, I don't like this.

BROWNE: Who does?

(*Pause.*)

SUSIE: It'd be better if I'd already seen him—

BROWNE: You'll be all right. All you have to do is stand there.

SUSIE: But isn't he raving?

BROWNE: No, no. He'll be calmer than any of us.

SIMPSON: The melancholy Dane. And he loves you, don't forget.

SUSIE: That's why I'm scared of him.

SIMPSON: You're the last person in the world he'd want to hurt, my dear.

BROWNE: And the whole thing will be over in seconds.

SUSIE: But what seconds! In the dark with a lunatic!

BROWNE: I'll be there too, remember. On the other pedestal.

SIMPSON: You've removed the statues?

BROWNE: Yes, it took ten men. (*To* SUSIE:) And all the others will be just outside. We two'll be on the pedestals, he'll pass through the room, that's your mother's cue, she enters, he looks up and sees two Ophelias—

SIMPSON: You sound like Sturm: are you going to be a psychiatrist when you grow up?

BROWNE: Well, let's not reopen *that* argument. I believe in the man.

SUSIE: So do I. I couldn't go through with it if I didn't.

SIMPSON (*ruminating*): . . . And sees two Ophelias, compares them, and figures out . . . . Lovely! Except for one little snag.

BROWNE: Who's playing the bright boy of the class now?

SUSIE (*nervously*): What snag do you mean?

SIMPSON: Sturm has figured it out, and he thinks James Hamlet Denmark will figure it out—forgetting only that lunatics *do not figure things out.*

BROWNE: It's not a matter of figuring things out. It's all done dramatically. A double image of his delusion, Sturm called it.

SIMPSON: Why, O why, do they graduate in medicine?

SUSIE: What?

BROWNE: Who?

SIMPSON: The psychodramatic shock troops.

SUSIE: Who?!

SIMPSON: Psychiatrists.

BROWNE: What should they graduate in? Military science?

SIMPSON: Theology.

SUSIE: They're doctors, aren't they?

SIMPSON: They're priests. Of a religion I don't believe in.

BROWNE: Nonsense, Sturm is the first to admit he's no faith healer—

SIMPSON: And that is precisely how he wins your faith.

SUSIE: But he knows he can't work miracles.

SIMPSON: Now *that's* a pity.

BROWNE: A pity?

SIMPSON: Yes: nothing short of a miracle can save James H. Denmark.

JACK (*who has been keeping watch at the door*): Sh! They're coming.

BROWNE: Coming in here?

JACK: He's showing them out or something—

BROWNE (*to* SUSIE *and* SIMPSON): We must leave. (*To* JACK:) You stay here.

JACK (*scared*): Stay?

(*But the three of them have gone without answering him.* MARTIN *shows* HAMLET *in.* HAMLET *is flanked by* STURM *and* MRS.

SIMPSON. JIMMY *follows on.*)

HAMLET (*to* MRS. SIMPSON): Strange that you should have to go to Wittenberg.

MRS. SIMPSON: Strange (*with an effort*), my lord?

HAMLET: Yes. I'd have thought you would stay in Elsinore and *I* would go to Wittenberg.

MARTIN: It could be so, my lord.

STURM: But also the reverse can happen.

HAMLET: Ha? You think a thing can both be and not be? (STURM *gapes.*) No, no, you don't *think*, you're a university man, aren't you, Polonius? You repeat what you've been told. (*He smiles at* MARTIN, *who sees an opportunity to make the occasion cheerful and grins, signalling to* JIMMY *to grin too.*) With your permission, Queen. (*He takes* STURM *by the elbow and draws him to one side.*) Where's your daughter?

STURM (*scared*): I . . . don't know.

HAMLET (*grinning again*): The cat is on the tiles, eh? Her own father doesn't know where she is? She doesn't love me, you know that?

MRS. SIMPSON: It's not true.

HAMLET (*turning swiftly*): What? *You* said that?

MRS. SIMPSON (*scared in her turn*): Yes, I did.

HAMLET: You don't believe those stories about my debauches?

MRS. SIMPSON (*as soon as she can speak*): No. No, I don't.

HAMLET (*mischievously*): Maybe you should. And don't defend Ophelia to *me*. (*Shouting:*) Don't do it!

MRS. SIMPSON (*driven by some strange necessity*): You don't—still love her?

HAMLET: *Still* love her? What do *you* know about it?

MRS. SIMPSON: Nothing of course.

HAMLET: Then mind your own business. (*To* STURM:) She insists on talking about Ophelia, I can't understand it.

MARTIN: Perhaps, Prince, she wishes Ophelia were in your good graces again—

STURM (*cottoning on*): Yes. Yes, Prince.

HAMLET (*to* STURM): You consider her my friend?

STURM: Oh, yes, my lord.

HAMLET: Are *you* my friend?

STURM: Most assuredly, my lord.

HAMLET: What *is* a friend?

STURM: Well, um—

HAMLET: I'll tell you what a friend is—No, I won't. You don't believe I ever really loved her. No one ever did believe it. And what is this thing: real love? Let's change the subject. Polonius, what about politics?

STURM: Politics?

HAMLET: Yes. Denmark versus Norway, Norway versus Poland. How's Fortinbras? And, by the way, you didn't answer my last question: how's Ophelia? She must be popular, all the other girls pretend they're her, did you know that? Yes, in comes a girl, and "What's your name, my dear?" I say, but why I say that I shall never know, the answer's always the same: "Ophelia, sir." After which the custom is to giggle. In bed, you understand? "Ophelia, sir"—then they giggle. I don't have clothes on, of course, and Ophelia doesn't have clothes on, isn't that strange?

STURM: Very strange.

HAMLET: What's strange about it? We don't ask who we are at times like that, do we? We leave our names on the chair by the bed—with our clothes. *I* think names and clothes are ghosts, do you agree? (*Before* STURM *can answer:*) And what are ghosts? Disorders of the mind. Images we can't quite hold within the bounds of sleep. They come charging towards me on horseback, laughing. Or maybe it's the horses that are laughing. And how their hooves beat on the cobblestones! Or maybe it's my heart throbbing, my blood pulsing in my veins like the dull sound of footsteps in distant rooms in the silence of the night! (MRS. SIMPSON *shudders.*) But I see I'm boring you. Your servant, lady. Your servant, Polonius.

(*He has brought them to the door and is showing them out. They go. He slowly shuts the door and comes back into the room. He sits. Pause. Then his shoulders begin to shake. He is laughing. Louder and louder. The three attendants are astonished. He abruptly stops.*)

They let me do as I like with them: tease them, tickle them, intimidate them, anything. Attendant to the Queen, ha!—I've scared the pants right off his ass. (JACK's *jaw has dropped.*) What's the matter? You don't catch on? I make people dress up when they come here *because I enjoy it.* I enjoy lording it over people, I even enjoy scaring them: it gives me a sense of power. What's your name?

JACK: Reynaldo.

HAMLET: That's a lie. But I approve of lies. Let me make you a present of my great idea: playing the madman, playing the madman to an audience and even alone, secretly, in front of a mirror—I *have* a secret mirror—year in, year out—

MARTIN: Hey, wait a minute—

JIMMY (*to* MARTIN): Do you hear what I hear?

JACK: Oh! Oh, I think I'm beginning to—!

HAMLET: Okay, be surprised, and get it over with! (*To himself*.) God, the effrontery of the woman—to come *here*—with *him* of all men! Pretending they hoped to keep me within bounds—as if I weren't beyond all bounds! Sure of themselves, aren't they? Sure that I can only be (*stressing each syllable*) what—they—think—I—am, neither more, nor less. Well, it's human, you're sure I can only be what *you* think I am, aren't you? You won't let me be anything else, will you? And *you* get your notion of me from *them.* You're what's called the general public. Somebody labels a man and *you* make the label stick. How would you like to be the man? The man who wakes up one morning to find himself labelled with one of their pet words? The word Crazy for instance. They say Crazy, echo answers Crazy, the whole world says Crazy! Meaning? Meaning he *seemed* crazy to one of the ones. Maybe to one of the ones who was crazy! Or to one that seemed crazy to him! Well, am I or aren't I? Ha? I am ! I'm crazy! (*Suddenly much louder.*) And so, by God, down on your knees before me! (*They obey.*) Ha! That's it! (*Laughing.*) That's great! Now do me a favor. Touch the floor three times with your foreheads. One, two, three. (*They obey.*) Oh, that's good! It does *you* good too, I bet. Get up! Off your knees, you cattle! (*They get up.*) Now isn't that nice? Obedience: another *word.* You obey me when you could have put a straitjacket on me. Aren't words wonderful—so light and yet so heavy? Can you seriously believe that Hamlet, father or son, king or prince, is alive today? Isn't it even a question whether he ever did live? Well then. Here is a dead man—or a man who never was alive—giving orders to the living. Good, ha? Now what I ask is: do you consider it comic, all this? It has its comical side—here—but, in the world outside, day is dawning, the sun just rising over the hill, the green earth stretching out to the river beyond. This day, you say, is yours, a day of your own making. *Of your own making:* if it were not for traditions and customs, the awful weight of the dead. You will not utter today one word that has not been uttered millions of times before. You think you're alive but all you do is go through the motions of the dead. (JACK *is again agape.*) What did you say your name was?

JACK: Reynaldo.

HAMLET: And what *is* your name?

JACK: (*weakly, and looking vainly to* MARTIN *and* JIMMY): Jack.

HAMLET: Jack! And you, Bernardo, are Martin, and you, Francisco, are plain Jimmy.

(Here MARTIN *and* JIMMY *are overjoyed and relieved.)*

MARTIN AND JIMMY: So you—?

HAMLET: So I'm not crazy. It was what is called a . . . joke. A joke on those who chose to believe it. Let's all have a big laugh about it, shall we? (*He starts laughing. The others hesitate at first, but then join in. When the laugh has burnt itself out,* JIMMY *and* MARTIN *turn to each other, asking: "Can it be true?" or stating: "He's cured!"* JACK, *however, has not laughed.*)

HAMLET: Sh! (*To* JACK:) Are you offended, Jack? It wasn't you I was mad at, it was the world, that *wishes* to believe certain people crazy.

JACK (*looks pathetic and starts to speak*): But why . . . ?

HAMLET: So it can lock them up! Why does the world wish to lock them up? Ha? (*He sighs.*) The madman says things that the others don't want to hear. Me, for instance. What would I say about today's visitors? I'd say: the woman has no passion, the man has no pride, the psychologist has no psyche . . . . Now don't go believing me. I'm crazy, remember. I'm the man you mustn't believe. The funny thing is—people still listen to me. They even get quite scared at the things I say. Why *is* that?

JACK: Well, um, I don't know, maybe they think . . . .

HAMLET: Be serious, Jack. Look into my eyes. No, no, really look. Ah! you have fear in your eyes, Jack. (*He sighs.*) You still think I'm crazy. That settles it.

MARTIN (*plucking up courage*): Settles what, sir?

HAMLET: Everything. For what does it mean, to be face to face with a lunatic? It means confronting a man who takes you—all that you've made of yourself through the years—takes you and shakes you till the logic of your life lies broken on the ground. Blessed are the lunatic—they construct without logic! Or with a logic that floats on air like a feather! They chop and change, here today and gone tomorrow. You stick to your guns, the lunatic takes to his heels. You say: "This cannot be." He says: "Can't it, though?" You say: "It's not true" because—it doesn't seem true to you or you or you (*pointing at the three in turn*) or a million others. Very well, my friends, we'll have to consider what seems true to each of the twenty billion people not considered insane, we'll have to see what they can tell us about the things they agree on, if any . . . ! (*Silence.*) All I know is, when I was a little child, the moon in the pond was true—to me. And the world was full of such truths. I accepted them all and I was . . . what is that word? yes: *happy.* Sufficient unto the day is the truth thereof. My advice to you, the advice of an old man, hundreds of years old, no? is this: hold on to what is true today, and, tomorrow, hold on to what is true tomorrow, even if it's the opposite, or there'll be trouble, and I wouldn't like you to be *engulfed—swallowed up* by a thought—like me. That might *really* drive you crazy. Yes, you might be with a woman sometime thinking you love her . . . . You look into her eyes, your souls about to meet, you look again, what's the matter, why is she laughing? A psychological problem? A woman that can't give herself? That's what *she* thinks, but you know what *I* thought, what the thought was that . . . *engulfed* me? (*Pause.*) The most "giving" woman in the world is still that remotest thing in the universe—another person. The place her eyes look out from is a prison, walled, moated, locked, barred, hermetically sealed. She is alone. You are alone. So what is love?

(*A long pause as the three attendants sense what* DR. STURM *calls the loneliness of the human situation.*)

How dark it's getting!

JIMMY: I'll bring the lamp.

HAMLET: My oil lamp! Do you think I don't know that, as soon as my back is turned and I'm in bed, you switch the electric light on?

MARTIN: Then you'd prefer us to—?

HAMLET: No, no. I prefer the oil lamp.

JIMMY: I have it. (*He gets it from upstage.*)

HAMLET (*taking the lamp and pointing to the large oak table*): Thank you. Now sit around this table, all three of you. No, not like *that*, be somebody, strike a noble attitude! You, like this. You, like this. And you, like this. (*He groups the three of them at the table.*) Now I'll sit here—with a view through the casement. You see how the moon is playing her part? *She* doesn't mind being a phoney, she poses for postcards and corny watercolors, doesn't admit that centuries have passed and that the man sitting at this table *cannot* be Hamlet.

MARTIN (*to* JIMMY): Just think! I feel now like we'd been the crazy ones!

HAMLET: What? What's that?

MARTIN: Well, I mean, only this morning I was telling this new guy (*indicating* JACK) what a pity it was—with us dressed for the play and all—

HAMLET: What was a pity?

MARTIN: Well, that we couldn't do any real acting, take it all as a play—

JIMMY: A comedy, quite a lark and all that—the way you now say it is!

MARTIN: Because we thought it was all in deadly earnest.

JIMMY: That's right.

JACK: Yeah, that's what they told *me*.

HAMLET: And now you find it was all a trick?

MARTIN: Yes, like you just told us—

HAMLET: A trick, but is that bad? A farce acted out before me, before visitors, *that's* bad, yes, that's trivial, contemptible, but a drama playing without intermission throughout your natural lives, a drama that stays with you in bed at night, that goes to the bathroom with you, is that bad? The point is to live in a distant century at Elsinore at Prince Hamlet's court—and to see the men of the twentieth century from the wrong end of the telescope of time. Would any man, looking through that telescope, say: "I want to go *there*"? For what is the twentieth century but chaos, menaced with total annihilation, *and yet not certain even of that*?

MARTIN: But—

HAMLET: The age of Hamlet was disordered too? Yes, my friend, what happens to Hamlet may be sad, but it has stopped changing, the end is not in doubt, *there is no uncertainty*! There his life stands—fixed and eternal as his statue! How pleasant to be in the past! You can sit back and marvel at each effect as it follows from each cause, coherent, consistent, definite, *known*: I call that living!

MARTIN: It does sound wonderful!

HAMLET (*smiling*): It is. (*Frowning*.) But you've spoiled it. It lasted only as long as you believed in it. So now it's over. (*He takes up the lamp, preparing to leave. To himself:*) She'll live to regret this! My mother, is she? Bringing a doctor with her, to study my idiosyncrasies? And an Attendant! Oh, that Attendant! A famous swordsman, is he? But he made a mistake to come here, a fatal error, that will lead right to the fifth act. Hamlet delayed. Delayed for twenty years—*but not forever, no*—

(*There is a knock at the door.*)

WILLIAM'S VOICE: It is I.

JIMMY (*to* JACK): That's William.

JACK: He might just as well say "it's me" now.

JIMMY: But he doesn't know. This is his evening visit.

MARTIN: He comes here *every* evening—in character.

JACK: I didn't know he was in the play.

HAMLET (*cutting angrily in*): He isn't. He's going to write it. He is William Shakespeare.

MARTIN: Taking down the reminiscences of Hamlet, Prince of Denmark.

JACK: They're not finished yet?

MARTIN (*nervously*): Um, no—

HAMLET: I could never get beyond the middle of Act Four.

MARTIN: Are we going to go through with it tonight? Not tell William anything's happened?

JIMMY: Yes, what a lark! Let's take William in!

HAMLET (*shocked*): What?

MARTIN: Shut up, Francisco! Can't you see he doesn't like it!

HAMLET: Let him talk.

MARTIN: But, sir, it's got to be just like it was true!

HAMLET: "Just like it was true?" Oh, that's good! Martin, my friend, you have found the only way in which the truth can be *more* than a lark. (*He lets* WILLIAM *in.* WILLIAM *is in Elizabethan costume—as* SHAKESPEARE.) Come in, Master Shakespeare, you are the last friend I have left.

MARTIN: What do you mean by that, sir?

HAMLET: A friend is someone who believes in you. Come, Master William. I have some new material for you. I'm coming to conclusions. Ready?

WILLIAM: Yes, sir.

HAMLET (*reciting with slow intensity*):
> How all occasions do inform against me
> And spur my dull revenge! What is a man
> If his chief good and market of his time
> Be but to sleep . . .

(*After the word* revenge, *the lights dim rapidly.*)

SCENE 2

The lights go up again at once. The scene is unchanged. HAMLET *is still dictating.*

HAMLET: . . . That for a fantasy or trick of fame
> Go to their graves like beds, fight for a plot
> Whereon the numbers cannot try the cause
> Which is not tomb enough and continent
> To hide the slain! Oh, from this time forth,
> My thoughts be bloody or be nothing worth!

(*He has spoken the lines quietly, monotonously, except for the last sentence. And now he sees that* WILLIAM *and the three young men are drowsy—so much so that when he stops, they do not notice. Pause.* HAMLET *rises and is about to leave when the others notice and jump up.*)

Don't get up! I can manage. Good night! (*And they watch him leave.*)

(At this point, the revolving stage starts to rumble;* the other set is being brought back on. HAMLET is on the turntable walking in the direction opposite to its movement; hence, in relation to the audience, he is stationary. The rumbling stops; we are in the other room. But the two pedestals no longer support statues. In the latter's stead stand SUSIE as OPHELIA and BROWNE as HAMLET.

HAMLET has walked right past both statues when a door opens and he turns to see who it is. It is MRS. SIMPSON, dressed exactly like her daughter, entering. Though hardly mistress of her actions, MRS. SIMPSON manages to raise her arm and point toward the statues. HAMLET's eyes follow. He gives a very slight and silent start, then, without warning, falls in a heap. The DOCTOR—for it is his cue— comes swiftly in, without his disguise, and crosses to HAMLET. SUSIE is down on the floor and in BROWNE's arms, trembling.)

MRS. SIMPSON: How is he?

STURM: All right! He's fainted but he'll be all right!

MRS. SIMPSON: You think it's worked?

STURM: We shall soon know. (*He gets* HAMLET *on to a couch.* MRS. SIMPSON *does what she can to help.*) We shall soon know. (*Suddenly,* SIMPSON *rushes in, also without his disguise, followed by the three attendants.*) Sh! Quiet, in Heaven's name! This man's fate is in the balance!

SIMPSON (*very excited*): Bosh! It was settled before we ever arrived. He's been sane for years!

STURM: What are you talking about?

SIMPSON: He said so himself. He told these three boys just now!

STURM: Told them what?

SIMPSON: That he knew their real names, knew this building has electric light, saw through our disguises this afternoon—

STURM: He said that?

SIMPSON: Yes, and a lot more of the same sort—didn't he?

MARTIN: Yes, sir, he did.

MRS. SIMPSON: He was just *acting* this afternoon.

---

* Alternatively, the curtains are drawn back.

SIMPSON: He's just been acting for years, it seems.

STURM: Sh! He's coming to.

MRS. SIMPSON: Is he—all right?

SIMPSON: Of course he is, I've been trying to tell you—

MRS. SIMPSON: You said he *was* sane. But now, after this shock treatment—

SIMPSON: You think it might work in reverse?

STURM: Sh! Here he comes!

HAMLET (*rising to a sitting position, looking around in silence. Pause*): I suppose I'll have to say something, that was obviously my cue.

STURM: You were listening?

HAMLET (*ignoring the query*): Now where did we leave off? (*Seeing* BROWNE *and* SUSIE *again.*) Oh yes, Hamlet and Ophelia—I never realized they so much resembled Romeo and Juliet. But who is everybody else? Who are these intruders in fancy dress? (*Pointing to the two men in modern dress.*) Who am I—partner of this older woman? I know. I'm Prince Hamlet's father, Old Hamlet, and, as such, no more than a ghost! (*Going over to* BROWNE *and taking hold of him:*)
>   I am thy father's spirit,
>   Doomed for a certain term to walk the night.
>   List, list, O list!
>   If thou didst ever thy dear father love—

BROWNE: O God!

HAMLET (*surprised at this correct answer*): Huh?
>   If thou didst ever thy dear father love
>   Revenge his foul and most unnatural murder!

BROWNE (*again, spontaneously, and in protest*): Murder!

HAMLET (*vehemently*):
>   Murder most foul, as in the best it is,
>   But this most foul, strange, and unnatural—
(*He breaks off and falls back on the couch as if in pain.*)

STURM: It *has* worked in reverse. Psychodramatic shock treatment has driven a sane man mad. I am ruined.

SIMPSON: Nonsense! He was acting before, he's been acting all his life, and he's acting now. Are we going to let him get away with murder?

HAMLET: What was that?

STURM (*nervously*): Nothing, nothing.

HAMLET: Get away with what?

STURM (*to* SIMPSON): You mustn't excite him, it could be dangerous at this time—

SIMPSON: But didn't you hear what these fellows (*indicating the attendants*) said?

HAMLET (*overhearing*): No. What did they say? (*Turning to them:*) What did you say?

MARTIN: Well, sir . . . we just said we thought you were cured.

SIMPSON (*petulantly*): So let's drop this comedy once and for all! (*To* BROWNE *and* SUSIE:) Go and get dressed, both of you!

MRS. SIMPSON: But—if he's cured—what does it matter what they wear?

HAMLET: No, no, he's right. Clothes make the man. (*To* SIMPSON:) And that's why I consider it insufferable that you come before me like that (*indicating his twentieth-century dress.*) For twenty years—

SIMPSON: Now look here, old boy, I did my bit of dressing up this morning, but then—

HAMLET: You thought I was crazy, and looked very glum. Now you find I'm, what's the word? sane, and her costume (*indicating* SUSIE) strikes you as comic. To me her present appearance—

STURM (*getting interested*): Yes, yes?

HAMLET (*interrupted*): Ha? Who are you? Oh, yes. Polonius—but in disguise—

STURM (*the German way of introducing oneself*): Theodor Sturm.

HAMLET: —the disguise of a German psychiatrist! All this (*pointing to the pedestals*) was your idea? Living statues, two couples, the old and the young—what in God's name did you hope would happen? (STURM*'s mouth opens.*) Don't tell me! I don't want to know.

SIMPSON: *I* said it was a lot of bosh from the start.

HAMLET (*coming over to him with a semblance of warmth*): You did? That's fine. You know what? I think I'll take this stuff off (*indicating his clothes*) and . . . slip into something comfortable? Let's say a boiled shirt, stiff collar, French cuffs—there must be some cuff links someplace—and I do hope my trousers have been properly pressed—anyway: I'm coming with you!

SIMPSON (*startled*): I say! Where to?

HAMLET: Oh—the Stork Club? Is it still there? Where are you living now? Sutton Place? Is *that* still there? Wherever you're living, let's go there and set up a nice little *maison à trois?*

SIMPSON (*petulant again*): Well, you can't stay here—now. What beats me is how you ever could.

HAMLET: Ever?

SIMPSON: Yes—after the accident—

HAMLET: Oh! (*Watching* SIMPSON.) But, you see, I *was* crazy—for quite some time.

STURM (*again interested*): Is that true? How long?

HAMLET: I haven't worked it out yet in hours, minutes, and seconds. In years, it came to twelve.

STURM (*making a mental note*): Ah!

HAMLET (*pressing forward, to* STURM): Can you imagine that? Not *going* crazy, *being* crazy. Day in, day out. Being a loony, the way the next man is a postman or a bus driver. No trade union to limit *my* hours: I was loony round the clock.

SIMPSON: Well now, really, I say—

HAMLET (*almost to himself*): The life we live! And the life we don't live! The things the little loony misses out on, not knowing who's dead, not knowing what's happened to his girl—but what *does* happen to girls?

SIMPSON (*trying somehow to get the upper hand*): Still, my friend, you've been here twenty years, not just twelve.

HAMLET (*smiling*): I should be thankful for small mercies? Trade in twelve mad years for eight sane ones? (STURM *is eyeing him intently.*) Stare away, Dr. Sturm, I'm an interesting case. (*He is shaking all over.*) Take a note of this. Go on, take out your notebook, and, everybody, do make yourselves comfortable. (*They all sit down as if hypnotized by him.*) One day—after twelve years of it—the trouble here (*he taps his forehead*) stopped. My eyes opened, as it were. The objects around me—I carefully touched them, one after the other, like this—they were real. (*He breaks off, and points at* SIMPSON.) I agree with him, you see. These clothes, this stage setting, they're a mask. Let's tear it off, open the windows, let in the daylight, let in the fresh breeze of life. (*Pause.*) No! Let's go *out* into the fresh breeze of life! Out of doors! I haven't been out of doors in twenty years, can you conceive of that? Come on, quick! (*He has pulled* SIMPSON *up from his chair and started to drag him toward the door. Suddenly, though, he stops, drops* SIMPSON*'s arm, and raises his own hand to his temple.*) But stop a minute, where are we going? And what are we going to do there? (*Into* SIMPSON*'s face, simply:*) You know, I wouldn't like all that nudging and pointing, all those Princeton men saying: "Hey, look, it's old Hamlet!"—and giggling like my thousand and one Ophelias, I wouldn't care for that.

SIMPSON (*trying to be solicitous because he is scared*): Now really, old boy, it wouldn't be as bad as all that—

MRS. SIMPSON (*hoping to be able to intervene*): Of course not! People couldn't be so cruel!

HAMLET (*quickly*): No? They called me crazy even *before* the little accident on the stairs!

MRS. SIMPSON: They didn't, they'd never have dared—

HAMLET (*snapping at her*): *He* did (*indicating* SIMPSON)!

SIMPSON: I say, if a man can't take a joke—

HAMLET: Joke? Look at my hair! (*They are all startled.*) No, not here (*indicating the crown of his head*) —here (*turning and holding his finger to the back of his neck*)!

SIMPSON: Steady on, old chap, you aren't the only one who's been getting a bit grey!

HAMLET: No. But *I* went grey here! Dying without ever having lived! How would *you* like to arrive at a banquet hungry as a wolf and find they'd cleared all the food away?

SIMPSON: Now, no one denies you've had a spot of bad luck—

HAMLET: I have, haven't I?

SIMPSON: But, then again, old chap, you couldn't expect people—to, um—um—

HAMLET: To sit around and wait till I was cured? No. Especially not the man who stuck his sword out so I'd trip and fall downstairs—!

SIMPSON (*icily*): I don't know what you're referring to.

BROWNE: What was that?

HAMLET: My little accident. I tripped over a sword. Someone else's sword. Not hanging loose from the scabbard. Held tight—and placed in my way . . . .

MRS. SIMPSON: I never heard of *that*.

HAMLET (*to* SIMPSON): Just a joke, of course, and if a man can't take a joke, eh?

SIMPSON (*very pale*): You're making all this up.

MRS. SIMPSON: But who was it? Didn't you see him as you fell?

HAMLET: He thought I didn't, but I did. (*Turning very serious at once.*) What do you all think I want? Pity? That's what you'll leave on the plate for me when the banquet is through—pity? No thank you! (*Wheeling round on the* DOCTOR.) Dr. Sturm, this case is rather new in the annals of insanity, this is a lunatic who *preferred* lunacy, chose madness for a mate, embraced madness as a bride! I took solitude—my solitude here—squalid as it seemed when my eyes first opened to it—and I clothed it in all the poetry of that distant day when I was Hamlet and you (*he addresses* SUSIE, *not* MRS. SIMPSON) were Ophelia. I had my little revenges too: I made my visitors return to a fancy-dress ball which—for them, if not for me—had ended long ago after a single evening. (*In a dream now.*) To go to the ball—and have it last forever—wonderful—but not so easy, eh? Well, *I* made it, ladies and gentlemen! And not in jest—in lunacy! In an illusion that was real! Elsinore! In Elsinore forever! (*His eyes close, his head drops, he is lost in reverie.*)

SIMPSON (*to the others*): It's true I tripped him on the stairs. I thought he didn't see me. But he seems rather pleased with the results.

MRS. SIMPSON: Hugh!

BROWNE (*to her*): He's lying! (*To* SIMPSON:) Hugh, don't be absurd!

MRS. SIMPSON: You didn't, Hugh, you didn't, you could never have—

SIMPSON: Have what?

MRS. SIMPSON (*stammering*): Have borne the shame of it, the guilt, without a sign—

SIMPSON: You told *him* I changed.

MRS. SIMPSON: You quieted down, put on that air of . . . .

SIMPSON: Self-abasement? Well?

MRS. SIMPSON: You *did* feel guilty?

SIMPSON: I felt that it was . . . funny to be the man who *didn't* feel guilty.

(*At this point,* DR. STURM *has walked over to* HAMLET *and is about to touch him to see if, perhaps, he has fainted, when the latter shakes himself out of his reverie.*)

HAMLET: Wait, Doctor, I'll get to you in a minute! (*Turning towards* MARTIN, JIMMY, *and* JACK:) Traitors! Idiots! What could you possibly gain by telling them I was cured? When I'm cured, I won't need you, you'll be fired. Then back to Greenwich Village with you, the poor man's Elsinore! Pah! (*He spits. They start to go.*) No, come back! (*Folding his hands.*) Father, forgive them, for they know not what they do! (*Wistfully, to everyone:*) For me, these clothes are a deliberate caricature of a fancy-dress ball that goes on all the time, attended by the whole human race! If my three young friends don't see it, why they must think their clothes (*pointing to the attendants' costumes*) are wildly out of character, not to say out of period. Well, that's their loss. *Eppur si muove!* The ball continues, may I have the next waltz? (DR. STURM *is staring at him and shaking his head.*) Now, Doctor, what's your name again?

STURM: Sturm.

HAMLET: Rest easy, Sturm, I'm cured. Really. I'm deliberately playing the fool—I avoid the words mad, insane, crazy, lunatic, depraved, deranged . . . .

STURM: You were listening?

HAMLET (*going right on*): Would you prefer me to live my . . . foolishness involuntarily, ignorantly—like some I could mention? (*He indicates with a broad gesture the others in the room and perhaps all the others in the world.*)

SIMPSON: So *we* are crazy! I hope you all get the implication.

HAMLET (*perkily*): If you weren't crazy—would you have come?

SIMPSON: I came to *see* a madman, not to *be* one.

HAMLET (*turning quickly on* MRS. SIMPSON): Will you endorse that remark?

MRS. SIMPSON: I? Certainly not! I came—

SIMPSON (*determined to take the offensive*): She's rather gone on you still, don't you know. Why don't you ask her to stay?

MRS. SIMPSON: I resent that!

HAMLET: Don't worry, I know what's eating him, I know what always did eat him—

SIMPSON: You know too much!

HAMLET (*again going right on*): Jealousy, that's his problem. (*To* SIMPSON:) But you forget: it's not mine. Do you think I bother my head about the events of twenty years ago—your part in them—or (*turning to* MRS. SIMPSON) hers? (*To them both:*) You think I sit here figuring out how you must look in bed together? (*Again, he spits.*) This is my life. You have grown old in a life I know nothing about—maybe *that* was what you wanted to prove with your little comedy, Dr. Sturm? (*Indicating* BROWNE:) But I do see he isn't Hamlet. You know why? He's too young for Old Hamlet, and, as for Prince Hamlet, I've been Prince Hamlet for twenty years, I still am, and (*bumptiously*) that's the way it's going to be! Now, listen carefully, Dr. Sturm—I really think you should be writing all this down—in those twenty years, she (*indicating* MRS. SIMPSON) has become someone else, I couldn's say who, she's a total stranger. (*Fixing* SUSIE *with his eyes.*) Ophelia is here. (SUSIE *is scared.*) Yes, jump, young woman, tremble like a fawn. You should: *you* haven't known Hamlet for twenty years, he's just noticed you for the first time, here he comes, straight from Wittenberg, his age is twenty, his hair is floppy and flaxen, he's the glass of fashion and the mould of form, and he is about to pay you his first compliment on your beauty. (*He is very close to her now. In a lower, more intense tone:*) But you shouldn't have let them play that trick on me, think of the impression it was bound to make! The statue come alive, the dream a waking reality, the word made flesh! (*And he takes her in his arms and kisses her passionately.* SUSIE *is limp with fear.*)

SIMPSON: Now, really, this is going a bit far! I'm afraid I must insist—

HAMLET: What—again? (SIMPSON *stammers.*) I let you "insist" the last time, wasn't that enough?

SIMPSON: That was twenty years ago.

HAMLET (*not listening*): After jealousy—revenge!

SIMPSON: I have my daughter to think of.

HAMLET (*brokenhearted, plangent*):
> I loved Ophelia! Forty thousand fathers
> Could not with all their quantity of love
> Make up my sum!

STURM (*in an urgent, low tone*): The man's raving! Stand back, everyone!

SIMPSON: Bosh! He's at it again, that's all, he always wants the woman and, by George, I always have to stop him—

HAMLET (*stopping dead*): What?

SIMPSON (*carried away*): And he's no more crazy than we are, he's just—

HAMLET (*like a military order*): William! (*All stand rigid waiting for the stroke of doom. WILLIAM must have been waiting just outside. He steps in.*) Ladies and gentlemen, meet Master Shakespeare! (*HAMLET is shaking all over.*) William, that little question of Hamlet's hesitation, I've got it licked, I'm past the end of Act Four now, I'm in the middle of the fifth and last act. (*It is as if he is reporting a dream.*) Osric comes and asks me to fight, I fight, now I can't see so clearly, but someone is shouting "the duel scene, the duel scene!"

STURM (*in a whisper*): Keep quite still, everyone, he's harmless, he has no weapon.

HAMLET: So how do I do it, William—without a weapon? Poison him?
> Here, thou incestuous, murderous, damned Dane,
> Drink off this potion!

And the stage manager provides a little colored water. Not good enough, William, for a play of yours. "We are such stuff as dreams are made on." Life is unreal. Good. But is death unreal? Is his chest unreal, and the heart inside it? (*He crosses like lightning to MARTIN, snatches his sword from its scabbard, and plunges it into SIMPSON's chest.*) Real sword, real chest . . . real blood! (*Everyone is petrified. The hall is still.*)

STURM (*moving over to SIMPSON*): He's mortally wounded. Help me.

(*BROWNE helps STURM move the body out of the room. MRS. SIMPSON and SUSIE follow, weeping hysterically. SIMPSON's voice is heard offstage weakly exclaiming: "He's not insane, I tell you, he's not insane at all!" Then silence. Then a scream: it is MRS. SIMPSON. The ATTENDANTS and WILLIAM are about to leave.*)

HAMLET: He got my point, ha? I'm sane! But sane people go to Sing Sing. To the electric chair. An insane man, on the other hand, can stay in . . . Elsinore forever. (*They all look at each other.*) Which is what I'll do. And you with me! H'm?

GERMAN REQUIEM

For Herbert Blau

Two households, both alike in dignity . . .

The time is medieval, the place is Swabia. Our story concerns two branches of the Schroffenstein family. One occupies a fortress in Rosset, the other a fortress in Varvand. A mountain lies between the two fortresses.

Schroffensteins of Rosset:

Count Rupert
Eunice, his wife
Otto, his legitimate son, aged 15
Johann, his natural son, aged 14

Schroffensteins of Varvand:

Count Sylvius, a blind old man
Count Sylvester, his son, and ruling count
Gertrude, his wife
Agnes, his daughter, aged 14

A Schroffenstein but not from these parts:

Jerome, a man in his thirties

Vassals of Rupert:

Aldo
Santing
Fintenring

A vassal of Sylvester:

Theistin

Ursula, a gravedigger's widow
Barna, her daughter, aged 14

The Rosset Priest

The Varvand Gardener

Two Wanderers

Servant to Rupert

Servant to Sylvester

A Rosset Chambermaid

The Twelve Scenes

1. Rosset. A Gothic Chapel.
2. Varvand. In the Castle.
3. On the Mountain. A Slope.
4. Varvand. In the Castle.
5. Varvand. Before the Gates.
6. On the Mountain. Same Slope as in Scene 3.
7. Rosset. In the Castle.
8. Varvand. In the Castle.
9. On the Edge of the Forest. Home of a Gravedigger's Widow.
10. On the Mountain. Another Slope.
11. Rosset. Prison. High in the Tower of the Castle.
12. On the Mountain. Inside a Cave.

ONE

Rosset. A Gothic chapel. Solemn music. A funeral procession which halts when the bier is stage center. On it, a child's body. A priest presides over a congregation that, in the theater, is imagined to be out front.

PRIEST: And so, to little Peter, on the eve of his tenth birthday, we bid farewell, his death a mystery that may never, on earth, be solved, our consolation—that he is gone to a better world than this. (*He looks up from the scroll he has read this from and speaks informally.*) The congregation will leave while the family pays its last respects. (*Crossing himself.*) In the name of the Father, the Son, and the Holy Ghost, Amen.

(Music plays as the congregation is imagined to depart and as the following enter and make a semicircle about the bier: COUNT RUPERT, *his wife* EUNICE, *their son* OTTO, *their kinsman* JEROME, *and* RUPERT's *herald* ALDO. *Family retainers stand in two groups, left and right, respectively, thus framing the tableau.)*

RUPERT (*after a silence*): And now what? (*Indicating each of his companions.*) Kinsman Jerome? Eunice, my wife? Otto, my son? My herald, Aldo?

ALDO: May I speak, my Lord?

RUPERT: Speak.

ALDO: This priest spoke of a mystery? What mystery?

EUNICE: Sh!

ALDO: Must I be silent, my Lord?

RUPERT: No.

ALDO: What mystery in sudden violence to the Schroffensteins of Rosset, its source forever the same?

EUNICE: Sh!

RUPERT: The Schroffensteins of Varvand.

ALDO (*nodding*): We therefore hold responsible for murder your kinsman Sylvester, young Peter's uncle.

RUPERT: But what do we do?

ALDO: What do you always do?

RUPERT: They say forgiveness is not in me. I hit back.

ALDO: Eye for eye, tooth for tooth.

RUPERT: But it hurts.

EUNICE: Yes. It hurts not just them, but you. Sometimes I think: you most of all.

RUPERT: It is a strain.

ALDO: But you're a man.

EUNICE: Are men not Christians too?

(ALDO *shrugs*).

RUPERT: Let me answer that, Aldo. Men are not Christians. They have a world to run.

EUNICE: To me, belief is real.

RUPERT: Belief *is* real. But not what is believed in.

EUNICE: Family is real. And trusting each other.

RUPERT: And mistrusting each other.

EUNICE: We're not beasts, we're human. And Sylvester is our cousin.

RUPERT: No, in bestiality, man outdoes the beasts. A lion has been known to spare a child, a she-wolf to give suck to son of woman. Only the man-beast is beast all through: an enemy to everything that moves.

ALDO: Now you're talking.

EUNICE: Sylvester—

RUPERT (*pointing to the bier*): Hark to the language that he speaks— the only language that he understands.

EUNICE: Rupert, I can't argue with you. But I love you. You love me. (*Pointing to the bier.*) Find out first just what happened. Find out what Sylvester is planning now.

ALDO: In other words: delay. Till Otto joins his brother there? (*Pointing to the bier.*) Till *you* join both? And you, Count Rupert, I, and all Rosset?

EUNICE: Rupert—

RUPERT: Silence, Eunice. Silence, Aldo, everyone. Here, following the solemn requiem mass, by the body and blood of the scourged and crucified Jew of Nazareth, we all swear: REVENGE. Otto, my son, step forward. (OTTO *does so*.) Swear!

OTTO (*drawing a deep breath*): May my heart take wing and bear my curse to God: I swear REVENGE.

RUPERT: On whom?

OTTO: Sylvester Schroffenstein.

RUPERT: In whose name?

OTTO: In your name, Father: Rupert Schroffenstein.

RUPERT: May your curse float straight into the arms of God. He will provide the thunderbolt to strike—whom, then—not Sylvester only?

OTTO: Every Schroffenstein in Varvand.

RUPERT: Even to the youngest?

OTTO: Even to the youngest.

RUPERT: Now, all together.

(Everyone on stage, except EUNICE, *sings the following Hymn to Revenge:)*

> If at nine years old our darling
> By the sword must bleed and die
> We demand, O God of Vengeance,
> Tooth for tooth and eye for eye.
>> *Vengeance is Mine, saith the Lord,*
>> *I bring not peace, but a sword.*
>
> Down in dust he tells the foeman
> 'Tis too soon to end a life
> Loving's what he craves, not dying
> But the answer is the knife.
>> *Vengeance is Mine, saith the Lord,*
>> *I bring not peace, but a sword.*
>
> In his coffin though still living
> Begs for mercy mild and meek
> Arms outstretched to the marauder
> The marauder does not speak.
>> *Vengeance is Mine, saith the Lord,*
>> *I bring not peace, but a sword.*

RUPERT: Aldo!

ALDO: My Lord?

RUPERT: Ride to Varvand. Tell Sylvester: WAR. Tell him I'll tear down his castle walls and raise a scaffold for him on the ruins. Tell him I'll drink his blood. He has one child left, his daughter Agnes. I'll drink her blood. Go tell him that.

(ALDO leaves. Everyone else follows except for OTTO and JEROME. While OTTO is only fifteen, JEROME is a man in his thirties who tries to counteract the impression made by his greying hair with dandified dress.)

JEROME: A word with you, young kinsman.

OTTO: Second cousin, or is it uncle? Where have you come from, Jerome?

JEROME: Varvand.

OTTO: No.

JEROME: Yes.

OTTO: How should I take that?

JEROME: Very simply. I'm on their side.

OTTO: Ah! Our enemy then?

JEROME: If you must all be so wrongheaded.

OTTO: Explain.

JEROME: *You* explain. Yes! Explain this charade we have both just witnessed. Quite a conjurer, your father—what does he want, to make clowns of us?

OTTO: You know something.

JEROME: Yes. I know Sylvester. Who's supposed to have killed a child. Not believable. The most this man ever killed was a fly, buzzing around his beloved daughter's head.

OTTO: The Varvand people make much of you. You're returning the compliment.

JEROME: And that's all there is to it?

OTTO: Also you're courting Sylvester's daughter, Agnes.

JEROME: You get around.

OTTO: She's a big fish but, as *his* daughter, may be said to feed on corpses.

JEROME: And I, to catch that fish, am killing my own honor to use as bait? You are offensive, kinsman.

OTTO: Who is our enemy? He who sits in Varvand and his kin. Who supports them? You do, kinsman.

JEROME: And I'll win others to their cause. As I ride through the fields and over the mountain, I'll stop at every castle and appeal to that which every good man has at heart.

OTTO: Namely?

JEROME: A sense of justice.

OTTO: We of Rosset have no sense of justice? *My* heart tells me my father speaks the truth!

JEROME: Pah! Even if you believed Sylvester innocent, you wouldn't dare tell your father!

OTTO: D'you see this knightly sword? I won it yesterday and came of age. I can't wait to use it!

JEROME: On me, boy? That's a challenge?

OTTO: As you wish.

JEROME: And if I don't wish, I'm a coward?

OTTO (*pointing to the body on the bier*): Any man who won't avenge *that* is, yes, a coward!

(Carried away with feeling, OTTO *rushes out.* JEROME *starts to follow him but then stops as he catches sight of the Rosset* PRIEST *who has returned to the chapel to put out candles and the like.)*

JEROME: Good day, Father. You have been priest here long?

PRIEST: More than a score of years, my Lord.

JEROME: I am Jerome. A Schroffenstein. But not from these parts.

PRIEST: So I had guessed: your face not being familiar.

JEROME: Will you talk freely with me?

PRIEST: Of what, my Lord?

JEROME (*pointing to the bier*): I can't believe that his own uncle slew this child . . . . Am I wrong?

PRIEST: Where to begin?

JEROME: At the beginning.

PRIEST (*sighing*): These troubles all go back to a certain contract, in which was written, about the two branches of the Schroffensteins, that of Varvand on the other side of the mountain and that of Rosset here: should either one die out, the vast estates—this part of Swabia for some fifty miles in each direction—will go to the survivor.

JEROME: Is this to the point—now?

PRIEST: Did an apple play a part in the Fall of Man?

JEROME: You're saying, then, it's all a battle for possession.

PRIEST: I'm saying what I hear.

JEROME: In Rosset.

PRIEST: You may allow for bias.

JEROME: Go on.

PRIEST: Neither—Rupert of Rosset, Sylvester of Varvand—had an heir. Then came Otto, Rupert's son. Sylvester winced at that event. But his wife soon bore him Agnes. A daughter, but better than nothing. She might rule Varvand one day, or marry another Schroffenstein.

JEROME: Sylvester had a son himself, though, later?

PRIEST: Philip, yes. Sickly from the start. Not living to be eight. Died just months ago.

JEROME: Of sickness?

PRIEST: Of course. But aggravating—again, I say what I hear—the spiritual sickness in his father.

JEROME: Sickness?

PRIEST: Resentment of Rupert. Who by now had two sons. Both healthy as young steers. Shooting up like poplar trees. The rest you know.

JEROME: I know?

PRIEST: Or can guess. Sylvester couldn't bear it. Coming upon Peter—Rupert's younger son—in the country, he grabbed an axe and felled him like a sapling.

JEROME: The body shows axe wounds?

PRIEST: I spoke metaphorically.

JEROME: And literally?

PRIEST: Walking in the fields, at the edge of the forest, Count Rupert stumbled on the body of his son, two men beside him, their knives dripping with blood. He draws his sword, strikes them both down—

JEROME: He struck them both down?

PRIEST: Killed one. The other lived—long enough to confess!

JEROME: He confessed?

PRIEST: Confessed all.

JEROME: Yes?

PRIEST: Sylvester hired him to kill the lad.

JEROME: He said that? You heard him say that?

PRIEST: As did everyone else.

JEROME: This was not a private confession—to you as priest?

PRIEST: Oh, no: he was under torture on the public square.

JEROME: So they tortured him, and he said—what?

PRIEST: It was so noisy on the square, it was hard to hear.

JEROME: Then you *didn't* hear him?

PRIEST: I heard one word.

JEROME: Which was?

PRIEST: Sylvester.

JEROME: One word that says everything. And then?

PRIEST: Nothing. He was dead.

JEROME: H'm. (*Gives him money. The* PRIEST *moves off to continue his labors. To himself:*) I was wrong. Otto was right. I will return to Varvand, confront Sylvester, then join the fight against him.

(*Exit* PRIEST *and* JEROME. *Enter* OTTO *and* JOHANN.)

OTTO: Brother Johann—

JOHANN: Half a brother. Half-brother Otto—

OTTO: My father's son's my brother. So, brother, why the tears?

JOHANN: The funeral—

OTTO: Which you did not attend. Where were you?

JOHANN: Outside, kneeling at the Virgin's shrine.

OTTO: Our Lady had a message for you?

JOHANN: I had one for her.

OTTO: About a woman's veil.

JOHANN: Ha?

OTTO: The one in your hand. Or did She give it to you?

JOHANN: I found it—near Her shrine.

OTTO: Whose is it?

JOHANN: I don't know—her name.

OTTO: I'll give you this ring in exchange for it.

JOHANN: Oh, no, I couldn't.

OTTO: What's your price?

JOHANN: It's worth more than my life.

OTTO: That little veil?

JOHANN: A single instant can be a foretaste of eternity!

OTTO: H'm. Tell me about that.

JOHANN: Some weeks ago Father led his huntsmen into the woods, me with them. Our horses shot into action like arrows from the bow. Mine was a Turkish mount, half wild. At the sound of barking dogs and cracking whips and hallooing horns, he panicked and outstripped the other steeds, taking the lead beside Father. Even then he refused to stop. I pulled at the reins but he hurtled down the valley, dove into the river where the current is swiftest, and dumped me where it's twenty feet deep.

OTTO (*laughing*): Thus Johann drowned and has not lived to tell the tale.

JOHANN: You laugh. But death *was* certain—I'd lost consciousness—

OTTO: But then an Angel appeared in the Heavens and—

JOHANN: How did you guess? But not in the Heavens. And not an Angel—

OTTO: A witch on a broomstick?

JOHANN: A goddess!

OTTO: Our Lady Herself—ah, *now* I see—

JOHANN (*smiling*): Only this goddess hadn't a stitch of clothing on. I caught her bathing in the river—

OTTO (*impressed*): Well!

JOHANN: A young girl. Beautiful. And modest too—

OTTO: Naked but modest?

JOHANN: And therefore not naked long once she'd caught sight of me. Her body covered, this veil over her face, she dragged me out of the water, laid me down, and stanched my wounds.

OTTO: I bet *that* felt good.

JOHANN: Ever seen a little girl gently holding a turtle dove and stroking its feathers? I was that dove.

OTTO: Did the goddess have a voice?

JOHANN: Musical as a bell. "What is your name, youth, and where do you hail from?"

OTTO: You said, "Johann from Rosset." And she said?

JOHANN: Nothing. But gave a violent start.

OTTO: Why?

JOHANN: God knows. But from then on was in a fearful hurry to get away. Ran, finally, as fast as her feet could carry her—leaving this veil behind.

OTTO: She'd removed it, so you'd see her face?

JOHANN: No, no, it fell off while she tended my wounds.

OTTO: What's her name?

JOHANN: There's a mystery about that. She won't tell me. "Please, please," I beg. "No, no, I *cannot* tell you," says she . . . .

OTTO: Now, stop a minute. This is her veil. And she won't tell her name . . . . I think I know the girl.

JOHANN: You? You know her?

OTTO: My dear Johann, d'you think the sun shines down on you alone? I'm interested in her.

JOHANN: Since when?

OTTO: Since last week.

JOHANN: Where?

OTTO: Let's just say: somewhere on the mountain . . . . But, you know, we both have to set aside romance and fight.

JOHANN: Fight who?

OTTO: At the funeral, we took a vow. War to the death. A war of extermination against those who killed our brother.

JOHANN: A whole family?

OTTO: A whole line—of our own family.

JOHANN: Those of Varvand?

OTTO: Who else?

JOHANN: It's impossible.

OTTO: For one so delicate as you, so Christian?

JOHANN: That's not what I mean.

OTTO: You just feel—you aren't one of us, being—

JOHANN: Illegitimate? Not that either. I *am* Rupert's son.

OTTO: Then what are you talking about?

JOHANN: I've been lying to you.

OTTO: Ha?

JOHANN: I do know her name.

OTTO: Whose?

JOHANN: The goddess's.

OTTO: If she told you her name . . . .

JOHANN: She didn't. Hearing I was from Rosset, she took to her heels. I followed. Her destination was Varvand!

OTTO: She's one of *them*?!

JOHANN: *The* one of them. There were people at Varvand's gates. "Who was that girl?" I asked. Can you guess the answer?

OTTO: Don't tell me.

JOHANN: I see I have told you.

(Silence.)

OTTO: You may not have taken the vow. But I did.

JOHANN: To kill them? To kill *her*?

(OTTO nods.)

JOHANN: It's not just barbaric, it's absurd. I know *your* secret, don't forget.

OTTO: Kill what one loves? It has happened before in this world's history!

JOHANN: That vow is your father's, not yours! He made you take it!

OTTO: I love Father. I'm sure he's right.

JOHANN: This is not real! You're not going to do it!

OTTO: Don't count on that.

JOHANN: Then let me beg one favor.

OTTO: Not to go ahead?

JOHANN: Not to go ahead—without verifying that Father is right.

OTTO: About what?

JOHANN: Them. All of them in Varvand. Especially Sylvester, her father. *Do* they hate us? *Are* they fighting a war of extermination against us? Is it *certain* one of them killed our brother? I love Father too, but he's not infallible! (OTTO *tries to speak but stammers.*) Besides, you're not just *interested* in Agnes—

OTTO (*the first time to say the name*): Agnes!

JOHANN: You love her. You are *in love* with her.

OTTO: How d'you know that?

JOHANN: I just know it. Otto, we both love her!

OTTO: You are asking me to break my vow, to break with Father, break with everything I—

JOHANN: I'm asking that you meet with Agnes. Find out—from her—if they're all of the same mind as Father. If Sylvester, too, is really such an avenger.

OTTO: And if not?

JOHANN: Don't kill her. Don't kill anyone. Return to Rosset and make Father see the truth.

OTTO: But then you love her too.

JOHANN: Ha?

OTTO: Left alive, is she mine or yours?

JOHANN: Or someone else's? Jerome maybe? Isn't that for her to say?

OTTO: I'll do it. At our meeting place on the mountain.

JOHANN: And won't betray me?

OTTO: You'll come with me and, from behind a tree, hear the whole exchange.

JOHANN (*kissing him on the cheek*): Brother!

TWO

Varvand. In the castle. AGNES *leading blind old* COUNT SYLVIUS, *her grandfather, to a chair.*

SYLVIUS (*when seated*): Agnes!

AGNES: Grandfather?

SYLVIUS: Where is my little grandson?

AGNES: Every day you still ask for Philip. What will keep you from forgetting?

SYLVIUS: What will keep me from remembering?

AGNES: Grandfather!

SYLVIUS: Agnes?

AGNES: Feel my cheeks.

SYLVIUS (*doing so*): Tears.

AGNES: Nothing can keep *me* from remembering.

SYLVIUS: But he's all right. He's up in Heaven now, little Philip. The priest has told you that.

AGNES: I only see that mound. Why a mound if there's no one under it?

SYLVIUS: Priests know better than we do.

AGNES: You really believe, don't you, Grandfather?

SYLVIUS: We have to, child. What else is there?

AGNES: Maybe I'll learn.

SYLVIUS: Fourteen, aren't you, now?

AGNES: Nearly fifteen.

SYLVIUS: Old enough to be confirmed in the Faith. Time for some young knight to lead you to the altar.

AGNES: I dream of that.

SYLVIUS: And dreams should come true. Have your mother send the Father Confessor to see you.

(*Enter* GERTRUDE, AGNES' *mother.*)

AGNES: Mother just came in, Grandfather.

SYLVIUS: Gertrude? Look at your daughter: this lovely head of hair invites a bridal wreath. (*He is running his fingers through* AGNES' *hair.*) You must have her confirmed!

GERTRUDE (*to* AGNES): Did Jerome put you up to this?

SYLVIUS: Courting her, is he, Jerome? Are you blushing, Agnes?

AGNES: No, Grandfather.

GERTRUDE (*to* AGNES): I'll talk to your father. Can you be patient till tomorrow? (AGNES *kisses her mother's hand.*) Here's the toy box you asked for—what for, by the way?

AGNES (*taking the box of toys*): To give to the gardener's children—whom Philip left behind.

SYLVIUS: Young Philip's toy soldiers? Let me hold them. (*Receiving the box, he takes out the soldiers. Unable to see them, he feels them, one by one.*) I don't see them, but when I feel them I see Philip—sitting down at my table, setting up the two opposing armies, starting the war, inventing the changing fortunes of battle . . . .

AGNES: The cavalry—that's our side, he'd say. The infantry here—they're from Rosset!

SYLVIUS (*shocked*): No, no, not "from Rosset." Just "the enemy."

AGNES: Same thing!

SYLVIUS: Agnes! Who says the men of Rosset are enemies?

AGNES (*evasively*): A lot of people.

SYLVIUS: Don't echo them, my child. The men of Rosset are friends and kinsmen.

AGNES: But, Grandfather, my brother Philip . . . was he not poisoned by them?

SYLVIUS: Poisoned by them? Certainly not! He died a natural death.

AGNES: But Mother says—

SYLVIUS: Ah, so *that's* the source—

GERTRUDE (*to* AGNES): You must learn to keep secrets.

AGNES: You never said it *was* one, Mother!

GERTRUDE (*hesitating*): It was . . . confidential talk between mother and daughter—

SYLVIUS: In which you asserted—

GERTRUDE: It looked *possible*—I'd *heard it said* that—

SYLVIUS: Rumor! Agnes, promise your grandfather never to spread rumors!

AGNES: I promise.

SYLVIUS: We are at peace with Rosset. Your father is a man of peace.

AGNES: Yes, Grandfather.

SYLVIUS: Don't forget it. Spread the news of it. To everyone you meet. (*To* GERTRUDE:) You shouldn't talk that way to the children.

GERTRUDE: What way? I accused no one!

SYLVIUS: You aired . . . a certain possibility.

GERTRUDE: Obviously. To die so fast . . . .

SYLVIUS: Gertrude!

GERTRUDE: Those marks on his body, where did *they* come from?

SYLVIUS: Oh, Gertrude!

GERTRUDE: Scarce does news of Philip reach their ears than their messenger's here, asking, in distracted tones, if the youngster's sick. We know what's on their minds: that contract, the inheritance . . . . (*A noise is heard offstage.*) Sh! Your father! He forbade me to speak of this.

(*Enter* SYLVESTER *and his* GARDENER.)

SYLVESTER: It can't be helped, though, Master Hans. Your turnips may, as you say, be sweet as sugar—

GARDENER: Sweet as figs, my Lord.

SYLVESTER: It can't be helped: they must be rooted up.

GARDENER: Rooting things up goes against the grain.

SYLVESTER: But if the aim's to plant something better? Look at the trees you've already planted. They dance like children as we pass. Take pride in them, Hans. They'll be your children's foster brothers: children and trees will grow up together and, when your daughter brings you your first grandchild, look! our barns are full to bursting with the fruit!

GARDENER: If we live to see the day.

SYLVESTER: Well, if *we* don't, our children will.

GARDENER: But will they? Pardon the liberty, my Lord, but I'd rather take on oak trees than your daughter.

SYLVESTER (*looking at* AGNES *with concern*): What *do* you mean, my dear Hans?

GARDENER: Well, sir, the north wind may beat down on them, but no one's going to come at them axe in hand—as they did at your son Philip.

SYLVESTER: Silence! Such talk in front of Agnes! These are wild dangerous rumors. Agnes, pay no attention!

GARDENER: Good, then: I'll uproot the turnips. I'll plant the trees. But if you don't live to eat the fruit thereof, my Lord (*he drops his voice to a whisper*), I'll be damned if I'll send any of it over to Rosset.

(*Exit* GARDENER. AGNES *is hiding her face in her mother's bosom.*)

SYLVESTER: You heard that, Gertrude? Preposterous! And all your handiwork. To the mistrustful eye, all things wear Satan's livery: all that's innocent is unravelled, then cunningly knit up into a guilty pattern. It's mistrust, Agnes, that's the cause of mischief: it's the black death of the soul.

GERTRUDE: If a light is lit, my Lord, one sees it.

SYLVESTER: One can shade it from the eyes of children.

GERTRUDE: Listen, my Lord—

SYLVESTER: Consider a red-hot cinder: an insect can carry it to a neighbor's roof and burn the house down.

GERTRUDE: An insect!

SYLVESTER: There's a parrot that repeats what others babble—

GERTRUDE: What parrot?

SYLVESTER: The common people like my gardener! Rumor's magnifying mirror!

GERTRUDE: They have eyes and can see.

SYLVESTER: Eighteen years ago, your sister was in childbirth with her first. You hurried over to Rosset where she lay. Her child was stillborn. Now suppose she'd said you stopped his breath? Seeming to embrace him, your hands had pressed down on the infant brain? Suppose, then, rumor had taken that up, the people's voice—*vox populi, vox dei*—suppose that voice had spoken, as it will, louder and louder—

GERTRUDE: Enough! I'll say nothing, accuse no one, just stand there and take it: if they but leave us our remaining child.

(She folds AGNES *in a passionate embrace. A knocking at the gate.)*

SYLVESTER *(calling to those without)*: Whoever it is, let him in.

SYLVIUS: Take me to my room, Agnes. (AGNES *does so.)*

GERTRUDE: Shall I prepare an extra place at table?

SYLVESTER: More if there's more than one. I'll go and see.

> *(Both leave.* AGNES *returns. She has taken* SYLVIUS *to his room. Now she looks around, throws a wrap about her, and prepares to leave the castle. Exit* AGNES. *Enter* SYLVESTER *with* ALDO.)

SYLVESTER: From Rosset, sir?

ALDO: You are Count Sylvester? I'm Aldo, Rupert's herald.

SYLVESTER *(as he himself sits down)*: Be seated. Beguile me with the Rosset news. The place is near enough but there's a mountain in between. A granite wall that reaches to the sky. And yet at christenings, weddings, funerals, a messenger will make the trip—up one side, down the other, and before he can get a word out he is asked what happened, what followed, and why not something else, how tall the eldest is, how many teeth the youngest has, if the cow has calved and such like . . . . So do sit down.

ALDO: I can talk standing.

SYLVESTER: Talking and standing belong as little together as riding and kissing.

ALDO: Count Rupert sent me here to break the peace.

(Silence.)

SYLVESTER: And why?

ALDO: On account of the murder of his son Peter.

SYLVESTER: Peter was—murdered?

ALDO: Count Rupert would not wish to prate of strife, struggle, battle, burning, ramming, raping, looting, laying waste, no, he's minded to tear down this castle and raise a scaffold on the ruins! He's minded to drink your blood! He's minded to drink the blood of your last remaining child!

SYLVESTER *(standing up, looking* ALDO *awkwardly in the eye)*: You'll sit down now, won't you? *(He places a chair for him.)* What was your name again?

ALDO: Aldo.

SYLVESTER: You're not from Rosset, are you, Aldo? You weren't born there?

ALDO: No.

SYLVESTER: Not Rosset, I knew it. You and I understand each other, don't we?

ALDO: What?

SYLVESTER: We can work something out, you and I, a peaceful solution.

ALDO: Ha?

SYLVESTER: Or, if it's to be war, fight side by side?

(Enter GERTRUDE.*)*

GERTRUDE: A place is prepared for you at dinner, sir.

ALDO: I won't be needing it, ma'am. (*To* SYLVESTER:) Ask the lady to leave.

GERTRUDE: I'll stay.

ALDO: Upon your head be it. Count Sylvester, the dogs in our yard know a murderer when they smell one. They wouldn't take food from him. Nor will I. War is declared. The cause: child murder.

SYLVESTER (*stopping him as he starts to leave*): Stop, Aldo. One of us two must be mad. If it's not you, it will soon be me: the ounce of sense that saves you from the madhouse will send *me* there. What was it you just told me? That rivers flow uphill and empty themselves in lakes on the mountain peaks? I'll try, *try* to believe that. But—if you are telling me—*I* killed a child, my own cousin's child . . . .

GERTRUDE: But, God in Heaven, who is it brings this dreadful charge? The Rosset people, those who themselves have murdered—

SYLVESTER (*quietly*): Hush, Gertrude. Now, sir, just tell me, did I hear aright. War is declared against me—because I killed a child?

ALDO: D'you want me to rattle it off a dozen times?

SYLVESTER: I heard you right. (*Calling to those without:*) Franz! Saddle my horse!—Slow-witted, I'm afraid: but who can comprehend what's not comprehensible?—Where's my helmet, where's my sword?

ALDO: I'll be going, then.

SYLVESTER: No, no, I'm riding with you, friend. (ALDO *stops, startled.*) I won't believe that message until I hear it from Rupert's own lips.

GERTRUDE: Don't place yourself in the enemy's power!

SYLVESTER: Let me be, Gertrude. Is Jerome back in Varvand?

GERTRUDE (*nodding*): He just returned.

SYLVESTER: Tell him I need him.

(GERTRUDE *leaves to look for* JEROME.)

ALDO: Don't fool yourself. At the very least, they'll chain you to the dungeon wall.

SYLVESTER (*donning things for a journey*): I go alone. A man alone has privilege. His life is sacred even among foes.

ALDO: In Rosset, *your* life is not sacred to anyone.

SYLVESTER: Yet, to me, *their* lives are sacred. Why not risk my own? If innocence is sacred to God, I shall return unscathed.

(GERTRUDE *returns with* JEROME.)

JEROME (*dry, reserved*): My Lord?

SYLVESTER: Good that you're back, Jerome. Stay with the womenfolk till I return.

JEROME: From where, my Lord?

SYLVESTER: Rosset.

JEROME: Rosset? What's happened? You've seen the light? You'll give yourself up there as a converted sinner?

SYLVESTER: What's this?

JEROME: Lay your head in Christian resignation on the block?

SYLVESTER: You amaze me, Jerome. You were in Rosset yourself. What have they been telling you?

JEROME: That you're a mountebank: you stand at the corner and deceive people with big words and conjuring tricks! What do you take *me* for? One more imbecile in your large following of imbeciles! I heard what this man (*pointing to* ALDO) called you—heard it through the wall, he has a loud voice—*SCOUNDREL!* You not only commit crimes, you cover them up, you pin them on others. Oh, you know nothing! You weren't there! You have an alibi . . . ! Dogs. What was it *you* said about dogs, Herald Aldo? Those dogs have the right idea, Sylvester. You smell. Of murder. (SYLVESTER *faints.* ALDO *looks quickly at him, quickly at* JEROME, *turns on his heel, and strides quickly out.* JEROME, *who had worked himself up into uncontrollable hysteria is now beginning to crumple and whimper.*) What have I said?

THREE

On the mountain. A slope. In the foreground, a cave. At one side of the stage, AGNES *sits weaving garlands. At the other side,* OTTO *and* JOHANN *enter unseen by her.* OTTO *conceals* JOHANN *behind a tree. He then paces up and down, "rehearsing," as it were, for the "scene" he will play with* AGNES. *When a twig breaks noisily under his feet, she hears it but pretends she doesn't.*

AGNES: He's here! And spying on me! Strange! Are there too many secrets here? His name's a secret from me but then so's mine from him . . . . He makes an impression, I must say. A face like a brisk morning storm! Eyes like summer lightning on the peaks! A lion's mane of hair secreting thunder like the clouds. Talk tumbles sparkling from his tongue like a mountain waterfall. —Speaking of spies, I think the sun would like to spy upon the night, break blazing into all that darkness, to witness night's great feasts of love! (*Sneaking a look at* OTTO, *she turns on him.*) What are you up to?

OTTO (*with a start*): Ha?

AGNES: Why all this prowling up and down?

OTTO: I'm getting myself ready. I have some things to ask you.

AGNES (*smiling*): Look what I've made for you! (*She holds up a crown of flowers.*) Let me try it on you. (*He sits, and she carefully puts the crown in place on his head.*) H'm. Interesting. (*She arranges garlands to fall about his shoulders.*) I wave my magic wand, and you're Queen of the May!

OTTO: I've been called The Girl before now. But watch! (*He gives her a leafy branch as scepter and sits her high up on a tree trunk as on a throne.*) Tableau! The Queen of the May meets the King of the Harvest! You're The Boy!

AGNES: The King who gives his blood for his people! (*She throws down the "scepter" and shows her fingers.*)

OTTO: Your fingers are bleeding!

AGNES (*with a laugh*): Every rose has its thorn. Each of *these* flowers had about three.

OTTO: Poor girl!

AGNES: Girl no longer. I'm about to be confirmed! And this is woman's work (*pointing to the garlands*). "A woman spares no pains," they say, and I've asked myself just where each flower should go, so that, how would Father put it? "the form and color of each may have its effect upon the whole." (OTTO *looks over his shoulder toward the spot where* JOHANN *is.*) What *is* the matter, today? (*She rises.* OTTO *takes her hand to reassure her.*) Ceremonious now? Are we still King and Queen? Do I understand you, young man?

OTTO: Does anyone understand anyone?

AGNES: And so bitter.

OTTO (*swallowing hard*): You said not to enquire and I didn't. But I happened to be told that, um, you are Agnes, daughter, only child now, of Sylvester, Lord of Varvand. (*Silence.*) Is that true?

(Silence.)

AGNES: Tell me *your* name, young man.

OTTO: The time will come for that. The time may come when *all* will be clear. But, first, make *yourself* clear to me.

AGNES: You know me without knowing me. You see into my soul.

OTTO: Then write your signature—that friendly invention which compresses the infinite into a word.

AGNES: You certainly have a way of putting things! But I too can only hope the time will come.

OTTO: What made you climb this mountain all alone when you know war is brewing and powerful neighbors, armed to the teeth, comb the countryside in murderous pursuit of each other?

AGNES: I know that, you say? I deny it. It is not so.

OTTO: A great family feud is the talk of Swabia. But you never heard of it?

AGNES (*hesitating*): I didn't say that.

OTTO: Ah! So there *is* a great family feud?

AGNES: No! There is much—too much—talk of one.

OTTO: Sylvester of Varvand lives it day and night, hates Rosset, is waging a war of extermination against all who live there, and has murdered Count Rupert's younger son.

AGNES: All quite untrue!

OTTO: So you do know the truth?

AGNES: Let's say . . . my presence is welcome in Varvand. And . . . let me invite you there. Do you know what will catch your eye? Dust, lying thick on all the weaponry and armor. (*Pause.*) You speak of Count Sylvester. Do you know him?

OTTO: By repute. By ill repute.

AGNES: Come to Varvand—I dare you to!—and I will show you a man with no enemies—unless it be the martens that invade his hencoops. Count Sylvester is a man of peace: he lives, and always has, at peace with his neighbors and with himself. (*Pause.*) Will you take me up on my dare? Or simply believe me?

OTTO (*slowly*): Simply believe you. If I do so slowly, it is because—this turns my world around. And yours.

AGNES: That is beyond me.

OTTO: We have known each other one week, you and I, have become more than friends. But I did not know your name. Well, Agnes, the man—boy if you will, but yesterday he won his knightly sword—the young knight who did not know your name is under oath to join the war of extermination against Varvand. (AGNES *gasps.*) Were that man, that boy, to meet Sylvester's daughter, he would have to destroy her unless—

AGNES (*jumping up*): You're an assassin!

OTTO: —Unless he should find that Sylvester has been misjudged. If, as you say, he is a man of peace—

AGNES: What am I to believe? You came here to kill me!

OTTO: Let me stay here to love you! You are more to me than life itself.

(*At this,* JOHANN *leaps from his hiding place in a fury.*)

JOHANN: No, this is too much! I'm to be idly looking on, while you press your own interests with the girl?

AGNES (*with a slight scream*): Who is this? There *is* a plot. You are *both* assassins!

JOHANN: Agnes—I shall call you that!—don't you remember me?

AGNES (*screams more loudly*): The boy I rescued from the river! Johann! Who admitted he was from Rosset!

OTTO: We are both from Rosset but— (*With the loudest scream yet,* AGNES *runs off in the direction of Varvand. They do not pursue her. But* OTTO *shouts after her:*) Be back tomorrow—usual time!

JOHANN (*to* OTTO): How dare you?

OTTO (*shrugging*): She treats us both alike. Refuses to tell me her name, as she did you. At the first hint that I'm from Rosset, flees from me, as she did from you. Puts on the same magic show for us both: suddenly appearing, suddenly vanishing, like a ghost.

JOHANN: With this small difference: yours the power to summon the ghost, mine the power to banish it.

OTTO: Johann!

JOHANN: Is there something wrong with my nose? My ear lobes? What is it about me that drives the blood from her cheeks?

OTTO: You're so aggrieved.

JOHANN: If someone told me of a horse he wished to buy, then behind his back I bought the beast myself, wouldn't he be "aggrieved"?

OTTO: Only that isn't what happened.

JOHANN: It is! I met her weeks before you did.

OTTO: But I didn't know that. You're determined to offend me!

JOHANN: I have few sources of amusement left.

OTTO: Johann, life has so much to offer you; and you, to it.

JOHANN: Flattery now! I throw it in your face!

OTTO: I refuse to be offended. This just isn't you.

JOHANN: Me? Can you see me? Do you see the open wound in my breast? A wound I intend to *keep* open? A wound I intend to prick with red-hot needles day and night?

OTTO: But why? Why in heaven's name?

JOHANN: In *earth's* name. The physical is real. I propose to keep in touch with what's real.

OTTO: That makes no sense.

JOHANN: What does? You? Me? God?

OTTO: Johann, you're impossible. I'm just going to walk away.

JOHANN: No, you're not: I'm not through with you yet!

OTTO: Through with me?

JOHANN: You and I, brother, are two spiders in a box.

OTTO: And?

JOHANN (*drawing his sword*): Draw!

OTTO: If we're to be Cain and Abel, I'll be Abel. Do what you want with me.

JOHANN: Coward! (*Silence.*) Fool! Don't you see it's *my own death* I'm after!

OTTO: Then drop your sword. We'll get it over fast.

(JOHANN, *trembling, drops the sword, stands there in total vulnerability. A pause while* OTTO *looks at him.*)

JOHANN (*feebly*): Draw, draw!

(OTTO *draws his sword, throws it on the ground, strides towards* JOHANN *with arms outstretched.*)

OTTO: My brother! My friend!

(JOHANN *can't take it. He holds his hands up to push* OTTO *away.*)

JOHANN: You're a snake but you refuse to sting me now because you've a more lingering death in view. I know who'll do it, though.

(*And he runs off, like* AGNES, *in the direction of Varvand.*)

FOUR

Varvand. In the castle. SYLVESTER *on a chair recovering from his fainting fit.* GERTRUDE *is with him. Also present: Sylvester's vassal,* THEISTIN, *and, standing farther apart,* JEROME.

GERTRUDE: He's coming to, thank God.

SYLVESTER: Gertrude!

GERTRUDE: Do you know me now, Sylvester?

SYLVESTER: The feeling I have is so . . . benign . . . is this the future life?

GERTRUDE: Indeed, and at the heavenly gate the angels stand—your own, your kith, your kin—to bid you welcome!

(*Pause.*)

SYLVESTER: Wasn't I standing? How did I get down on this chair?

GERTRUDE: You fainted, dear.

SYLVESTER: What made me faint? How strangely you all look at me. Agnes!—Is all well with Agnes?

GERTRUDE: Yes, yes, she's in the garden.

SYLVESTER: Then what *is* it? Gertrude! Oh, oh, it's coming back to me now . . . . Where's Jerome?

JEROME: Here, my Lord.

SYLVESTER: Not yet in Rosset?

GERTRUDE: You must lie down, Sylvester.

SYLVESTER: The human spirit—how poor a thing it is!

GERTRUDE: To bed, Sylvester, your body needs rest.

SYLVESTER: Is my body even weaker than my spirit?

GERTRUDE: Take some of that Austrian medicine.

SYLVESTER: For my body, yes. And for my spirit?

GERTRUDE: Double the dose of Austrian medicine!

SYLVESTER: D'you put more stock in a salve than in a soul?

GERTRUDE: The spirit, as you said, is weak.

SYLVESTER: It deserts us, too, sometimes, the spirit. But it is only flowing back to the fountainhead, the Godhead, to renew itself and to return in strength. Can you believe that, Gertrude? Can I? The spirit is a misery—but also a glory. And this is a moment for glory! For heroism! (*Noticing* THEISTIN *for the first time:*) My vassal Theistin, am I right?

THEISTIN: We've been waiting for you to reach that conclusion, Count.

SYLVESTER: We?

THEISTIN: Your people.

SYLVESTER: Even the people are ahead of me?

THEISTIN (*crudely*): Ahead? Ha! They *have* a head—allow the pun—they have the head that brought the news from Rosset.

SYLVESTER: Their herald, Aldo, is still here?

THEISTIN: Here—without his head.

SYLVESTER: Killed by—?

THEISTIN: Stoned to death. The people could not be held back.

SYLVESTER: His head—? Where is it?

THEISTIN: You recall where two dead owls are nailed to the gateway? (SYLVESTER *nods slowly.*) His head is nailed there too—between the owls.

SYLVESTER: Theistin, that's horrible. And horribly—unjust. A herald's head is sacred. And it was our job—your job—to protect it.

THEISTIN: He'd lost it before I arrived. It was as much as I could do to save Jerome from the same fate.

JEROME: It's true, my Lord. I owe my life to him.

SYLVESTER: "Who touches pitch shall be defiled," and war is blackest pitch. How shall we justify ourselves, Theistin, to our grandchildren?

THEISTIN: *You* won't have grandchildren, Count, unless you do what's *un*justified.

SYLVESTER: Can good come of evil? Can the evil that flared up to kill a herald fuel a fire that burns for honor and for right?

THEISTIN: What's done is done. Make the best of it.

SYLVESTER: Yes. We must, mustn't we? Yes. Ride out, Theistin. Bring me some of these killers . . . heroes, I would say. Meanwhile I'll speak to the . . . heroes already here.

THEISTIN: Your words will light a fire, holy or otherwise.

SYLVESTER: We'll halt the first onslaught. Later, when stronger, we'll advance—pursue the wolf into his lair.

THEISTIN (*leaving*): Before the day is out, those heroes will be here!

SYLVESTER: Good. (*Exit* THEISTIN. *Calling into the wings:*) Call my steward! My armorers! (*To* JEROME:) And, my dear Jerome, if it's your wish to be in Rosset, go there: I will provide an escort. As for my weakness, Jerome (*smiling*), the encroaching senility, the sick and dying oak tree rides out a storm that fells the young and healthy trees, gripping, as it does, their lavish leaves. When I'm hurt I scream. Silent serenity is for gladiators: they're paid for it. I'm content if I'm still on my feet. To stand up for an hour or two and then good night: what more is possible? (*Silence.*) Ha? But I won't hold you any longer. (*Silence.*) Ha?

JEROME: I'm tongue-tied. My words are children hiding in the dark, refusing to come out.—If you are senile, Count, I am not yet born!—Let me be plain. Theistin saved my life. You leave me my own master. Free to go to Rosset, I am also free to stay here at your side. Call for me when you need me, Count. My life is yours. (*He leaves the room.*)

GERTRUDE: Jerome! (*But he is gone.*) Call him back, Sylvester.

SYLVESTER (*abstracted*): They say life is a dream.

GERTRUDE: You trust him?

SYLVESTER: Jerome? Of course.

GERTRUDE: The man's a turncoat: that's been proved already. Who knows what he'll do next?

SYLVESTER: They upset him. For a matter of days. He's been ours for years.

GERTRUDE: Sylvester, don't you see how far things have gone? Suspicion's everywhere. It's fallen even on you.

SYLVESTER: How?

GERTRUDE: Rupert's son Peter *was* slain—and by your people on the mountain.

SYLVESTER: By my people?

GERTRUDE: One of them confessed you hired him to do it.

SYLVESTER: He confessed that?

GERTRUDE: Under torture. And died one minute later.

SYLVESTER: In death no man's a liar. Who heard him confess?

GERTRUDE: All Rosset. He was tortured on the public square.

SYLVESTER: And who told *you*?

GERTRUDE: Jerome.

SYLVESTER: Whom you don't trust.

GERTRUDE: It could all be confirmed by a hundred others.

SYLVESTER: So it's not deceit.

GERTRUDE: We need to show it *was* deceit. But how?

SYLVESTER: Ask God!

GERTRUDE: Because if it's not deceit—we're suspect.

SYLVESTER: The burden of proof's on us—to prove we did not do it.

GERTRUDE: It's hopeless.

SYLVESTER: Yes. No. Not if I can speak with Rupert.

GERTRUDE: At just this moment? When news of his herald's death will have driven him to frenzy? Don't stick your head in the rabid lion's mouth!

SYLVESTER: Jerome, who's been so friendly with them, will act as mediator. Send him in to me.

FIVE

Varvand. Before the fortress gates. JOHANN *has chased* AGNES *down the mountain, only now catching up with her.*

AGNES (*as she feels he will take hold of her*): Help, help!

JOHANN (*gripping her*): Ah! At last. But what made you run like that? And all this way?

AGNES: Monster! Leave me alone!

JOHANN: "Monster?" Am I some rapist on a rampage?

AGNES: You are from Rosset! That's enough! Go back there!

JOHANN: May I not speak three words to you?

AGNES: No.

JOHANN: I love you. Yes, *those* three words. Too feeble, much too feeble. I worship you!

AGNES: You seem to be a raving lunatic.

JOHANN: My . . . mental stability is not all it should be . . . but what have *you* to fear? I'll touch you—for one moment—then goodbye.

AGNES: You're threatening me!

JOHANN: You're . . . someone I once knew. That's all. Let me hold you in my arms!

AGNES (*again trying to make herself heard to others*): Help!

JOHANN: By tomorrow, I'll be underground. Can you say no to a dying man? (*While she is trying to take this in, he kisses her on the lips. She is petrified. Silence.*)

AGNES: Save me, all ye saints above.

JOHANN: Save *me*, my little saint here below. You have stabbed me to the heart. Do it again. But this time—with this. (*He unsheathes a dagger.*)

AGNES (*not following the words but seeing the action*): Murder! Help!

JOHANN: Yes, help! Help *me*! (AGNES *sees the dagger but does not notice it is the hilt, not the blade, that he holds out to her. She faints.*) With the same passion that I kissed your lips, my breast will kiss this knife. Up, girl! Do it for me, do it!

(Enter JEROME through the gate. He is responding to AGNES' cry of murder.)

JEROME: Agnes! (*He sees her body on the ground, and JOHANN dagger in hand, screaming:*) Agnes! (*He draws his sword and cuts JOHANN down. The dagger is on the ground.*) So much for that. Now, Agnes? (*He lifts her head and shoulders.*) She's unconscious only. I see no wound.

(Having heard the noise, SYLVESTER and GERTRUDE come through the gate. SYLVESTER's SERVANT follows.)

SYLVESTER: Agnes' voice first, but then, much louder, Jerome's. My God! (*They take in the scene.*)

GERTRUDE: Agnes, my last, my only one!

JEROME: She is not dead.

GERTRUDE: No, no, she breathes.

SYLVESTER: Is she badly hurt?

JEROME: I arrived in the nick of time, cut him down before he could touch her.

GERTRUDE: From Rosset, is he?

JEROME: I blush for shame, but yes.

SYLVESTER: You've saved my girl, Jerome: I think we understand each other now.

JEROME (*accepting his hand*): I know we do.

GERTRUDE: Her eyes are opening.

AGNES (*jumping up*): Mother! Father! Is he gone, that monster?

GERTRUDE (*pointing at JOHANN*): There he lies, dead.

AGNES: Oh? On my account? How hideous!

GERTRUDE: Jerome saved your life, but tell us—

AGNES: He'd followed me down the mountain. Fear drove me fast.

But something drove him faster.

SYLVESTER: Did he say anything?

AGNES: He said he worshipped me. Called me a saint! But then called me a corpse! And drew his dagger!

SYLVESTER: To kill you?

AGNES: So I felt. Though now I recall—he said I should kill *him*!

SYLVESTER (*having felt* JOHANN's *pulse*): He is still alive. (*To his* SERVANT:) Help him into the castle. Call the surgeon. (*The* SERVANT *helps him off.*) Come back when there's news.

GERTRUDE (*sitting* AGNES *down on a bench*): Agnes, how could you venture so far up the mountain?

AGNES: It's a favorite walk of mine, Mother.

GERTRUDE: But to stay so long! All by yourself!

AGNES: I was going to meet a boy—a young knight!

GERTRUDE: Running headlong into danger! That boy must have been from Rosset, too.

JEROME: Young Otto often climbs the mountain, I've heard that.

AGNES: You mean that—

JEROME: Count Rupert's eldest son. Don't you know him?

AGNES: I've never seen him in my life!

JEROME: He knows you, they tell me.

AGNES: How could he?

GERTRUDE: Knows our Agnes?

AGNES (*hiding her head in her mother's bosom*): Oh, Mother—

GERTRUDE: You must be more careful, Agnes. A man like that could pluck an apple off a tree—and poison you with it!

JEROME: At the requiem mass for his brother Peter, he vowed your death.

AGNES: He vowed my death?

JEROME: Death to all Varvand.

GERTRUDE (*to* AGNES): From now on, you must never leave my side.

(SYLVESTER's SERVANT *reenters.*)

SERVANT: My Lord, the wound is slight. The man is conscious and talking—

SYLVESTER: Talking? About what?

SERVANT: No one can make sense of it.

JEROME: He must be faking madness.

SYLVESTER: You know the lad?

JEROME: I believe it's Johann, Rupert's natural son.

SYLVESTER (*to the* SERVANT): Leave us. (*The* SERVANT *does so.*) I'd have forgiven their affronts and accusations, their avowal of revenge, their declaration of war within the family. Had they then burned my castle down, slain my wife and child, these are acts of war: I would have tried to forgive even these. But that they should send a hired assassin to Varvand—if they *have* done this—

GERTRUDE (*moving over to him*): They did that before!

SYLVESTER: You mean—with Philip?

GERTRUDE: You see it now, then? At the time, when I spoke of *my* certitude, you called it female guesswork. I could tell you more—

SYLVESTER: More?

GERTRUDE: Two years ago you had a fever. When you were recovering, Eunice sent you pineapple preserves.

SYLVESTER: A trooper brought them over from Rosset, yes.

GERTRUDE: On some pretext, I asked you not to eat them, and brought you *peach* preserves from my own stock. But you insisted, spurned my peaches, took the pineapple. There followed a fit of vomiting.

SYLVESTER: Which proves you right again?

GERTRUDE: Yes.

SYLVESTER: No. The cat knocked the pineapple jar over and Agnes gave me the peaches instead. Remember, Agnes?

AGNES: Yes, Father.

SYLVESTER: The pineapple did the cat no harm. But the peaches, prepared by you—

GERTRUDE (*furious*): Oh, everything can be turned around—! (*And she returns to* AGNES' *bench.*)

SYLVESTER: Indeed! So I ignore what *you* turn around. No more of Philip. We don't know he was poisoned.

GERTRUDE: We know we have no son and heir.

SYLVESTER: Agnes will inherit.

GERTRUDE: And bear a husband's name.

SYLVESTER: Remain single. Or marry a Schroffenstein.

JEROME: But can we—excuse me, Count—ignore Peter, even if he was not murdered? Don't we then have to ask why murder was confessed falsely?

SYLVESTER: Explain.

JEROME: It's possible that Peter just died but that Rupert, seeing a chance to grab the inheritance, knew how to make your men *seem* guilty. That way he had a pretext to declare war and root out your whole line.

SYLVESTER: But if one of my own people, at death's door, confessed I hired him to murder Peter?

JEROME: The priest I spoke to only heard one word.

SYLVESTER: Which was?

JEROME: Sylvester. (*Silence.*) One of your own people. Now don't you have in your power, right now, one of *their* own people?

SYLVESTER (*after a short pause*): Johann? But he's not going to say—

JEROME: He tried to kill Agnes? (*Silence.*) How did the Rosset people extort their confession?

SYLVESTER: By torture.

JEROME: Stretch Johann on the rack, don't you suppose he'll say he was Rupert's paid assassin?

SYLVESTER: But that's the logic—believing evidence extorted under torture—by which *I* am proved a murderer.

(*Silence.*)

JEROME: Oh, if you are raising moral difficulties . . . .

SYLVESTER: I puzzle you? I have not renounced all faith like Rupert. God is in this! He puzzles *me*!

JEROME: So you conclude?

SYLVESTER: I can't torture Johann. I have scruples. I'll speak with

Rupert.

JEROME: And return alive? *He* has no scruples.

SYLVESTER: Men risk the thought of frightfulness but not the frightfulness itself.

JEROME: He *has* risked frightfulness itself.

SYLVESTER: When very much provoked.

JEROME: As you are now.

SYLVESTER: But if I act as if I were not? Mightn't just that have an effect?

JEROME: Such as?

SYLVESTER: You hardly dare hope someone will do a certain thing. He notices you hardly dare hope that, and for that reason—does it.

JEROME: You propose to count on this?

SYLVESTER: I'd like to be the kind of man who would.

JEROME: But are you?

SYLVESTER: I do want to confront Rupert. To ride straight over is too rash?

JEROME: Yes.

SYLVESTER: Yes. I need a safe conduct. Get me one.

JEROME: Me?

SYLVESTER: They know you. You were their advocate.

JEROME: By now they must also hate me. *I* struck down Johann.

SYLVESTER: *Must* hate you? Hate is always a must?

JEROME: Still, if *I* go, that at least stops *you* from going.

SYLVESTER: It will enable me to go—in peace.

JEROME: You trust them.

SYLVESTER: Trust them to receive my ambassador, our common kinsman? What is left to trust in life, if not these things?

(Pause.)

JEROME: Very well. I'll do it.

SYLVESTER: Thank you. You are a living proof to Rupert that the world is not as bad as he thinks.

JEROME: I'll do my best. God keep you.

SYLVESTER (*embracing him*): God *will* keep you.

GERTRUDE (*embracing him*): You will be in our prayers. (JEROME *leaves. Meanwhile* AGNES *has picked up* JOHANN's *dagger from the ground.*) Agnes! That's your assassin's dagger—it may be poisoned! (AGNES, *shocked, drops it. Changing into a gentler key:*) We are only trying to preserve you, my darling. Without you, remember, our whole family's extinct.

SIX

On the mountain. The same slope as in Scene Three. But this time OTTO *has arrived first and is waiting. Enter* AGNES.

OTTO: So you made it.

AGNES: You thought I wouldn't?

OTTO: We didn't part on the best of terms.

AGNES (*smiling sadly*): That was the least of my worries. I'm under orders not to leave Varvand.

OTTO: I *am* privileged.

AGNES: It's just . . . I was brought up. . . Father always says: "Go through with it to the end."

OTTO: My!

AGNES: Yes, walking up here, I was asking myself: what qualities will I need for this . . . experience?

OTTO: And you answered yourself?

AGNES: Steadfastness, "turn neither left nor right": Father again. Strength, though girls aren't supposed to have that. Most of all: courage.

OTTO: You're so disturbed!

AGNES: You did say to come?

OTTO: Are you going to trust me . . . Mary?

AGNES: Mary?

OTTO: Have you agreed to be Agnes?

AGNES: Oh, no.

OTTO: I christened you Mary one lovely day when you were sleeping in your cradle.

AGNES: Cradle?

OTTO: This slope. Its branches wove a roof of leaves. The waterfall sang a lullaby. Light breezes were fine feathers, fanning you. An angel stood guard till you woke and saw me. "What's your name?" I asked. You hadn't been christened yet, you answered. I cupped a little spring water in my left hand, sprinkled your brow with my right, and said: "Then I christen you Mary. You are the earthly image of God's Mother." (AGNES *turns towards him in some agitation.*) Your soul lay open before me like some great book which first merely touches the spirit but finally takes hold and won't let go. Oh yes, at times, the day's demands distract the reader but he returns to that book: it explains the world in the language of the gods. (*Silence.*) Mary . . . .

AGNES: I don't feel well. (*She sits.*)

OTTO: Is there anything I can do?

AGNES (*loudly*): Yes! Leave me! (*Softly:*) Can you leave me for just a moment?

OTTO: Shall I bring you a little spring water?

AGNES (*loudly*): No! (*Quietly:*) Well, if you must . . . . (*Exit* OTTO. AGNES' *face is transformed into a tragic mask. Suddenly standing:*) It is the moment, Agnes, the crown—do you see it there?—the crown is falling. Falling into the sea. It sinks. What can the un-crowned queen do now but—throw herself in after it? (*She sits again.*) What he brings me now may really only be water. But be ready for anything, Agnes: this man has vowed your death.

OTTO (*returning, carrying water in his hat*): Feel any better?

AGNES: Much stronger.

OTTO: Drink this.

AGNES: It isn't too . . . cold?

OTTO: No, I don't think so.

AGNES: Taste it yourself.

OTTO: Why?

AGNES: You don't want to? I understand. (*She reaches out for it.*)

OTTO: Careful, don't spill it.

AGNES: Won't one drop be enough?

(She drinks, with her eyes on him the whole time.)

OTTO: How is it?

AGNES: Cold. *(She shudders.)* Cold.

OTTO: Drink it up, anyway!

AGNES: Why?

OTTO: It's as good as medicine.

AGNES: To put one out of one's misery?

OTTO: What!?

AGNES: Sit down with me till I feel better. A doctor like you doesn't do it for money, does he?

OTTO: Do what for money?

(He sits down.)

AGNES: I'm babbling to pass the time. Terminal cases love to babble.

OTTO: Terminal cases?!

AGNES *(stands, walks away, turns)*: I have things to tell you.

OTTO *(rising)*: Yes?

AGNES: First: you are Otto Schroffenstein.

(Pause.)

OTTO: Who told you?

AGNES: Second: at the requiem mass for your brother Peter, you vowed my death.

OTTO: My God!

AGNES: Third: you have carried out your vow: with this poison.

OTTO: Poison?

AGNES: Which now I'll finish.

OTTO: Stop! Let me drink that. *(He drinks what's left. Pause.)* Now, are we both dying?

(Pause.)

AGNES: Or was this my mother's delusion? Or—? *(Pause.)* We are not dying, are we?

OTTO *(embracing her)*: We are not dying.

AGNES: Though dying together has its appeal.

OTTO: You wouldn't rather—live together?

AGNES: You'll still take me?

OTTO: After what?

AGNES: After I've accused you of attempting murder!

OTTO: I'll make one condition.

AGNES: Yes?

OTTO: That you confront this specter of mistrust that haunts the Schroffensteins: that you trust *me*.

AGNES: I accept!

OTTO: However much appearances may be against me?

AGNES: However much.

OTTO: Through all eternity?

AGNES: Through all eternity.

OTTO (*smiling*): Amen. Because that's how long we'll need to do the explaining! Things like—my brother Peter slain by your father!

AGNES: You really believe that?

OTTO: I'm afraid there's no doubt: one of the murderers confessed.

AGNES: Then *you* must believe it.

OTTO: And you?

AGNES: Well, one can suspect something, one may even think one knows it, yet . . . the *conviction* of someone's—of what someone is like—their *integrity* . . . is more than the suspicion, more than the "knowledge."

OTTO: But can you ask me to see through your eyes?

AGNES: Can you ask me to see through yours?

OTTO: Must I trust my father less than you do yours?

AGNES: Must I trust *my* father less than you do yours?

OTTO: Agnes, my dear, I'm not going to make you pay for another's sins. Are you your father?

AGNES: As little as you are yours—or how could I swear to love you forever?

OTTO: Faced with the murder of his son, my father declared a feud against the murderers. Was that wrong?

AGNES: That he sent a hired assassin to Varvand was *very* wrong.

OTTO: Hired assassin?

AGNES: I should know. It was me he drew his dagger on. If Jerome hadn't instantly cut him down I'd be dead.

OTTO: Who was this . . . "assassin"?

AGNES: You saw him chase me down the mountain! Yesterday! Your friend Johann!

OTTO: My half-brother. But you've made a gross mistake.

AGNES: So I do have to see things through your eyes!

OTTO: My father is an angry man but he never did anything vile in all his life.

AGNES: So I should trust him more than *my* father?

OTTO: My father did not pay Johann to—

AGNES: My father did not pay those who slew Peter—

(Silence.)

OTTO: If only Jerome hadn't been so quick to attack Johann, there would have been no puzzle.

AGNES: If only your father hadn't been so quick to slay the men he found by Peter's body . . . .

(Silence.)

OTTO: Only, Agnes, *that* deed can hardly be denied. One of the murderers confessed.

(Silence.)

AGNES: Johann is feverish and mentions many names. If my father were hot for revenge, he could just pick the name that suits his purpose . . . . *(Silence.)* And so, on and on.

OTTO: Is it possible, Agnes, that I have blamed your father—overmuch?

AGNES: And I yours? Those who think falsehoods must learn to take them back, be they of Varvand—

OTTO: Or of Rosset, yes. We're beginning to learn, you and I.

AGNES: The sun is rising—in our souls.

OTTO: We . . . trust each other at long last.

AGNES: If only our fathers could do that!

OTTO: Separate, each thinks his own one thought. What if each could bring himself to . . . think the other's thought?

AGNES: Two thoughts are better than one! And lead to a third thought that might save the day!

OTTO: My father could never make the first move. Could yours?

AGNES: I think he already has.

OTTO: Ha?

AGNES: He must be on his way to Rosset right now.

OTTO: A remarkable man.

AGNES: Thank you.

OTTO: And one who knows how to forgive?

AGNES: Who makes a habit of forgiving.

OTTO: Count Rupert's habit is retaliation: "Hit back, it's the only language they understand." Count Sylvester must not arrive in Rosset without warning.

AGNES: He won't. Jerome is going to get him a safe-conduct.

OTTO: Jerome! *He'll* need a safe-conduct for himself!

AGNES: Because he—?

OTTO: Because it was he—you told me—who cut Johann down.

AGNES: How would your father know that?

OTTO: He has spies. And his own suspiciousness amounts to second sight.

AGNES: Still, he loves you? (OTTO *nods*.) And he needs you—if his family's to have a future. Plead with him. Wear him down.

OTTO: What can wear down the cliffs on the ocean shore? The ocean itself, maybe, in a thousand years! In our family, Rupert's the ocean, the rest of us small boats tossed this way and that . . . .

AGNES: You're saying: we are helpless.

OTTO: Except for one small weapon, yes.

AGNES: One small weapon—!

OTTO: The truth. We can remove certain errors that stand in its way.

AGNES: Such as?

OTTO: Johann seemed to threaten *my* life too, drew his sword on *me* as well as you, but only to provoke me, to make me draw on him. So what's his secret?

AGNES: He wants to die!

OTTO: Not to kill.

AGNES: He even muttered something of the sort—

OTTO: So, bit by bit, the truth can come to light!

AGNES: I still don't understand. Yes, he played the madman, forced the dagger into my hand, yet, when I refused to take it, he declared I'd already stabbed him through the heart—

OTTO: Well, you had!

AGNES: Ah! With Cupid's arrow!

OTTO: For Johann, the sharpest arrow of them all.

AGNES: Yes. Yes. And what a lack of sympathy I showed! Even now I let the poor boy languish in my father's dungeon—wounded—

OTTO: In mind as well as body. I fear for that boy's sanity. Can you get him out?

AGNES: I must.

OTTO: There is a second error. From my dead brother's hands, both of them, the little finger had been severed. Why? What use are such fingers to a murderer? This must be looked into, and on the scene of the crime. People live there—on the edge of the forest. I must go talk to them.

AGNES (*as the pair prepare to leave, in opposite directions*): And I to my father. Sylvester is the most magnanimous—the most Christian, gentleman—in the world. All will yet be well.

SEVEN

If the play is given in two parts, the second part would begin here. The entire cast, their costumes covered by cloaks, should again sing the Hymn to Revenge in front of the curtain. Scene Seven is set in Rosset. The castle. RUPERT *is alone in a room from which he has a view of any who approach the castle gates. At rise, he is pacing the room and taking an occasional look through the window. At a certain point he stops in his tracks and whistles (two fingers in mouth). His* SERVANT *enters.*

RUPERT: Where's Aldo, my herald?

SERVANT: I don't know, sir.

RUPERT: I've kept watch all day. No Aldo.

SERVANT: There are rumors, of course.

RUPERT: The Swabians are a people of old women. What rumors?

SERVANT: Of death.

RUPERT: Whose death?

SERVANT: The rumors don't say. Or cite so many different names—

RUPERT: Death where, then? From what cause?

SERVANT: Death in Varvand. From . . . what always *is* the cause.

RUPERT: Ha?

SERVANT: Their hatred—their mistrust—of us.

(A bang at the door.)

RUPERT: Come in.

EUNICE *(entering)*: Rupert, have you heard? *(When she sees the* SERVANT, *she stops.)*

RUPERT *(to the* SERVANT): And where's my son Johann?

SERVANT: Not in the castle.

RUPERT: Find him. *(Waves the* SERVANT *out.)* Heard what? Your old woman's rumors? Death to persons unnamed?

EUNICE: This one's name is Aldo.

RUPERT: Who told you such a cock-and-bull story? The many-headed multitude?

EUNICE: A man straight from Varvand.

RUPERT: What kind of man?

EUNICE: A travelling man. A wanderer over the face of the earth.

RUPERT: Maybe it's his mind that wanders! *(Another bang on the door.)* Who is it?

SANTING *(outside)*: Santing, your loyal vassal.

RUPERT: Come in. (SANTING *does so.*) It's written all over your face, Santing: you too bring news of death. Give me no rumors! Tell me your source before you tell the news.

SANTING: A man straight from Varvand.

RUPERT: Not a wanderer over the face of the earth?

EUNICE: I have the story from such a one. It must be the same man.

SANTING: He's someone I believe, Count.

RUPERT: Believe they'd murder my ambassador—?

SANTING: What's that, Count? It's much worse than that.

EUNICE: No, that's exactly what he said.

SANTING: Then it's another wanderer .

RUPERT: What's *your* report, in Heaven's name?

SANTING: That they have slain your son Johann.

(A stunned silence.)

RUPERT: It's not so, is it, Eunice?

EUNICE: No, it's not!

SANTING: My God, Count, I'd have to be a murderer myself to bring you news like that if it wasn't true—!

RUPERT: Bring me your wanderer! Both, if there are two! (SANTING *and* EUNICE *leave.* RUPERT *whistles. The* SERVANT *reenters.)* You've found Johann?

SERVANT: No, sir.

RUPERT: And Aldo's still not back?

SERVANT: That's right, sir.

RUPERT: Where's young Count Otto?

SERVANT: Also not here, sir.

RUPERT: Find him.

*(*RUPERT *waves him away. Reenter* EUNICE, *this time with a* WANDERER.*)*

EUNICE: This is my wanderer.

RUPERT: You were in Varvand?

WANDERER: Yes, sir.

RUPERT: What did you see there?

WANDERER: Your herald Aldo slain.

(Pause. RUPERT *clenches his fists.)*

RUPERT: By whom?

WANDERER: All Sylvester's people fell upon him at once. A hundred to one.

RUPERT: Was Count Sylvester present?

WANDERER: Not until Aldo's body lay in pieces in his courtyard.

RUPERT: What did he say to that?

WANDERER: He said he was against it, but, um—

RUPERT: Yes? Yes?

WANDERER: None of them believed him. He was calling them his loyal retainers the day after.

EUNICE: Had Aldo offended the Count in some way?

RUPERT (*cutting in*): Of course. He was the pincers I pinched Sylvester with—for that he must die? (*To the* WANDERER:) You are dismissed.

(*The* WANDERER *leaves.*)

EUNICE: Aldo died. But was Sylvester behind it? Why would he needlessly enrage you further?

RUPERT: To see how far I'll go. To test my skills in this high science of revenge!

(*Enter* SANTING *with another* WANDERER.)

SANTING (*pushing him forward*): This is *my* wanderer, Count.

RUPERT: And he's going to tell me . . . ? (*Addressing* WANDERER II:) Are you in league with the Devil?

WANDERER II: No, sir. But there are them that are.

RUPERT: Is that all you have to say?

WANDERER II: What would you wish to know, sir?

RUPERT: Was Aldo—my herald—was he slain by Count Sylvester's men?

WANDERER II: Yes, sir, he was.

RUPERT: Ah!

EUNICE: You see?

SANTING: I must ask him another question, Count. (*The* COUNT *nods, reluctantly.*) Did they slay anyone else, later?

WANDERER II: A boy. A young knight. Name of Johann.

(Again the pause. Again the clenching of the fists.)

RUPERT: You are dismissed. (WANDERER II *leaves, and* SANTING *is leaving with him.*) Not you, Santing. Why believe *either* of these . . . dirt-carrying insects?

SANTING: In the house where I met this man, there was another wandering man, unknown to him. He gave the same report.

RUPERT: Aldo, the herald, it's monstrous, yet I could believe it. But my Johann? He would never have been in Varvand in the first place!

SANTING: Unless he went there to slay Sylvester's daughter as they say.

RUPERT: My boy—murder a young girl? Are they insane?

SANTING: They say he was drawing his dagger to stab her when Jerome arrived and cut him down.

RUPERT (*pacing up and down*): Jerome, that greybeard fop . . . he's courting the girl himself. (*He stops in his tracks.*) I refuse to believe any of this. Go straight to Varvand and get a report firsthand!

SANTING: Aldo, Johann—and Santing, ha? If I'm not back tonight, you'll know they got me too.

RUPERT: No, then. That, no. Where's this third wanderer? Bring *him* in.

SANTING: He's sick in bed.

RUPERT: Then take *me* to *him.*

(They both leave. Enter EUNICE *and* JEROME.*)*

EUNICE: Jerome, my husband would never—

JEROME: Send his son to sneak in behind Sylvester's back and murder his daughter?

EUNICE: No, I tell you—

JEROME: When Rupert's vengeance is as foul as the offense avenged, is he better than those he accuses?

EUNICE: You don't know the whole story. You—

JEROME: I know enough. Enough to put me squarely on their side.

EUNICE: Did our side plan an attack on Agnes?

JEROME: Obviously! Johann himself confessed.

EUNICE: Sylvester's men confessed they murdered our Peter!

JEROME: You haven't listened to Sylvester!

(Silence.)

EUNICE: "Admissions," "Confessions." These are much, but what the heart feels is more.

JEROME: Well put! But that's exactly what Sylvester thinks: and I trust *Sylvester's* heart.

EUNICE: If the murder of Peter is like this attack on Agnes—

JEROME: As far as Peter goes, I'll vouch for Sylvester's innocence.

EUNICE: And as far as Agnes goes?

JEROME: Your side have still to clear yourselves.

EUNICE: Then tell me *what* Johann confessed.

JEROME: You tell me what Peter's murderer said—when he was tortured—tell me the exact words.

(Pause.)

EUNICE: I wish I knew. They just say: he confessed. When I ask: confessed what? No one, even Rupert, can report more than a single word.

JEROME: Namely?

EUNICE: Sylvester.

JEROME: If that one word was enough for Rupert, he must have known beforehand.

EUNICE: Call it a . . . premonition. He did suspect.

JEROME: So even the one word wasn't needed: a look would have sufficed.

EUNICE (*breaking down*): Oh, Jerome, Jerome, I was never really convinced! Yet a person can only fly the way the wind blows . . . . What did Johann confess?

JEROME: Also: one single word—Rupert. But it was quite enough—for anyone less scrupulous than Sylvester.

EUNICE: He didn't believe it?

JEROME: Still finds excuses for Rupert. The only man in Varvand who does.

EUNICE: And that one word—was it extorted by torture, as with that other?

JEROME: Sylvester would not allow it. No, poor Johann is delirious. This hatred, Eunice, that divides Rosset from Varvand, what foundation has it?

EUNICE: A long battle for possession—possession of the land.

JEROME: I don't see it. I don't see the hunger for the other man's food.

EUNICE: What do you see?

JEROME: Fear of having one's own snatched from one's mouth. Fear of deprivation, of *dis*possession.

EUNICE: The terrible mutual mistrust, what can ever be done about it?

JEROME: I'll tell you. Johann revealed something of great importance— to you, to me, perhaps to everyone.

EUNICE: What?

JEROME: For him, the mountain's hell; for Otto and Agnes, it is heaven.

EUNICE: Which means?

JEROME: He's unloved, rejected, but Otto and Agnes love each other like a pair of angels.

EUNICE: Don't tell me Otto and Agnes are in love.

JEROME: They are.

EUNICE: How could they have met? He's been here all the time; she is at Varvand.

JEROME: *All* the time?

EUNICE: The afternoons, perhaps, afforded a few hours . . . .

JEROME: Quite enough—to meet by chance—somewhere between Rosset and Varvand.

EUNICE: On the mountain?

JEROME: Beside some stream, in some cavern.

EUNICE: You lose her.

JEROME: But when Otto gets her? A family united at long last! The endless blood feud ended! The sound of these marriage bells will be heard from one end of Swabia to the other!

EUNICE: Yes. Yes. I am for it. So will Gertrude be. Will Sylvester consent?

JEROME: Consent? He'll be enraptured. If there's an obstacle, it'll be your Rupert.

EUNICE: Sh! Here he is.

(RUPERT *and* SANTING *enter. When* RUPERT *notices* JEROME, *he turns pale, wheels around, and leaves, saying:*)

RUPERT: Santing. A word with you.

(SANTING *follows* RUPERT *out.*)

JEROME: What was all *that* about?

EUNICE: Had you met with him earlier?

JEROME (*shaking his head*): I felt I had to speak with you first.

EUNICE: He turned pale when he saw you. With him, that's a very bad sign.

JEROME: Does he know I was Johann's assailant?

EUNICE: God knows what Santing may have told him.

JEROME: That could wreck our plan entirely.

RUPERT (*reentering, without* SANTING): Leave us, Eunice.

EUNICE (*whispering to* JEROME): Be very careful. (*Exit* EUNICE.)

JEROME: Greetings, Count.

RUPERT: What brings you to Rosset?

JEROME: I beg your pardon?

RUPERT: You come from Varvand, don't you?

JEROME: I was in Varvand, briefly.

RUPERT: And heard of the new trouble with Rosset?

JEROME: Ha?

RUPERT: You have a mission to me? In the cause of peace, in the sacred role of herald?

JEROME: I'm Eunice's guest. And yours, Count.

RUPERT: My guest, eh? No errand from Varvand?

JEROME: None that can't be performed by a friend.

RUPERT: When?

JEROME: Whenever we have the chance to talk.

RUPERT: We have the chance to talk right now.

JEROME: Well and good, Count: Sylvester wants to meet with you.

RUPERT: Wants to . . . meet with *me*?

JEROME: If you need proof of your cousin's innocence, this is it.

RUPERT: His innocence.

JEROME: There's a puzzle, I agree. The murderers having confessed, Sylvester's suspect.

RUPERT: You see that much.

JEROME: Yet a confession extorted by torture is dubious. And this confession is a single word that leaves everything quite vague. Your cousin submits some mistake must lurk here.

RUPERT: Some mistake.

JEROME: Some error.

RUPERT: Some error.

JEROME: To uncover which, he needs to meet with you.

RUPERT: Ever the man of peace.

JEROME: The sword's decisions are bloody.

RUPERT: You are reason itself.

JEROME: You will see him?

RUPERT: Why, yes, if ever again he and I should be in touch—

JEROME: Ever again? I'm going to Varvand now.

RUPERT: Tell him I'll be pleased to see him any time.

JEROME: Bless you. I'll ride posthaste to Varvand and bring him back with me. May he find you half as kindly and mild as I have.

RUPERT: God be with you then.

JEROME: I understand your suspicion. I shared it. Meeting with Count Sylvester changed my mind. So I say—if I may presume—wish him innocent and you will find him so.

RUPERT: You have done a good job. Goodbye.

JEROME: First, I must clear up two ugly rumors.

RUPERT: Ha?

JEROME: Your son Johann lies sick in Varvand—

RUPERT: Sick unto death.

JEROME: No! No: his life is not in danger, Count!

RUPERT: So *you* would have me believe.

JEROME: I beg your pardon?

RUPERT: Nothing.

JEROME: While Johann did draw his dagger—

RUPERT (*loudly*): Which I, of course, had paid him to do!

JEROME: What?!

RUPERT (*quietly*): I paid him to do that.

JEROME: Of course, you didn't.

RUPERT: Is it for you to deny it? He confessed.

JEROME: He spoke your name. Imputed nothing.

RUPERT: Sylvester's convinced—and why shouldn't he be?—that I'm as much a murderer as he!

JEROME: Just the opposite. Everyone else in Varvand has been misled by the appearances but not him. He holds you blameless; and he cannot be moved.

RUPERT (*screaming all of a sudden*): A trick! A fiendish trick!

JEROME: Count Rupert! I don't understand.

RUPERT (*sitting down*): So much for the first rumor. What's the second?

JEROME: May God give me the strength! And may you, kinsman, give me . . . trust!

RUPERT: Let's hear you first.

JEROME: Your herald Aldo—

RUPERT: Was betrayed and slain.

JEROME: But—

RUPERT (*raising his hand*): But of course Cousin Sylvester is not to blame!

JEROME: That's right. He fainted. Wasn't even conscious when it happened. He now asks what satisfaction you demand for a crime he deplores.

RUPERT: I don't demand a thing.

JEROME: What?

RUPERT: What's a herald?

JEROME: What is a herald? For one thing, his *head* is sacred—

RUPERT: Aren't you a herald right now?

JEROME: And guest. My head, thus, doubly sacred.

RUPERT: But what is sacred to me?

JEROME: What?!

RUPERT: At the crucial moment I intend to faint.

JEROME: My God!

(He hurries to the door. RUPERT *does not move. Silence. Then a noise from the courtyard below.* EUNICE *rushes in. Opens a window. The noise, much louder now, is that of a lynch mob.* RUPERT *does not move.)*

EUNICE: It's Jerome. They've fallen upon him at once, your men, they're clubbing him. Send some troopers out to stop this! Quick, quick! Come see for yourself. They've got him down on the ground now: they're going to kill him.—No, he's on his feet again, he's drawn his sword, he advances, they retreat. *Now* send help, Rupert, he can still be saved!—They're pressing forward again now, he defends himself like a wildcat.—Come to the window, Rupert, shout down to your people, one word from you is enough!—Oh, oh! What a blow *that* was. He's staggering, tottering.—Another! (*Pause.*) He's keeling over. (*Pause.*) He's dead. (RUPERT *has never moved. She strides over to him.*) This was *our* Jerome! And you just sit there?

(Enter SANTING.*)*

SANTING: We've finished, Count.

EUNICE: Finished what? (RUPERT *turns away.*) I see. You are my husband. Father of my children. I love you. I fear you, too. But there is also justice. Justice! You are a murderer, Rupert.

RUPERT (*stands up*): I disown this deed. Whoever struck Jerome first I hereby sentence to death.

SANTING: But Count, your own orders were to—

RUPERT: Silence! Who says so?

SANTING: Who—?

RUPERT: Misinterpreting my words, distorting my will, you face a similar penalty, my good man. I hereby consign you to my dungeon.

SANTING: A last request.

RUPERT: Yes?

SANTING: A private conference of one minute.

RUPERT (*to* EUNICE): Return in one minute, Eunice. (*She leaves.*) Well?

SANTING: I do know what it is to serve.

RUPERT: Yes. It is to give me what I need. *Do I need remorse?* This deed, done in my name, is repugnant to me. It's not mine, it's yours, and you must suffer for it.

SANTING: Yes, master.

RUPERT (*whispering in his ear*): You'll be released in two weeks. Secretly. (SANTING *goes down on one knee. Still whispering:*) That secluded mountain estate you've had your eye on so long—on your release, it's yours. (SANTING *rises; stands discreetly awaiting further orders. Pause.*) This is the curse of power: the revocable will *grows an arm*—which acts irrevocably. My servants can plan evil to their heart's content: no evil will result. But if I, their master, think an evil thought, hey presto! it's an evil action. (*Pause.*) That minute's up. (*He whistles. His* SERVANT *enters.*) Where is Count Otto?

SERVANT: Out.

RUPERT: Out where?

SERVANT: Last reported near the spot at the edge of the forest where his brother perished.

RUPERT: Have my dogs catch his scent and find him.

SERVANT: Your vassal Fintenring holding them in leash?

RUPERT: That's the man. Old Fintenring. Now lock Santing in my dungeon.

(*The* SERVANT *withdraws with* SANTING. *A* CHAMBERMAID *rushes in and embraces* RUPERT'*s knees.*)

CHAMBERMAID: Help, gracious Lord! Mercy! They're taking him to his death.

RUPERT: Taking—? What are you talking about?

CHAMBERMAID: My husband—he was first to hit him—Jerome the herald whom you ordered slain—

RUPERT: Silence! That is a lie. It was Santing.

CHAMBERMAID (*rising to her feet*): But he had his orders, my Lord.

RUPERT: Leave the room.

CHAMBERMAID (*standing her ground*): He had his orders, and I heard you give them, my Lord.

RUPERT: Absurd. You weren't even there.

CHAMBERMAID: I was just behind you, cleaning up in the hall, you were so mad you didn't notice—

RUPERT: Lies, lies. (*Pause.*) —Look, a single witness against *me* counts for nothing.

CHAMBERMAID: There were three of us.

RUPERT (*very quietly*): Woman, don't you realize I can kill you where you stand?

CHAMBERMAID: No, you can't. The other two know where I am.

(Silence.)

RUPERT: What do you want?

CHAMBERMAID: A reprieve.

(Silence.)

RUPERT: You won't go screaming the news all round Rosset?

CHAMBERMAID: The mistress says I'm discretion itself. (*Silence.*) He gets the reprieve?

RUPERT (*nods abruptly*): And you get out.

CHAMBERMAID (*blithely*): Oh, his life is yours now, my Lord, he'll die for you any time, any time, God bless you!

RUPERT: Out!

(Exit CHAMBERMAID.*)*

EUNICE (*entering*): Lord and master—

RUPERT: Are you continuing your indictment?

EUNICE: If I did you wrong—

RUPERT: What more can I do? Capital punishment for the ringleader, chains and a dungeon cell for Santing?

EUNICE: But, husband, I rejoice to find you on the side of justice!

RUPERT: You know how it happened, don't you?

EUNICE: Yes. Santing worked the mob up to a frenzy!

RUPERT: But I should have sent a rescue party?

EUNICE: No. Things went so fast, it would have arrived too late.

RUPERT: I should have shouted from the window?

EUNICE: By then, they wouldn't have heard you—too much noise.

RUPERT: What if I'd shown myself at the window?

EUNICE: Who was looking? No one. No one would have seen you.

RUPERT: Thank you, Eunice.

EUNICE: Oh, I take back my dire accusation.

RUPERT: I don't say my hands are clean. This is war.

EUNICE: A man is never better, says the priest, than when he admits he's bad: repentance is the innocence of sinners.

RUPERT: Now, Eunice, you aren't trying to make me "feel fine" by any chance?

EUNICE: What better cause is there—than to make someone—someone one loves—feel "fine"? A crime has been committed: you were in it but you disowned it and punished the criminals. They say the moment after a crime can be the finest in a man's life.

RUPERT: It can.

EUNICE: Ha?

RUPERT: If he has what it takes to commit a bigger crime.

EUNICE: (*aghast*): What?

RUPERT: I disgust you, ha? Me, too. Would you offer balm for my wounds? Balm in Gilead? Don't. That's all gone, that's all lost and gone. There is one thing I want, and it's not God.

EUNICE: What is it?

RUPERT: To get my own back.

EUNICE: Who—?

RUPERT: Who made me disgusting? Oh, I can answer that one. It's not true life's problems are unanswerable. Who made me disgusting? Sylvester.

EUNICE: Peter died. If it was murder, Sylvester was not a party to it!

RUPERT: Nor was I a party to the attack on Agnes!

EUNICE: Quite right! The cases are alike. You found a suspect, they found a suspect. Sylvester's name was mentioned in a so-called confession, your name was mentioned in a so-called confession . . . . Only one circumstance, in these two sorry tales, is different: the character of Sylvester. You're his accuser but he's not yours, and, when you're in the wrong, he can forgive you!

RUPERT: He forgives me to demonstrate that I *need* forgiveness. Forgiving me for Jerome's death, he convicts me of murder.

EUNICE: Will you give him a chance? Is there anything Sylvester can say that you won't twist and turn against him?

RUPERT: Appearances are against me: he *has* to believe me guilty. But *he* needs forgiveness, too. He forgives *me* to force me to forgive *him*. A miscalculation: Rupert cannot be forced.

EUNICE: What can he do?

RUPERT: Get even with Sylvester. Better than even. He can win. At a price.

EUNICE: What price?

RUPERT: I do "feel fine," now the decision is reached.

EUNICE: Decision?

RUPERT: To do what Johann left undone.

(Silence.)

EUNICE: Kill Agnes? Kill a young girl? Your own niece?

RUPERT (*withdrawing deep into himself, he begins to pant like a dog that's been running hard*): Trees—

EUNICE: What?!

RUPERT: Trees can be planted much too close together, Eunice. Their branches interlock and destroy each other. A whole forest can die out that way . . . .

(Silence.)

EUNICE: Give me your attention, Rupert. What would you think of a man who should kill Otto, your son and heir?

RUPERT: The same that I think of those who did kill Peter. Maybe worse.

EUNICE: Because, now, to kill Agnes would be to kill Otto. Or, which is the same, to earn his undying enmity.

RUPERT: Ha?

EUNICE: God is showing you a way to save your son and end this unholy family feud before it ends the race of the Schroffensteins!

RUPERT (*with tired sarcasm*): Really?

EUNICE: Your son Otto and Sylvester's daughter Agnes are in love.

RUPERT (*laughing out loud*): Love! Love is the subject now! And God!

EUNICE: God brought them together on the mountain.

RUPERT (*suddenly paying attention*): On the mountain?

EUNICE: Jerome told me. Inspired by his great hope: to reconcile the parties—by marriage. Even at the cost of his own happiness. He would surrender his beloved to your son. Honor that hope of his in death, Rupert! Give your son the wife his heart desires, give lasting peace to all the Schroffensteins!

RUPERT (*coldly*): On the mountain is where they meet?

EUNICE (*after a pause, in which she has "realized"*): God in heaven!

(RUPERT *whistles. His* SERVANT *enters.*)

EUNICE: No! No!

RUPERT: Has Fintenring returned yet with my son?

SERVANT: No, sir.

RUPERT: Where is Santing?

SERVANT: In your dungeon, sir.

RUPERT: Of course. Then take me to him.

(*The two men quickly leave.*)

EUNICE (*feebly*): Rupert!

EIGHT

Varvand. In the castle. SYLVESTER *at a window. Enter* AGNES.

AGNES: Father! (*No answer.*) Father! (*She realizes he hears but is choosing to be silent.*) Johann lies wounded in your dungeon. Wounded, we fear, in mind as well as body. Your men will let no one in but Grandfather Sylvius. So I appeal to you. The truth is: it was all a misunderstanding, he never meant me any harm. (*Silence.*) Father!

GERTRUDE (*entering*): Sylvester! Has the news reached you? (*She notices* AGNES.) You here, Agnes? (*Turning quickly back to* SYLVESTER:) It seems you haven't heard: they killed Jerome. They cut him to bits.

(AGNES *gives a little cry.* SYLVESTER *shows no reaction at all.*)

AGNES: Father, what is it? Why don't you say anything—feel anything?

SYLVESTER (*turning from the window, but still as if in a world of his own*): It *is* a dismal day, Agnes. Wind, rain, the whole sky in turmoil. (*Rambling now:*) Strange how, sometimes, everything seems . . . driven, driven in the same direction, dust, clouds, waves—

GERTRUDE: Sylvester! Don't you hear me?

SYLVESTER (*glancing at her, then looking back through the window*): Oh, yes, Gertrude, I saw it too.

GERTRUDE: Saw it?

SYLVESTER: On the lake there. That little sailboat. Still rocking so wildly. Will it make the shore?

GERTRUDE (*swallowing*): You sent Jerome to Rupert—herald, friend, and kinsman, on an errand of peace. Rupert had him slaughtered. That was a desecration of all you hold sacred, a betrayal of all you live for (SYLVESTER *turns and meets her gaze*) and it's just the beginning, Jerome a single branch on a trunk from which this Rupert plans to strip all branches, so the sap will push the treetop— his overweening self—higher and higher. What do you say? (*Silence.*) Do you refuse to know all this, or do you know and propose to ignore it?

SYLVESTER (*holding up his hand*): Give me time.

GERTRUDE: There is no time.

SYLVESTER: Three seconds.

GERTRUDE (*counting them out*): One, two, three.

SYLVESTER: I am ready. It was not easy, Gertrude, making myself ready. Dropping, shall we say, the prejudices of a lifetime? is . . . not so easy.

GERTRUDE: So you knew.

(SYLVESTER *nodding.*)

GERTRUDE: And you do nothing.

SYLVESTER (*shaking his head*): Where is Theistin? I have been a thunder cloud all this time hovering uneasily on high. I am about to descend. As forked lightning. (*A bang on the door.*) Come in, Theistin. (*And it is indeed* THEISTIN, *who now enters.*) Well?

THEISTIN: Success, Count. I have five vassals with me. They have thirty troopers in tow.

SYLVESTER: That will do it. Cousin Rupert's word shall now be mine.

GERTRUDE: Cousin Rupert's word?

SYLVESTER: Revenge!

GERTRUDE: So, Sylvester—

SYLVESTER: Now comes the cloud burst. Let the lightning strike! Leave us, women.

GERTRUDE (*taking* AGNES *out with her*): For Varvand and Sylvester, victory!

SYLVESTER: Your thirty troopers are ready to go?

THEISTIN: Like bended bows. The slaughter of Jerome has roused their ire.

SYLVESTER: Ire! We can use ire! I can add twenty troopers more. With the morale we've got, fifty such men are an army. So, since Rupert has aimed at my head, let's take aim, now, at his!

THEISTIN: Yes, now. This very night. So they won't expect us. Seven country bumpkins will be keeping a sleepy watch.

SYLVESTER: So?

THEISTIN: Give me fifteen men to break down their gates. Then you follow with the rest.

SYLVESTER: Yes. That will be vengeance. Around Jerome's body we will hold a festival of death: Rosset in flames will be the torch to light it.

THEISTIN: Vengeance!

SYLVESTER: Vengeance! Let's join our fifty heroes.

NINE

On the edge of the forest. Peasant cottage. Two rooms. URSULA, *a gravedigger's widow, is making the bed in the bedroom. Her daughter* BARNA *is in the kitchen stirring a pot over the fire.*

BARNA (*taking a deep breath*): So here goes. For my father. First, may he find peace in his grave, may no impious hand scatter his bones over fen and field. Second, an easy rebirth, that, when the last trumpet sounds, he may lift his head from the grave in joy! Third, eternal bliss: that celestial light may pour down and the gates of heaven open wide to him!

URSULA (*calling from the bedroom*): Barna! Are you stirring the pot?

BARNA: Yes, mother, with both hands! (*Smirking:*) Want me to use my feet as well?

URSULA: I don't hear you reciting the Three Wishes!

BARNA: God wouldn't hear if He was as deaf as you! Listen hard now! For my mother. First, success in everything: let no witch with poisonous glance kill the calf in the cow's womb. Second, health to her body. Let not cancer strike! And the rag, red with her blood, let it vanish from the rubbish heap! Third, life that defies death: may no devil intercept her prayers as they fly up to God! Now, for myself. First, joys aplenty: may a handsome lad, pulling with all his strength, get me onto his marriage bed. Second, merciful pain: that—

URSULA: Barna! Did you remember the seeds from the deadly nightshade?

BARNA: Yes, Mother, and the broth's so thick my ladle stands upright in it.

URSULA: What about the unlaid eggs cut from the pike's belly?

BARNA: Shall I cut up another pike?

URSULA: First I must prepare some elder blossom. But let no one in the kitchen, do you hear? And go on stirring, do you hear? And reciting the Three Wishes, do you hear?

BARNA: Yes, yes. Now where was I? Joys aplenty—No, I said that. Merciful pain: when the dear fruit winds its way out of my womb, let it not be all pain and woe! That's all. Now, starting over: For my father. May no impious hand strew his bones over fen and field— Oh! (OTTO *has just entered the kitchen by the outside door. He had knocked gently during her speech.*) Oh! Did you knock?

OTTO: Yes. But you were busy talking to your pot. Are you a witch?

BARNA: Of course not.

OTTO: I wouldn't mind—you're so pretty.

BARNA: I'll have to ask you to leave, sir. No one's allowed in here just now—not even Mother.

OTTO: Except you, eh?

BARNA: Because I'm a virgin.

OTTO: Then I'm allowed in too: *I'm* a virgin.

BARNA: H'm. What's your name?

OTTO: Otto. And yours?

BARNA: Barna.

OTTO: Barna and Otto! Virgins both!

BARNA: Otto and Barna! Keepers of the Cauldron!

(They laugh.)

URSULA: Who's that in the kitchen?

(OTTO makes a sign of entreaty. BARNA plays along with him.)

BARNA: What's that, Mother?

URSULA: Was that you? Are you reciting the Three Wishes?

BARNA: Of course! *(She starts stirring the pot again.)* But now, really, you must leave, sir. If the impure are looking, Mother says, the broth "comes to naught."

OTTO: But only the pure are looking.

BARNA *(grinning)*: You're a wag, you are. Anyhow, don't disturb me. This is the Good Fortune Broth, and I must recite the Three Wishes.

OTTO: What's in the broth?

BARNA: A small boy's finger. *(She laughs.)* Now you *will* call me a witch.

OTTO: A small boy's finger?

URSULA: Barna! Bad girl! What are you laughing at?

BARNA: Just having a good time, Mother—reciting the wishes.

URSULA: The one about cancer?

BARNA: *And* the one about the calf inside the cow!

OTTO: Did I hear you aright: a small boy's—

BARNA: Look, I must recite the wishes, or mother will get mad and the broth will be spoiled.

OTTO: See this purse? (*He has taken one out.*) Show it to your mother. Tell her it fell down the chimney, then come right back.

BARNA (*taking and opening the purse*): Hey, there's money in it.

OTTO: Don't tell your mother who gave it to you.

BARNA: You are an angel—Archangel Otto!

(He pushes her gently into the bedroom, then walks excitedly up and down the kitchen.)

OTTO: A boy's finger. Maybe—Peter's little finger! I feel a warm breeze blowing through my soul. Rock me, O Hope, on your enchanted swing! (*He closes his eyes, as if to let this happen.*) —But I must find out for sure. (BARNA, *who has been talking excitedly in dumb show with her mother and showing off the purse, now returns to the kitchen.*) Barna, how did you come by this little finger?

BARNA: We found it, my mother and me.

OTTO: When? Where? Tell me the whole story.

BARNA: Mother told me not to but—

OTTO: But?

BARNA: I like you, so I will. We were picking herbs by the stream on the mountainside. The water had thrown up a drowned child on the bank. Mother cut that little finger off—the left one, of course, the one that's useful in dealing with the Devil, especially when your husband's passed on and you're alone in the world . . . .

OTTO: Did you see anyone around?

BARNA: No sooner had we stashed that finger safely away than two men from Varvand came along and, when they saw the body, they wanted the other little finger, the right one, no good against the Devil . . . . We made off. And that's all I know.

OTTO: It's enough. Now, will you do something for me?

BARNA: Of course.

OTTO: Go to Varvand, and tell someone "a certain person" awaits her in "the cave." Go with her. She'll know which cave.

BARNA: What do I tell Mother?

OTTO: That the purse had a letter in it, sending you on a little errand. The letter also said your mother must return lost property. To that same cave.

BARNA: Lost property?

OTTO: One little finger.

BARNA: How will *she* find the cave?

OTTO (*taking out a bit of parchment*): With this. I've drawn the path.

BARNA (*taking the parchment*): And how am I to find your "someone" in Varvand?

OTTO: Ask anyone there for the young lady of the house.

BARNA: The "certain person" is you? (OTTO *smiles.*) I thought you liked *me*.

OTTO: I do. (*He kisses her.*)

BARNA: But you like her more? (*Again,* OTTO *smiles.*) Her name?

OTTO: Agnes.

BARNA: Will she believe me?

OTTO (*handing her his scarf*): If you give her this, yes. Goodbye. (*He leaves by the outside door.*)

BARNA (*sighing, then opening the door to the kitchen and addressing her mother*): Mother, there was a letter in the purse . . . .

TEN

On the mountain. Another slope. RUPERT *and* SANTING *looking around.*

SANTING: This is the area where Otto's been seen, says your forester, an experienced spy. And if Otto's on the mountain, so is Agnes, and we'll catch two birds with one stone. If not, Old Fintenring has Otto locked up by now in the tower, and we'll catch Agnes on her own.

RUPERT (*exhausted, sitting down on a stone*): I'm hot. My tongue is dry.

SANTING: That's funny, there's such a cool breeze.

RUPERT: The trouble's all within.

SANTING: You mean you're falling sick?

RUPERT: I'm thirsty.

SANTING: There's a spring over here.

RUPERT (*dully*): Can it quench a thirst like mine?

SANTING: It's crystal-clear water, you can see yourself in it, take a look! (RUPERT *lumbers heavily over to the spring, takes a long look in, then suddenly pulls back.*) What's wrong?

RUPERT: What looked back at me was . . . the face of a demon!

SANTING (*grinning*): Just your own face, Count!

RUPERT: You know me well.

(He sits on the stone again. BARNA *enters.)*

BARNA (*seeing* SANTING *first*): This *is* the path to Varvand, gracious knight?

SANTING: You have business there, lovely child?

BARNA: I have a message for Miss Agnes of Varvand!

SANTING: Really? (*He exchanges a look with* RUPERT.) I don't know her but if she's half as pretty as you, I'd like to go with you! What's the message?

BARNA: Oh, no real message, just that I'm to bring her up here on the mountain.

SANTING: Today?

BARNA: Do you know her?

SANTING (*with coarse flirtatiousness*): I know you better, and I'd like to know you better still. Today, you said?

BARNA: Yes, right away. —I *am* on the right path?

SANTING (*nodding*): So who sent you?

BARNA (*cautiously*): My mother.

SANTING (*doubting it*): Really?

BARNA: Really!

SANTING: Well, stick to the path and you can't go wrong.

BARNA: God keep you, sirs!

(Exit BARNA.*)*

SANTING: So Agnes will be here today. And this peasant girl was sent by—her mother?

RUPERT: Or my son? (SANTING *nods, knowingly.* RUPERT *rises.*) Agnes will fall into our trap.

SANTING: Thank God!

RUPERT: Thank the Devil! They have wanted me a murderer. I shall now give them their own way. (*Trying to be casual:*) Where do they meet, those two, do you know the spot?

SANTING: I know the terrain. And there'll be tracks. And tracks can be followed.

RUPERT: Let's go then. (*And he starts to go in the same direction as* BARNA *had gone.*)

SANTING: No, this way.

(*And they walk on in the opposite direction,* SANTING *keeping a lookout for tracks.*)

ELEVEN

Rosset. A prison high in the tower of the castle. A key turns in a lock, and a cell door opens. OLD FINTENRING, *another vassal of* RUPERT's, *enters the cell.* OTTO *lingers in the doorway.*

FINTENRING: Pray come in, Count Otto. Look around. Take your ease.

OTTO: "Won't you come into my parlor?" said the spider to the fly.

FINTENRING: Tell yourself it's a great adventure.

OTTO: You're quite a character, my dear Fintenring.

FINTENRING: I'm not sure I know that expression.

OTTO: Do you believe your own act? That's what people wonder about you.

FINTENRING: That's what people wonder about everybody.

OTTO: Let's hear your version of this escapade. Why?

FINTENRING: Why what, Count Otto?

OTTO: Why come hunting me with snarling mastiffs? Why rush me back here? Why tell me we're going to "explore" the castle? It's my home after all.

FINTENRING: Excuse me, Count. Have you ever been up here before?

OTTO: Not this high in the tower. It's a jail, isn't it? Why would the son of the house be "exploring" its jails?

FINTENRING: You're a big boy now.

OTTO: Not so big you didn't rattle on about secret corridors and sliding doors.

FINTENRING: Not to mention a concealed arbor and grotto where fair maidens will bedeck you with lilies and roses!

OTTO: The lilies and roses—ropes and chains?

FINTENRING: Afraid to come in and find out? Is it true, Count, that the boys call you The Girl? (*This taunt brings* OTTO *through the doorway into the cell.*) Dressed as a great lady, you have made quite an impression at Carnival time! (OTTO *is looking around the interior of the cell.*) And here there's nothing to scare the daintiest of females. What more chaste than such a bedchamber? Why, the stone flags of this floor would cool a satyr's lust!

OTTO: In short, I'm to be imprisoned.

FINTENRING: All great men have done time. It took prison to drag their great thoughts out of them! Were you going to write that great drama, *The Schroffenstein Family*?

OTTO: No.

FINTENRING: Well, now you may as well.

OTTO (*in the tone of an order to a servant*): Take me to my father.

FINTENRING (*blocking the doorway with alacrity*): What's that? Old Fintenring is hard of hearing.

OTTO: There is urgent news.

FINTENRING: Urgent to you?

OTTO: Urgent to him.

FINTENRING: To weigh such an allegation on the scales of justice, one needs to know what the news is.

OTTO: That is between the master of this house and his son.

FINTENRING: Tell me anyway. I'm in on all the secrets of this place.

OTTO: No.

FINTENRING: You say no. I say no. (FINTENRING *steps outside the cell and locks* OTTO *in. They now speak to each other through the bars.*) Your father's not home, by the way.

OTTO: Why couldn't you have said that?

FINTENRING: My Mum called me a Child of Fantasy.

OTTO: It makes no difference. I must go to him.

FINTENRING: I don't know where he is.

OTTO: Others do. The Master of Rosset can't fly away on a broom-stick.

FINTENRING: I'd have to consult the Rosset witches about that.

OTTO: Find out where my father is!

FINTENRING: He and Santing set out some hours ago "for an undis-closed destination."

OTTO: Only hours ago? Then how far away can he be?

FINTENRING: On a broomstick?

OTTO: I'll send out search parties.

FINTENRING: How?

OTTO: Let me out.

FINTENRING: 'fraid not.

OTTO: I'll bribe you.

FINTENRING: I value money. I value my head more.

OTTO: Every man has his price. What's yours?

FINTENRING: A price your father can pay, and you can't.

OTTO: Nothing can corrupt you, Fintenring!

FINTENRING: Hey, thank you!

OTTO: So let me out.

FINTENRING: Why?

OTTO: For telling you nothing can corrupt you.

FINTENRING: So *you're* the Child of Fantasy, ha? I like you, Count. Now I can do my good deed for the day.

OTTO: What's this?

FINTENRING: Talk of *my* Mum reminded me of yours. And she's *here*. Thinks about you all the time, moans, groans, wrings her hands, calls on the Deity. I think you and she should have a little *tête a tête*.

OTTO: Fine. Open that door.

FINTENRING: No, no, Mrs. Mohammed will come to the Mountain. Hold on.

(*Exit* FINTENRING. *He is going to descend the tower and bring* EUNICE.)

OTTO (*alone*): Fintenring! (*Silence. Screaming:*) Fintenring! (*The sound echoes through the tower in echo-diminuendo: Fintenring, Fintenring, Fintenring.*) What can I make a noise with in here? No door to bang on. Walls, floor, ceiling, all stone. Let's bash the table about a bit. (*Beats on the table with his fists. Hits the table with the one stool in the place, which soon breaks. Tries Fintenring's name once more, this time with a more controlled loudness:*) Fintenring! (*Silence.*) A man that only one key can open: his master. The perfect poodle! (*Silence.*) Very well, I who am called The Girl will study that female virtue, Patience, the art of leaving everything undone but not taking it hard. You begin by counting up to ten. (*When he has counted up to ten a couple of times, there is a sound of people approaching.* FINTENRING *unlocks the door, lets* EUNICE *in, locks the cell door behind her.*)

EUNICE (*to* FINTENRING): Later, I'll make this worth your while.

FINTENRING: Now there's a bribe I can accept. (*He withdraws.*)

OTTO: Mother!

EUNICE: Otto, Jerome is slain.

OTTO: God in Heaven!

EUNICE: And Rupert knows about you and Agnes.

OTTO: Who could have told him?

EUNICE: I did. Jerome told *me* and, in misguided zeal—I'd never known him as pure tyrant, outright barbarian—

OTTO: Known who?

EUNICE: Your father.

OTTO: Tyrant? Barbarian?

EUNICE: He killed Jerome.

OTTO (*hands to head*): I can't take it in. But let me tell you something, Mother: that mystery—it's solved, the riddle of my brother's murder. The men they found by Peter's body had themselves just found the body. All they did was cut a finger off it. Sylvester is as blameless as the sun.

EUNICE: But, God help us, he's going to kill Agnes now!

OTTO: Who is?

EUNICE: Your father! If she's on the mountain, she's done for. Rupert and Santing are up there hunting her down!

OTTO (*again screaming*): Fintenring!

EUNICE: Fintenring can't let you out, it would cost him his life.

OTTO: And you—my Mother?

EUNICE: I'm helpless.

OTTO (*looking about him in the cell*): Help me then, Mother of God! (*He spots a heavy cloak on the floor, picks it up and wraps it round him.*) This heavy cloak will cushion my fall. (*He clambers onto the sill of an unbarred window.*)

EUNICE: Otto, you mustn't jump from here. The tower is fifty feet high, and nothing but paving stones below.

OTTO (*from the window ledge*): When I jump, keep very quiet, or they'll be on my heels.

EUNICE: Otto, don't jump! Don't treat life with such contempt!

OTTO: Life, my dear Mother, is worth while when you despise it.

(*He jumps.*)

EUNICE (*soundlessly*): Fintenring!

TWELVE

On the mountain. Inside the cave which we previously saw only the mouth of. Stage magic or mechanics has turned this cave through 180 degrees, so that now the mouth is at the back of the stage. In the downstage area, we are deep inside. Indeed the auditorium itself can now be regarded as even deeper inside, in which case we are all, actors and audience alike, in the cave together. Not much light comes in at the mouth of the cave, since night is falling. AGNES and BARNA are well inside the cave (i.e., downstage) to one side.

AGNES: But you should have told me about *them* before, Barna, I would never have come here. Run to the mouth of the cave and see if anyone's there.

BARNA (*does this, moving upstage*): Not a trace of those two knights!

AGNES (*with a sigh of relief*): God be thanked!

BARNA: No trace of the beautiful boy either.

AGNES: You're sure you know him when you see him?

BARNA: Oh, I'll never forget him!

AGNES: Take another look down the path.

BARNA (*still at the mouth of the cave*): It's growing dark now in the valley—yellow candles flickering in the windows—red fires in the fireplaces—

AGNES: I don't understand how he can be so late.

BARNA: And if anyone *was* coming, I'd hear. You hear the slightest sound up here on the heights.

AGNES: I think I should go back home, Barna. Come with me.

BARNA: Sh! A sound! Sh! Again! Oh, but it's the waterfall. The sound of rushing waters was carried all the way here by a sudden gust of wind.

AGNES: Just the waterfall?

BARNA: No, there's something moving, dark, in the mist—

AGNES: A man? Two men?

BARNA: Not sure. But it *is* human. Oh!

(BARNA *runs back to* AGNES. OTTO *appears in the mouth of the cave, looks around, sees* AGNES, *and rushes into her arms.*)

OTTO: So you're alive! That angel must again have stood guard over you.

AGNES (*trembling*): The unknown messenger. And you so late. And two knights lurking about!

OTTO: Two knights?

AGNES: Who asked after me.

OTTO: Asked who?

AGNES: Barna, here. They got out of her that she was taking me up the mountain.

OTTO: God forbid!

AGNES: You know who they are?

OTTO (*to* BARNA): Do they know Agnes is here? In this cave?

BARNA: No, no!

AGNES: They're not from Rosset, are they? And on my trail? They're not murderers, are they?

OTTO (*coming out of his blue study*): Agnes, the big secret is cleared up. Barna here had Peter's finger. He wasn't killed, he drowned. Your father is blameless. While we can, let's enjoy . . . an hour of silent beauty.

AGNES: Is beauty silent, Otto?

OTTO: Yes! Grief, like boredom, talks: happiness is mute. (*And a moment of magic silence is "heard."*) Let's make this night a festival of love. (*Releasing her from his embrace, he draws her over on to a seat.*) The gross error having been uncovered, our fathers can be reconciled. (*He kisses her.*) With this kiss we are betrothed. (*He whispers something to her about* BARNA, *as we note from a gesture, then stands up and goes over to talk to* BARNA *in an undertone which* AGNES *will not overhear.*) Stand at the mouth of the cave. If you see anyone, call. And something else: Agnes and I will exchange clothes. If anyone takes us by surprise, they'll think she's a man, and you can sneak her away.

(*BARNA nods and goes upstage.*)

AGNES: Where's she going?

OTTO (*sitting*): And thus the future opens up its gates! Can you take the measure of such bliss?

AGNES (*smiling*): You'll teach me.

OTTO: The great day—or rather, night—is not far off. Light comes to lovers in the night. Right now, in this dark cave, I see you're blushing.

AGNES: Your *cheeks* tell you that mine are glowing!

OTTO: So who needs eyes to see? Not lovers. Let's close our eyes and look into that future. (*He closes his eyes.*) Among the thronging guests, whose eager glances follow us like wasps, I approach. You shyly say two words, then turn to chatter with the prude beside you. I don't resent her, for when she leaves, your eyes catch mine and twinkle . . . . Now, *all* the guests have left. Only our parents remain. "So good night, children." Smiling, they kiss you. (*Opening his eyes, he kisses her.*) I take a candle and climb the stairs, as calm as if we'd nothing on our minds. No sound save the rustle of your skirts until—Are you falling asleep, Agnes?

AGNES: Falling asleep!?

OTTO: You're so quiet.—I gently open the bedroom door, then gently close it, as if forbidden to: the grown man trembles at what's forbidden to a child. We sit. I press your lips to mine, all my love in one long kiss. (*He kisses her, then breaks away and runs to the mouth of the cave. To* BARNA, *in a whisper:*) Well?

BARNA: Two men . . . creeping by . . . as if on tiptoe.

AGNES (*to* OTTO *as he returns*): Why do you keep talking to Barna?

OTTO (*sitting*): Where were we? Ah yes: the one long kiss. (*He is now starting to remove her clothing, so that she can be disguised as a man.*) —Now love grows bolder and, because you're mine—you *are* mine, aren't you, Agnes?—I take your hat off for you. (*He does so.*) Disturbing the neat order of your curls, I take away the neckerchief. (*He does so.*) "At least put out the light," you murmur. I do so. Night weaves its veil around our love and—

BARNA (*from the mouth of the cave*): Count Otto!

OTTO (*cutting in, as* AGNES *looks anxiously around*): I now untie this knot. (*He unties a knot.*) Then this one. (*Another.*) Then lightly strip unwelcome covering from your back. (*He strips off her outer garment: a cloak. And that, in one style of production, is as far as the stripping need go. In another style of production, both performers would be naked while* OTTO *speaks his next words.*) And now, like swollen waters in the spring, emotion breaks all bounds—

AGNES: What are you at? (*She falls upon his neck.*)

OTTO: —Our bodies interpenetrate! Love comes into its own!

BARNA: Count Otto! One of them just passed! Quite near! Quite slowly!

OTTO: Did he see you?

BARNA: He might have.

AGNES: Why did she shout?

OTTO: Oh, it's nothing.

AGNES: I know it's something.

OTTO: All right, two farmers have got lost.—But you're freezing, put these on.

AGNES: *Your* clothes?

OTTO: While I wear yours!

(OTTO *is now donning* AGNES' *clothes.*)

AGNES: Are we turning into each other?

OTTO: Who'd think this mannish cloak covered a young girl's body? If I cover your curls with this helmet (*and he does so*), women will be my rivals for your hand.

AGNES (*looking at him, now female*): And men for yours!

OTTO: King of the Harvest!

AGNES: Queen of the May!

(*This tableau is held for a moment.*)

BARNA (*running from the mouth of the cave*): They're coming!

AGNES: Who? Who's coming?

OTTO (*putting the finishing touches on his disguise, but also changing his tone to "level" with her*): My father, Agnes. My father and . . . a friend.

AGNES: Then what on earth are we about?

OTTO (*calmly*): They are hunting a girl. If you leave this cave as a boy—act the part, plucky, cocksure—but don't say anything—no one will touch you.

AGNES: But you—dressed as a girl?

OTTO: He's *my* father: leave him to me.

AGNES: But—

(*Before* AGNES *can speak,* RUPERT *and* SANTING *appear.* OTTO *lowers his voice.*)

OTTO: Now go. And remember: don't speak.

(*Both girls start to leave, but* RUPERT *blocks their path.*)

RUPERT (*to* SANTING, *speaking of* BARNA): This farm girl is not Agnes. Who are you, young man?

OTTO (*steps into* RUPERT'*s line of vision and speaks in a woman's voice*): Did someone ask for Agnes? (*The two girls take the hint, and slip out.* RUPERT *must now give them time to get clear away.*)

SANTING (*with rough sarcasm*): Think carefully before you answer.

OTTO: Will you give me a minute to think *very* carefully?

RUPERT: You need a minute to think of your own name?

OTTO: I have something else to tell you—that takes a minute.

SANTING: There's something fishy here.

OTTO (*quickly, to forestall doubts*): If you're from Varvand, take me home to Father.

RUPERT: Home to Father, eh? (*He draws a short sword.*)

OTTO (*in his own voice, but no attention is being paid now, even by SANTING*): One moment! I am—

RUPERT (*bringing the sword down on OTTO like a dagger, straight into his heart*): Let this send you home to your Heavenly Father! (OTTO *falls without a sound. Astounded, terrified, at his own violence,* RUPERT *goes limp, stares blankly at the body before him. Nervously, to* SANTING:) Did that do it?

SANTING: Snakes die hard, but this one has nine inches of sword in her bosom.

(Silence.)

RUPERT (*numb, quiet*): Why did I do that?

SANTING: I beg your pardon.

RUPERT: Remind me why I did it.

SANTING: This was Agnes.

RUPERT: Agnes, that's the name. She did me wrong. (*Silence.*) What wrong did she do me?

SANTING: The girl herself did you no wrong.

RUPERT (*horrified, shrieking*): Then why have I murdered her? (*Silence.*) Don't glare at me like that, you basilisk! Speak! If you don't know the answer, tell a lie.

SANTING: It was because she was Sylvester's daughter.

RUPERT: Sylvester, right: the fellow who murdered my Peter.

SANTING (*nodding*): Your herald Aldo and your beloved Johann.

RUPERT: Aldo. Johann. Yes, Sylvester's lies made me out a monster, and now I am one. (*He plucks the sword out of* OTTO's *chest.*) Take this, generation of vipers. (*He plunges the sword back into the body.*)

SANTING (*who has slipped to the mouth of the cave*): Danger, Count! We must head straight back home!

RUPERT: Ha?

SANTING: A lot of people. With torches. Moving in procession. It's an army! From Varvand! Moving silently up the mountain! And this path leads only to Rosset! Come!

RUPERT: One thing. Was that Otto leaving the cave as we entered?

SANTING: It may well have been.

RUPERT: Then—

SANTING: He'd be on his way home, we'll overtake him. Come!

(They both leave the cave. AGNES *and* BARNA *return to it, and are seen in its mouth.)*

AGNES: What is it? A gigantic funeral procession? The blood-red light of torches fills the valley. I can't walk home through this army of spooks, Barna! If the cave's empty, let's return.

BARNA: The two knights just left.

AGNES: Then Otto is still here. (*They walk on.*) Otto, Otto!

OTTO (*very feebly*): Agnes.

AGNES (*tracing the source of the voice, and catching sight of* OTTO *on the ground*): A sword still in his chest, O God! (*She throws herself down beside him.*)

OTTO: My plan succeeded: they let you go. Now fly! (*He dies.*)

BARNA (*to* AGNES, *who is overcome*): Pull yourself together, and follow!

BARNA *runs off. Enter* SYLVESTER *and* THEISTIN *with* SERVANT *carrying a torch.*)

SYLVESTER: Halt! Pass the word along, Theistin. (*Word is passed to troops—offstage, of course—to halt.*) Is this the right cave?

THEISTIN: Yes, my Lord. Johann described it to me. Your daughter must be here.

SYLVESTER: Bring me a torch. (*The* SERVANT *comes forward with the torch. He will stay downstage with it for the rest of the scene.*) Can you make anything out, Theistin?

THEISTIN: Too much. Agnes prostrate. Otto towering threateningly above her.

SYLVESTER (*seeing the sight now, letting out a cry*): Aaah! He's already done it! There's a sword in her bosom! Agnes!

AGNES (*hearing her name, turns towards her father, who of course takes her for* OTTO): Who's there?

SYLVESTER: Murderer! Hell is here! (*He stabs her. She stumbles across the cave and falls dead.* SYLVESTER *hardly notices her body but turns at once to* OTTO*'s:*) Agnes! Agnes!

(An outcry without, "Holla," etc.)

THEISTIN (*stepping to the mouth of the cave*): Two prisoners have been taken. Men of rank. They must have been lurking in the undergrowth.

*(*RUPERT *and* SANTING *are pushed into the cave by the men outside.)*

SYLVESTER: Let me see them. (*He looks.*) No, it cannot be. Rupert himself!

THEISTIN: And Santing, his evil conscience.

SYLVESTER: Rupert.

THEISTIN: And in this way Heaven has placed the malefactors in the executioner's hands.

SYLVESTER: Ha?

THEISTIN: When these heads are off, Rosset itself has neither head nor trunk nor limbs!

SYLVESTER: You want me to—

THEISTIN (*drawing his big two-edged sword*): Let me behead them, here and now! We then sweep down on Rosset and leave not a man, not a stone, standing.

(Silence.)

SYLVESTER: No.

THEISTIN: No?!

SYLVESTER: No. It was all for her, Theistin: only Agnes could give me grandchildren, only Agnes gave Varvand a future. Put up your sword. (THEISTIN, *if grudgingly, has to sheathe his sword.*)

RUPERT (*having seen* AGNES' *body and taken it for* OTTO*'s*): Let me be with my son. (THEISTIN *shakes his head but* SYLVESTER *silently bids him stay his hand.* RUPERT *staggers over to what is actually* AGNES' *body, kneels.*) My Otto!

GERTRUDE (*entering*): My Agnes dead in this cave, is it true? (*She finds* OTTO*'s body.*) Mother of God, Agnes! (*She kneels.*)

EUNICE (*heard offstage coping with the obstruction offered by* SYL-VESTER's *men*): Sylvester! Order them to let me through!

SYLVESTER: Grief, if nothing else, is free to come and go! (*He gives a sign, and she is admitted.*)

EUNICE (*entering, seeing both bodies*): My Otto! And your Agnes, too, Sylvester? Is *this* their wedding?

(She kneels before what she takes for OTTO's *body. Enter old* SYLVIUS, SYLVESTER's *father, lost and senile, led by the hand by* JOHANN, RUPERT's *son, now quite mad. In his other hand* JOHANN *carries a torch.)*

JOHANN: Good day, good people. We two were headed for the City of Misery—

SYLVIUS: Where little Agnes lies buried—

JOHANN: Is this it?

SYLVESTER: Ha? Oh, yes, and you're just in time for our Family Reunion. Welcome, Father, this is your son Sylvester.

(Goes down on one knee to him.)

SYLVIUS: I knew him well. Well.

SYLVESTER: And welcome, Johann. Your father and your brother are here already.

(RUPERT *does not heed this.*)

SYLVIUS: I want to go home.

JOHANN: What's that, Grandfather?

SYLVIUS: I don't like it here.

JOHANN: Home! Home is the City of Bliss. We passed it, but couldn't get in: it was locked on the inside. We're stuck with this City of Misery.

SYLVIUS: Where little Agnes lies buried.

JOHANN: Only they don't bother about burial. Just strew their corpses around. I think I *see* Agnes'. Can you *smell* it? (*What he has seen is* OTTO *in* AGNES' *clothes.*) I'll take you to her. (*He takes* SYLVIUS *by the hand to* OTTO's *body.*)

SYLVIUS (*en route*): Can anyone spare a penny for a blind old man quite lost in the forest? (*They are now at* OTTO's *body.*) How much further, boy?

JOHANN: Six inches. From up to down.

SYLVIUS (*whom* JOHANN *has brought to a kneeling position where he can feel the body*): A sword! Still in her bosom!

JOHANN: And to think! She was good, that girl, and beautiful!

SYLVIUS (*feeling further*): This is not Agnes!

JOHANN (*torch in hand, looking the body over*): How clever you are, Grandfather! You know the difference between a girl and a boy!

GERTRUDE (*standing*): This is a boy?

SYLVESTER: A torch here! Is this Agnes or not? (*The torch throws its light.*) It is not, it is not!

JOHANN: Oh, well, don't worry, there's no lack of corpses: I see a lovely one right there!

SYLVIUS: I've guessed it: the City of Misery is a charnel house!

JOHANN: So cheer up, Uncle Sylvester, one of 'em must be Agnes. How about that one? (*He points at* AGNES' *body, dressed as it is in* OTTO'*s clothes.*)

SYLVESTER (*rushing over to verify*): Agnes? Yes, this *is* Agnes! And this is the one I—! Then it was not Rupert who—!

GERTRUDE (*who has also rushed over*): Agnes, Agnes.

JOHANN (*to* GERTRUDE): Stroke her cheeks, they were always soft as gossamer. (*Turning now to* RUPERT, *who has not yet noticed his presence, lost, as he is, in his own agony.*) Hey, Dad, aren't you in the wrong shop?

RUPERT: Are you talking to me?

JOHANN: Which would be natural: I'm your natural son.

RUPERT: I don't have a son.

JOHANN: Just a dead daughter.

RUPERT: Are you mocking me?

JOHANN: Life is mocking you.

RUPERT: Never mock the helplessness of an imbecile.

JOHANN: How can it hurt?

RUPERT: Even if he's in chains, he can spit in your face.

JOHANN: Everyone does.

RUPERT: But *his* spittle's infected with the plague! Leave me with my Otto.

JOHANN: Even if he's a she?

(RUPERT *pulls back some of the clothing on* AGNES' *body.*)

RUPERT: Aaah! Then . . . then where is *he*?

JOHANN: All in place for the Family Reunion: Agnes, here; Otto, there.

RUPERT (*going to* OTTO's *body, followed by* EUNICE): This is Otto? Yes, yes? But this is the one I—I—and twice! Pierced him twice, right through the heart! (*Silence.*) Devils are moving in on us. They're all around. See that one, there—the demon I saw in the spring, Santing—he's sticking out his tongue at me!

(*Above the voices of soldiers offstage, a shrill feminine voice is heard.*)

URSULA (*who has pushed her own way in*): Everyone here? (*She looks around, to assure herself that all concerned must be present.*) Contrary to rumor, me and my daughter are not witches! I'm an honest woman, come to return lost property! (*Holding something up.*) A small boy's little finger.

EUNICE: My Peter, he—

URSULA: You're the mother?

EUNICE: Oh, yes.

URSULA (*giving her the finger*): Then it's yours, and yours only. Bye! (*She leaves.*)

EUNICE (*who has examined the finger closely*): And it *is* his. I know it by the scar, the only scar on a perfect body.

RUPERT (*suddenly roused, shouting to people offstage*): Bring that woman back! (URSULA *is pushed back on stage by unseen hands.*) How did you come by this finger, woman?

URSULA: I cut it off. But he was dead, my Lord. Oh no, not murdered or anything: drowned. The body was thrown up on the river bank.

RUPERT: But why, in God's name, cut a finger off?

URSULA: In the Devil's name, pardon me. To keep the Devil away! I kept it on my threshold.

RUPERT: But when I came upon the body, you weren't present.

URSULA: No. That was later.

RUPERT: Two men from Varvand were there, their knives dripping with blood.

URSULA: Yes. They'd been hacking away at the other little finger, ignorant fools!

RUPERT: Go! (*She does so.*) Sylvester was innocent.

(While the four parents kneel in grief before the two bodies at each side of the cave, SYLVIUS *talks with* JOHANN *in the center.)*

SYLVIUS: What's going on, boy?

JOHANN: People are cutting their little fingers off, Grandfather.

SYLVIUS: That all?

JOHANN: They're stabbing their sons and daughters right and left.

SYLVIUS: There must've been a misunderstanding.

JOHANN: A miscalculation.

SYLVIUS: Someone guessed wrong.

JOHANN: But cheer up: everything's solved now.

SYLVIUS: The Schroffensteins?

JOHANN: Nothing to solve there. Eunice and Gertrude are too old to have children. Rupert and Sylvester are—the last of the Schroffensteins.

(His torch, which has been burning low, now goes out.)

SYLVIUS (*an idea striking him*): I know: it's the end of the world.

JOHANN: Ha? It can still end beautifully: a reconciliation. (*To* RUPERT:) Father! Talk to Uncle Sylvester.

RUPERT (*standing and addressing Sylvester*): Sylvester! Could all this (*he indicates the two bodies*) serve to bring us together at last?

SYLVESTER (*who does not rise or move*): Ha? No.

RUPERT (*feebly*): Why not?

SYLVESTER: Force is the only language I understand.

RUPERT: I said that.

(SYLVESTER simply leaves a silence.)

RUPERT: Tell me what to do.

SYLVESTER: Too late.

RUPERT: The loss of Agnes—the loss—

SYLVESTER: Of everything.

RUPERT: You don't trust me.

SYLVESTER: Don't trust anyone, anything.

(RUPERT *again kneels by* OTTO's *body. The cave is dark except for the* SERVANT's *torch and a faint ray of moonlight which lights up the faces of* SYLVIUS *and* JOHANN.)

SYLVIUS: The end of the world.

JOHANN: Ha? Oh, I don't know, Grandfather. Some idiot might declare me legitimate. I might get some idiot pregnant. The world may yet have a future.

DONA NOBIS PACEM

Afterword

Tragedy and non-tragic drama are the confession which this salvation army must make (army of both salvation and perdition, as it is) . . . this salvation army which we call Humanity. . . . Not only in the private confessional but also in public, without any reticence and at the top of its voice, for the echo of this voice is more distinct, more real than the voice itself. Let's not kid ourselves, the kinship of theater and religious solemnity is quite evident, and it is no accident that, at one time, performances were presented, on any and every occasion, in front of our cathedrals. (This area was known as the Parvis, the courtyard before Saint Peter's in Rome having been called Paradise). On gala evenings of theater, it is to this Paradise that the audience proceeds to see and hear the illuminated confession of its destinies, both petty and grand. Calderon is Humanity confessing a yen for eternity; Corneille confesses Humanity's dignity; Racine its weakness; Shakespeare is Humanity confessing a yen for life itself; Claudel confesses Humanity's state of sin and salvation; Goethe confesses Humanity's . . . humanity; KLEIST, ITS FLASHES OF LIGHTNING. Such is theater, the public recall of unbelievable prodigies, visions of which will upset and even topsy-turvy all those gala evenings. Such is the perfomance of a play, the living and unconcerned spectator's sudden awareness of passion and death.

—Jean Giraudoux (translated by Eric Bentley, emphasis added)

Notes

LORD ALFRED'S LOVER

1.

Many of the books on Oscar Wilde are richly illustrated. Anyone who wishes to find out what the people of my story actually looked like should consult at least Sheridan Morley's *Oscar Wilde*, Martin Fido's *Oscar Wilde*, Rupert Croft-Cooke's *Bosie*, and H. Montgomery Hyde's three books on Wilde.

Am I intimating that an actor playing Oscar Wilde should get hold of photos and drawings and then try to become a look-alike? No. Such mimicry, in the theater, is apt to distract from the drama. It is not exact imitation of the historical material that is needed but adaptation, transposition. Given *my* face, the actor must say, how can I make it up to suggest something of the *character* (not the dimensions) of Oscar Wilde's? Obviously, this calculation cannot be made in ignorance of the historical Wilde: my play needs the pictures.

Is it important that Wilde be played by a fat man? Fatness could help, I think, not as a sight gag, but as providing a certain physical clumsiness contrasting with the mental sprightliness of the man; but a thin actor, declining to pad himself out, might get that effect another way.

Another matter is age. At his trial, Wilde was only forty, but his many pounds made him look more. A fifty-year-old actor might play the role but should seek to give the impression of an old forty.

If the actor playing the young Alfred Douglas need not resemble the actual man, it *is* necessary that (a) he look some sixteen years younger than the actor playing Wilde and (b) have the flowerlike loveliness that is one gay archetype. On the other hand, he should look some ten years *older* than Maurice, the teenage beauty of the final scene.

How old are Oscar Wilde's sons in the one scene where they appear? I have purposely left the date of the scene vague so that my director will not feel tied to exact ages. The children should be about a year apart—one might be eight, the other nine—but the scene would make sense with children of eleven and twelve.

What about the *passage* of time? Although I have not tied the earlier scenes to particular dates, and have sometimes played hob with real-life chronology, even the most casual reader or spectator will notice that the action of the play covers between five and ten years. Should we see the characters *age* during this time? Actually, the problem, if it is one, only applies to Oscar, as no one else is seen through that whole time span, and my answer, as to him, is that his body should show the marks, not so much of time, as of shock. Certainly, his death is being hastened by what happens. He "dies" once during the play—in Reading Gaol—and is not far from a second or "real" death in the final scene.

Douglas we do not see aging but in dual images: "crabbèd age and youth," respectively. Some young actor will want to play both Douglases, I am sure. But then the stunt itself will become obtrusive. Better an old actor and a young.

The actor playing Robbie Ross should have in mind—and body—another gay archetype: not flowerlike beauty, but a certain soft charm. Another aspect of Ross is suggested by Wilde's own description of him: "puck-faced."

The photos and drawings are, of course, an infallible guide in another area: costume. The costume designer will see from the graphic material just what degree of dandyism to give Oscar in contrast with the austere formality of, say, the lawyers.

And the appearance of the stage as a whole? On this, different directors will, quite legitimately, have different ideas. One approach would be to use very little scenery but a certain number of projections showing (a) photos of such locales as 16 Tite Street, the Mitre Hotel, the Café Royal, Reading Gaol, and (b) photos, paintings, and drawings of the persons depicted. The fact that these sometimes contrast with the actors in the roles could be not only acceptable but interesting.

2.

What is true? Where Pontius Pilate threw up his hands—or at least washed them—it is not for the author of *Lord Alfred's Lover* to do anything with his hands except sit on them. But—coyly, or otherwise—he can cite other people.

Here is Max Beerbohm describing Oscar Wilde: "Luxury—gold-tipped matches—hair curled—Assyrian—wax statue—huge rings—fat white hands—not *soigné*—feather bed—pointed fingers—ample scarf—Louis Quinze cane—vast *malmaison*—catlike tread—heavy shoulders—enormous dowager—or schoolboy—way of laughing with hand over mouth—stroking chin—looking up sideways—jollity overdone—But real vitality . . . ."

Beerbohm was a caricaturist. Frank Harris was a notorious liar: if one quotes him at all, it is only because one can suspect there may be an interesting grain of truth behind the exaggerations: "His [Oscar's] hands were flabby, greasy; his skin looked bilious and dirty . . . . He was overdressed rather than well-dressed; his clothes fitted him too tightly; he was too stout . . . . His jowl was fat and pouchy . . . . I lay stress on this physical repulsion because I think most people felt it . . . . His grey eyes were finely expressive, in turn vivacious, laughing, sympathetic, always beautiful. The carven mouth, too, with its heavy, chiselled, purple-tinged lips, had a certain attraction . . . in spite of a black front tooth . . . . He looked like a Roman Emperor of the decadence . . . ."

And here is something probably just as exaggerated about Lord Alfred Douglas toward the end of his life. It is by Hugh Walpole: ". . . a rather bent, crooked-bodied, hideous old man . . . a nose as ugly as Cyrano's with a dead-white bulbous end. He talks ceaselessly on a shrill almost-broken note, agitated, trembling . . . .

When someone he hates . . . is mentioned, he gets so angry that all his crooked features light up, and his nose achieves a sort of somber glow . . . listening to no arguments, screaming like a parrot . . . ."

3.

Lord Rosebery? It is H. Montgomery Hyde who has revealed that the Queensberry family did not believe Drumlanrig's death to have been accidental: they assumed that he sacrificed himself to save a future prime minister. But what prime minister? Even Hyde's books give us no "leads" on him. But in *Love in Earnest*, by Timothy d'Arch Smith, this passage is to be found:

> It is curious to note that Corvo wished to dedicate . . . *Stories Toto Told Me* to Lord Rosebery, the former Liberal Prime Minister, for in him he would have found a reticent but sympathetic reader. According to a well-informed writer on the phenomenon of 'similisexualism' as a social problem, Rosebery was himself inclined to Uranian ideals. '[Rosebery] . . . is a constant absentee in his beautiful home in Southern Europe whence only gentle rumours of his racial homosexuality reach his birth-land.'

The well-informed writer is "Xavier Mayne" in his 1908 book *The Intersexes*.

4.

Anachronisms in *Lord Alfred's Lover*. History plays are anachronistic from beginning to end since they are put together by writers, not by antiquarians or linguists. Although there are many quotations from the actual Wilde in the play, and some from the actual Douglas and others, the speech is not consistently Victorian: it is twentieth century with an occasional archaism for flavor. As for the order of events, chronology has sometimes been flouted not only in the Wilde story itself, but in references and citations: The actual Wilde could not have mentioned H. G. Wells's *Invisible Man* where he does, as it had not yet been written. "Will you love me in December?" had not yet been composed in the period when the playwright has Arthur Marling sing it . . . and so on.

H FOR HAMLET

In the early Fifties, I was always encouraging British and American theater people to do Pirandello's *Enrico IV*. At one point, Alfred Drake and, at another point, Alexander Knox, were very interested in undertaking the title role. But both made the same objection: the German and Italian history in the play is too remote and unfamiliar, audiences in London and New York will never get interested in any Henry IV who is not Henry IV of England. I racked my brains for a familiar historical figure who might be analogous to Pirandello's *tragico imperatore*. Nothing doing. But then it struck me that there were strong analogies with the Hamlet story, which itself has an at least quasi-historical basis. And if one gives up

Germany, one may as well give up Italy, so I chose a setting that would be familiar at least to New York Americans (and, through Scott Fitzgerald, more): Long Island. The result was *H for Hamlet*, which also Messrs. Drake and Knox did not do.

In the Sixties, Charles Laughton said it was definitely something he should and would have done—several decades earlier. So it comes before a public for the first time, not on stage, but in print, and more than thirty years later. A little changed perhaps, since change is the law of life. (Non-change is the law of death.)

The idea of escaping from reality, that was Pirandello's idea, was it not? Surely the greatest idea in the world, for reality asks for nothing so much as to be escaped from. Gallantly the theologians and poets try to make us an offer we cannot refuse: Heaven, Utopia, etc. They are all the same thing, but alas, to accept any of the well-meant offers is to learn, and to learn the hard way, that the toads in their imaginary gardens are real . . . . Anyway, here is a play about an imaginary emperor who commits a real murder. And the dead man is not the one who is monstrously martyred.* The murderer is.

Ha? Who says so? Pirandello? Eric Bentley? Have it your way. It's "as you like it." *Così è se vi pare.* The martyrdom remains monstrous, whoever the martyr.

GERMAN REQUIEM

1.

The list of characters (page 163) comprises seventeen male and six female roles but judicious doubling (in one case, tripling) can reduce the number of actors from twenty-three to seventeen. The actress playing Barna can also play the Chambermaid. The actor playing Aldo can also play First Wanderer and Fintenring. The actor playing Santing can also play the Gardener. The Priest can be doubled with the Second Wanderer. One actor can play both Servants. When a stage direction in the first scene indicates that retainers of Rupert sing a hymn, these retainers can include everyone not otherwise needed in the scene, each with a cloak over his costume. Thus twelve actors and five actresses can perform the play without omitting any characters, even those with the fewest lines.

Four of the characters (Agnes, Barna, Otto, and Johann) are teenagers. Performers in their twenties like to think they are still "right" for such roles but usually they are not. It is desirable to cast high school students for these four parts.

2.

The stage designer of this play has to make visible the macabre world which its people live in. As this is not the real, historical Middle Ages, the best guide in art will not be work of the medieval period but rather of the Kleist period: the

---

* A possible subtitle for *H for Hamlet* would be *A Pirandello Variation*, on the lines of the already published *Kleist Variations*.

romantic painters such as Caspar David Friedrich, John Martin, and maybe Gustave Doré. The best stage for such a play is the traditional proscenium stage of the eighteenth and nineteenth centuries with its pictorial backdrops, though today these should be executed not on painted canvas but by projected photographs. It is often as well if the projected picture is smaller than the back wall of the stage so that the actors are not excessively dwarfed thereby. I say "excessively," since a degree of dwarfing is called for: this is a world in which mere people can only be lost, in the way in which the Bard is lost in John Martin's picture with that title.

Otherwise, the main point for the stage designer to take hold of is that the images stand in bold contrast, one with another: mountain slope contrasts with castle, and chapel with both. One "high" moment is reached in a very high place, a tower; the final catastrophe is claustrophobically enclosed in a cave. On the other hand, the two castles might well be horribly alike.

3.

As in the stage design, so in the music, medievalism should be avoided.

Certain sounds from Prokofiev's score to *Alexander Nevsky* might prove suggestive, as might particularly the opening passage in Benjamin Britten's *Sinfonia da Requiem*. But an orchestra should not be used (nor recordings of same). The job is best done by three musicians, either on the stage or near it. One should play percussion, mainly a military type of drum; one, brass, a primitive-sounding horn, which might appropriately sound to battle; and the third, a pipe—perhaps a flute—which can "musicalize" the lovers' retreat(s) on the mountain. (For the scene of the "witches' cauldron," three instruments might be grotesquely mingled.) A single musician might even suffice, provided he is a very good pianist and has a very good piano on hand. In this case, all the incidental music should be drawn from the works of Liszt, especially *Les Funérailles* and *Waldesrauschen*.

The playwright is not suggesting that the amount of musical "background" be maximized, as in the movies. Rather, it should be used sparingly—chiefly to mark breaks and transitions in the scene.

The hymn in Scene One presents a particular problem. Though sung in a church, it is highly unchristian. It should savor less of Christian piety than of the neo-pagan ferocity of the K.K.K. or the S.S.

4.

History plays have come to be called costume plays: their people wearing "costumes," not clothes. This makes of historical drama a pageant or party game or fancy-dress ball. What should have evoked a time and a place evokes only operetta.

German Requiem is not a history play, but if its "past" is more imaginary than actual, what is imagined should not be in the operetta vein. It needs a solid human reality, if not an historical one. And the epoch evoked must not be picturesque like that of traditional operetta, etc., but harsh, violent, guilt-ridden, barbaric—like the twentieth century.

The late twentieth-century theater is ready for such manifestations. It was made ready by Eisenstein's films (especially *Nevsky* and *Ivan*) and Brecht's stage productions (especially *Mother Courage*). Shakespeare's history plays presented in London today are much harsher, earthier, and consequently more real than they were up to and including Olivier's pretty picture-postcard version of *Henry V* filmed in 1944.

I have said the stage designer should be guided by artists like John Martin, not by medieval work. Make-up and costume should be modeled on the work of nineteenth- and twentieth-century illustrators, not on medieval painting or stained glass. Also on movies. Eisenstein again. And such things as the Dreyer *Passion of Joan of Arc* (so wonderfully contrasted with our stage Saint Joans, whose model is Rosalind in tights).

5.

German Requiem is a variation on the play *The Schroffenstein Family* by Heinrich von Kleist. Those who wish to know what I have appropriated and what I have changed will have to check with the Kleist play.

This note simply records my lack of sympathy with another variation on the play that appeared on TV screens in West Germany while my own script lay in MS awaiting publication and production.

The German producers had plenty of money and hired very good actors, but their production was Artaud rather than Kleist, surreal rather than romantic. Because its emphasis was sexual, not political, it came across as a private affair, more ugly than expressive. In mistakenly trying to make explicit everything that Kleist left implicit, these producers also made explicit a great deal that is not even implicit. It would seem that the director took the opportunity to empty out for all to see the dismal and dismaying contents of his own still adolescent fantasy. The film was rejected not only by my brain and taste but by my nervous system: it gave me such a headache, I had to stop watching it about two-thirds of the way through.

It aroused none of the envy I thought might be aroused by a rival effort. The sibling rivalry between myself and Hans Neuenfels, the director, is nil. At the same time, after seeing this atrocity, I tremble at my rashness. Kleist's play deals with atrocity, and the danger, felt by Kleist himself, is that, from an atrocity, one may easily *make* an atrocity. Placed on the defensive, I will only say, first, that I was always aware of the hazard and, second, that I always found a contrary element in the gruesome tale, a "romanticism" in the popular sense, namely a naively charming eroticism in the midst of all the hideous violence. Thus (if I am in the right) Neuenfels' key mistake was to be sophisticated about all the sex, and turn the beauty that is there into nastiness. Certainly he could quote precedent: our Theater of Cruelty has done this sort of thing with *Macbeth* and *Lear*. But there too—again I can only give my own opinion—the results were dire. Enough: I must leave reader and spectator to judge.